Welfare Reform
in America

MIDDLEBURY CONFERENCE SERIES
ON ECONOMIC ISSUES

Welfare Reform in America

Perspectives and Prospects

Paul M. Sommers

Editor

KLUWER·NIJHOFF PUBLISHING
BOSTON/THE HAGUE/LONDON

DISTRIBUTORS FOR NORTH AMERICA:
Kluwer Boston, Inc.
190 Old Derby Street
Hingham, Massachusetts 02043, U.S.A.

DISTRIBUTORS OUTSIDE NORTH AMERICA:
Kluwer Academic Publishers Group
Distribution Centre
P.O. Box 322
3300 AH Dordrecht, The Netherlands

Library of Congress Cataloging in Publication Data

Main entry under title:
Welfare reform in America.

  (Middlebury conference series on economic issues)
  Papers presented at the second annual Middlebury
Conference on Economic Issues, held in April 1980.
  Bibliography: p.
  Contents: Goals and purposes of social welfare
expenditures / Robert J. Lampman — Welfare reform /
William P. Albrecht — The war on income poverty /
Sheldon Danziger and Robert Plotnick — [etc.]
  1. Public welfare — United States — Congresses.
2. Public welfare — Government policy — United States
— Congresses. I. Sommers, Paul M. II. Middlebury
College Conference on Economic Issues (2nd : 1980)
III. Series.
HV91.W47   361.6′8′0973   81-13677

ISBN 0-89838-079-0   AACR2

CONTENTS

VOLUME EDITOR'S
INTRODUCTION

This is the second in a series of books growing out of the annual Middlebury College Conference on Economic Issues. The second conference, held in April 1980, focused on goals and realities of welfare reform. The objectives of the conference were threefold: (1) evaluation of the antipoverty effort so far; (2) discussion of welfare reform alternatives; and (3) prediction of how new initiatives would change work behavior and productivity.

During the time this country has been engaged in a "war on poverty," two massive efforts to reform welfare, Richard M. Nixon's Family Assistance Plan (FAP) and Jimmy Carter's Program for Better Jobs and Income (PBJI), were proposed. Both defined national benefit levels and featured a negative income tax. Both measures were defeated in Congress.

More modest efforts at reform have, however, changed the economic landscape. Because of the rapid growth in cash and in-kind transfer programs, income poverty is no longer the serious problem that it was in 1964. In fact, looking at the proliferation of programs and the substantial surge in participation rates, some politicians have even advocated a period of government retrenchment. In 1971, the governor of California proposed (and implemented) a major welfare reform in an attempt to stem the rapid growth of welfare caseloads that began in his state in 1967–68. He argued that savings from administrative improvements could be used to raise benefits for the "truly needy." The governor's "blueprint" for reform also included legislation that would bring more people — including many AFDC and food stamp recipients — under the "workfare" umbrella and would stiffen the penalties for not working. Ablebodied welfare recipients either worked for, or lost, their benefits. Not surprisingly, President Ronald Reagan's initiatives today have a familiar ring.

Improving the efficiency, equity, and responsiveness of antipoverty programs continues to be a politically significant issue. The patchwork nature of current programs, the attendant administrative inefficiencies, and the equally serious inefficiencies in the targeting of benefits on those most in need have nurtured a growing skepticism about government in general and about welfare policy in particular. New approaches to policy such as negative income taxes, wage rate subsidies, and public employment programs offer some advantages over the programs already in place, but their superiority is at best controversial. However the debate is resolved, whether through incremental reform or a basic overhaul, it is clear that public confidence in the welfare system needs to be restored.

This volume puts into perspective nearly two decades of federal antipoverty programs and considers the prospects for reform. The authors are from universities, independent research organizations, and government. In addition to the contributors to this volume, others who provided stimulation and added to the discussion of the issues were: Orley C. Ashenfelter, Samuel Bowles, Richard V. Burkhauser, Patricia DuBuclet, Irwin Garfinkel, Richard W. Hurd, Michael C. Keeley, Juanita Kreps, Mark Plant, Bradley R. Schiller, Timothy M. Smeeding, Thomas Sowell, and Michael Wiseman. The papers have been revised with an eye to the January 1981 change in the federal government and the new era of austerity. It is hoped that the information and analysis presented here will prove useful to teachers and practitioners in indicating the direction toward which antipoverty policy should proceed.

Currently, there is no up-to-date book of readings for an undergraduate or a public policy school course on poverty and welfare issues. This book attempts to fill the void.

Welfare Reform
in America

I POLITICAL ECONOMY OF WELFARE REFORM

The paper by Robert J. Lampman reviews four closely interlocked, distributional goals of social welfare expenditures: (1) offsetting income loss, (2) helping people to buy essentials, (3) reducing income poverty, and (4) sharing the tax burden fairly. While there may be wide agreement that these goals should serve as the basis for evaluating any welfare reform, there is less agreement about the priorities among them. However priorities are ordered, social welfare expenditures show unmistakable signs of slackening.

William P. Albrecht is prepared to administer the last rites to welfare reform. The "inexorable conflicts" among income adequacy, target efficiency, and enhanced work incentives exist in one way or another for all redistributive plans. Achieving a desirable balance among these objectives is no longer (if it ever was) politically possible. Perhaps we should now be prepared to entertain the possibility that the welfare system that has evolved is reasonably satisfactory, a theme more thoroughly developed in part II.

1 GOALS AND PURPOSES OF SOCIAL WELFARE EXPENDITURES

Robert J. Lampman

In this paper we look at *welfare reform* in the context of *social welfare expenditures* (SWE). Both terms have a variety of definitions — there is no universally accepted, standard usage. We will use the term *SWE* to cover what Ida C. Merriam, formerly of the Social Security Administration, originally defined as

> cash and medical benefits, services, and administrative costs for all programs operating under public law that are of direct benefit to individuals and families. Included are programs providing income maintenance and health benefits through social insurance and public aid, and those providing public support of health, education, housing and other welfare services. (McMillan 1979, p. 7)[1]

SWE were $394 billion in 1978, equal in amount to 19.3% of GNP. (Cash transfers are, of course, not part of GNP.) Table 1.1 shows that since 1950 these expenditures by the federal, state, and local governments

Research for this paper was funded in part by funds granted to the Institute for Research on Poverty at the University of Wisconsin (Madison) by the U.S. Department of Health and Human Services pursuant to the provisions of the Economic Opportunity Act of 1964. The opinions expressed are the author's.

3

Table 1.1. Social Welfare Expenditures under Public Programs as Percentage of Gross National Product, Selected Fiscal Years, 1950–1978

Fiscal Year	GNP (in billions of dollars)	Social Welfare Expenditures as Percentage of GNP									Total Health and Medical Expenditures as Percentage of GNP[b]
		Total[a]	Federal[a]	State-Local[a]	Social Insurance	Public Aid	Health and Medical Programs	Veterans' Programs	Education	Other Social Welfare	
1950	264.8	8.9	4.0	4.9	1.9	.9	.8	2.6	2.5	.2	1.2
1955	379.7	8.6	3.9	4.7	2.6	.8	.8	1.3	2.9	.2	1.2
1960	498.3	10.5	5.0	5.5	3.9	.8	.9	1.1	3.5	.2	1.3
1965	658.0	11.7	5.7	6.0	4.3	1.0	.9	.9	4.3	.3	1.4
1970	960.2	15.2	8.1	7.1	5.7	1.7	1.0	.9	5.3	.4	2.6
1974	1,361.2	17.6	10.1	7.5	7.3	2.3	1.1	1.0	5.2	.5	3.0
1975	1,452.3	19.9	11.5	8.4	8.5	2.8	1.2	1.2	5.6	.5	3.5
1976	1,625.4	20.4	12.1	8.3	9.0	3.0	1.2	1.2	5.4	.6	3.6
1977c	1,838.0	19.7	11.9	7.8	8.8	2.9	1.1	1.0	5.1	.5	3.7
1978c	2,044.0	19.3	—	—	8.6	2.9	1.2	1.0	5.0	.5	3.7

SOURCES: McMillan 1979, p. 10, Table 3; U.S. Department of Health, Education, and Welfare 1980.

aIncludes housing, not shown separately.

bCombines health and medical programs with medical services provided in connection with social insurance, public aid, veterans' services, vocational rehabilitation, and antipoverty programs.

cPreliminary estimates.

have risen much faster than GNP. In fact, they more than doubled as a percentage of GNP in the past three decades. The principal categories of SWE are social insurance and education. SWE now amount to 60% of all combined government expenditures.

Welfare, it appears, is used by many writers to cover some or all of the expenditures classified in Table 1.1 as public aid and other social welfare, as well as public housing. These three classifications accounted for 2.9%, .5%, and .1% of GNP, respectively, in 1978. However, some writers use the term more narrowly to mean only the cash benefits payable under Aid to Families with Dependent Children (AFDC) and General Assistance (GA). Supplementary Security Income (SSI) is also a cash benefit program, but it has received less critical attention because, unlike the others, SSI reaches those traditionally regarded as "truly needy," that is, the aged, blind, and disabled. Cash benefits under these three programs amount to about 1% of GNP.

Table 1.2 shows more detail about what may or may not be counted as welfare. All of these expenditures are funded out of general revenues, unlike social insurance, which is largely paid for out of payroll taxes. Most of them are targeted to lower-income people, and many are income- or means-tested. Only about a third of these expenditures take the form of cash benefits. A larger part is used to provide health care, food, and housing. (Note that Medicaid is the largest single welfare program.) The remainder is largely devoted to a range of social services from counseling to day care to training (note the overlap with education).

WELFARE REFORMERS AND THEIR GOALS

Welfare reform is another term that lacks a precise and agreed-upon meaning. Undoubtedly, the most famous of many reform efforts was that which led to adoption of a new poor law in early nineteenth century England. At that time, *reform* meant division of the poor into two groups, namely, those expected to work and those not: denial of "outdoor relief" for those in the first category and enforcement of responsibility of relatives to contribute to the support of those in the second category. This reform was partly a reaction to the alleged failure of a kind of negative income tax known as the Speenhamland scheme, which paid benefits to the working poor. The reaction emphasized the need to deter malingering and to encourage work and thrift.

On the other hand, welfare reform in the later years of that century came to mean separating out groups of the poor for special consideration.

Table 1.2. Expenditures for Public Aid, Public
Housing, and Other Social Welfare, by Type, 1977
(in billions of dollars)

Type of Aid	
Cash (total)	20.4
AFDC and GA	13.6
SSI	6.8
Health care (total)	18.0
Medicaid	17.6
Institutional care	.4
Food (total)	8.7
Food Stamps	5.4
Child nutrition[a]	3.3
Public housing	2.8
Social services (total)	5.8
Nonmedical services	3.1
Child welfare	.8
Vocational rehabilitation	1.3
Special OEO and Action programs	.6
Other public aid[b]	5.9
Social welfare, not elsewhere classified[c]	3.2
Overall total	64.8

SOURCE: Derived from McMillan 1979, pp. 4–7, Table 1.
[a]Surplus food for schools and programs under National
School Lunch and Child Nutrition Acts.
[b]Work relief, other emergency aid, surplus food for the
needy, repatriation and refugee assistance, and work experience training.
[c]Indian welfare and guidance, aging and juvenile delin-
quency activities, antipoverty and manpower training programs, day care, child services, legal assistance, care of
transients, and other unspecified welfare services.

Criminals, mentally ill persons, orphans, widows, veterans, the aged, and the disabled were among those singled out for study, concern, and legislation. This categorical approach to welfare guided the federal government in the United States when it adopted the public assistance and social services titles of the Social Security Act in 1935. Since that time we have seen several themes competing for the label of welfare reform. One theme has introduced new categorical programs to make existing welfare programs more generous and to allow more people to qualify for them. Some of these reforms have been accomplished by the courts in extending the constitutional rights of due process and equal protection under the law to welfare recipients. Others have come about through congressional establishment of national minimums in specific programs, for example, SSI, which was adopted in 1972.

A second theme of recent years has been to cut back on eligibility for welfare benefits by pushing for relative responsibility and work-tests. This theme is, of course, reminiscent of the previous century, but is focused this time on the AFDC program and its population of families headed largely by divorced and separated women. Unlike some earlier themes, this one carries the emphasis on work to the point of creating public jobs for those on welfare and of subsidizing child care to enable the welfare mothers to take the jobs.

The third theme to claim the title of welfare reform is distinct from the other two. It emerged in the 1960s under the flag of the negative income tax (NIT). It featured elimination of categories among the poor, a minimum income for all (including the "working poor" who were not eligible for AFDC), no work-tests, and a moderate benefit-reduction rate designed to avoid strong disincentives to work. Some enthusiasts of NIT saw it as a replacement for all existing cash and in-kind social welfare benefits. President Nixon incorporated some NIT ideas in his 1969 welfare reform package of SSI (which ultimately passed) and the Family Assistance Plan (which did not). The latter, FAP, deviated from a pure NIT in that it was categorical (it excluded single persons and childless couples as well as the aged and disabled persons eligible for SSI); it featured a work-test; it had a high benefit-reduction rate (FAP, food stamps, and other programs together produced a combined benefit-reduction rate of 70% or more); it was not strictly a cash program (it offered child day care services to working mothers); and it proposed to create public jobs.

With FAP, NIT became identified as a substitute for AFDC. As such, it emphasized the second theme identified above. Alternatively, President Nixon could have designed NIT as a substitute for GA, the unemployed

fathers segment of AFDC, and the minimum-wage law. This would have
meant a new categorical program for the working poor.

While the failure of FAP and the rejection of Senator McGovern's tax
reform, which featured a $1,000 per person guarantee and a 33⅓% benefit
reduction rate, are often said to have signaled the demise of NIT, it is
plausible to argue that its theme is not dead. It lives on in SSI, the Food
Stamp Program, the Basic Education Opportunity grant program, the
earned income tax credit, and other income-tested benefits.

It would appear that everybody is for welfare reform, but that there
are contradictory ways to be a reformer. One is to create new categories
of beneficiaries and new types of benefits, and to make eligibility easier
to attain. For some observers, the welfare explosion of the 1960s and
early 1970s *was* the reform.[2] A second way is to tighten up on eligibility
and to push people out into the world of work, even if this means creation
of special jobs.[3] A third is to abolish the maze of special welfare programs
and replace them with a single cash benefit program based upon progressive income tax principles.

Clearly, the adversaries in this several-sided debate have different
goals in mind. The first emphasizes compassion for the poor, who are
seen as victims of systemic social and economic failure. The second
highlights the loss of self-respect and withdrawal of potential labor time
associated with welfare dependency. The third claims that the goal is to
release the poor from paternalistic guidance and bureaucratic restrictions.
"You pays your money and you takes your choice" of adversarial positions, or you may take some of each and develop your own unique
version of welfare reform.

GOALS OF SOCIAL WELFARE EXPENDITURES

We said earlier that welfare programs are part of a broader pattern of
SWE. The welfare programs listed in Table 1.2 in fact amount to only
16% of SWE. We may gain some new insights into the welfare reform
controversies if we look at the goals and purposes of the larger system
represented by SWE and the taxes levied to pay for it.

Economists are wont to characterize the purposes of public expenditures as pursuit of equity and efficiency. Government can presumably
improve upon market outcomes by redistributing income and reallocating
resources. Textbooks often relate equity gain to reduction in the inequality of the size distribution of income accomplished by expenditures and
taxes. Efficiency has to do with gains in output associated with reallo-

cations toward production of consumer goods most highly valued, and toward productive investments in physical and human capital. It is likely that there is a trade-off between equity and efficiency. Indeed, the lesson of economics is that there is no such thing as a free lunch.

It seems to be the general view of economists that SWE accomplish a considerable amount of redistribution, but relatively little reallocation. That is to say, the distribution of final income — including nonmoney income — is less unequal than the distribution of market income, but the allocation of resources among goods and services is not much different from what it would be if all SWE took the form of cash transfers. (For example, the consumption of food would be about the same if food stamps were converted to cash.) However, economists generally believe that SWE result in some loss of GNP because they increase the attractiveness of leisure, and because the taxes paid to finance SWE reduce the capacity of people to save and thereby to increase the capital stock.

That particular formulation, which highlights the equity-efficiency trade-off, is perhaps more prescriptive than descriptive of any nation's decision-making with reference to SWE. An alternative formulation is more inductive, based upon the record of announced purposes and of formulas of existing SWE programs and tax laws. In this approach the goals are thought to be revealed by legislative behavior. Thus the immediate goals of the American system of SWE would appear to be:

offsetting income loss,
helping people to buy essentials,
reducing income poverty,
sharing tax burdens fairly.

More than half of SWE in the United States are motivated by concern for losses of income associated with old age, disability, unemployment, and loss of a family breadwinner. This concern is not limited to those made poor by events beyond their control; the mere fact that income falls below its customary or expected level is deemed a sufficient basis for social intervention. Social insurance, which features contributions by workers and employers and benefits payable as a matter of contractual right, is a preferred method for offsetting loss. However, the same risks are also protected against by public assistance as a second level of defense. For example, an unemployed worker may receive unemployment insurance benefits first and public assistance benefits later. This goal is associated with the sharing of income loss during a recession, which may have the side effect of automatically stabilizing the economy.

Another substantial part of SWE is devoted to helping people buy essentials.[4] The leading example under this heading is public spending for education, which amounts to 5% of GNP (see Table 1.1). Free public education at elementary and secondary levels is provided as a civil right and funded out of general revenues. Parents are, of course, compelled to send their children of specific ages to school and hence must meet certain noninstructional costs of school attendance, including the forgone earnings of children, out of their own pockets. Higher education is typically not free, but governments may subsidize tuition and otherwise help students and their families meet the costs of going to college. Such help may or may not bear any relationship to financial need in the narrow sense, but it is given in recognition of the difficulties most families have in planning for — or borrowing for — the costs of college, and also in the faith that there are external benefits to be captured from encouraging more people to seek higher education.

The point about external benefits raises the question of whether the goal is simply to help people buy what they, as individual consumers, want, or whether the goal, and hence the standard for evaluation, is to provide education that will improve their capacity to produce. Should one count education benefits in the year the expenditure is made or in the year that extra income due to education is realized? Should health care expenditures be counted only if they result in lower mortality and morbidity? Interestingly, few writers ask whether one should count cash transfers for the sole purpose of making the recipients happier.

Similar considerations to those for education seem to underlie government expenditures for health care, which now amount to 3.7% of GNP, or about a third of total health care outlays. We appear to be moving toward the view that health care, like education, should be available as a civil right. On the other hand, housing and food are less touched by the civil rights concept, but are apparently seen as essentials meriting public support. SWE for the latter two items combined amount to less than 1% of GNP and are highly concentrated on the poor. It is interesting that housing outlays make up a much larger part of SWE in some welfare states other than the United States (e.g., the United Kingdom and Sweden).

The third immediate goal of American SWE is to reduce income poverty. This goal, which was enunciated by President Johnson in 1964, encourages a tilt of SWE in the direction of those whose incomes fall below a recognized national minimum. Hence, we must ask whether SWE that offset income loss or help people buy essentials really do reach the poor as well as other social groups. Can we design cash transfers to help those who have chronic low earnings, but have not suffered an income loss? Also, are these programs, which we have traditionally addressed to specific categories of the poor, the best that are possible? Can the whole range of SWE be managed so as to contribute, along with growth in pretransfer income, to year-by-year reduction in the number of Americans with incomes below the poverty line? At present, almost 40% of SWE, that is, about $150 billion worth of the goods and services and cash transfers provided under these public programs, go to people whose pretransfer money income is below the poverty line in the year of receipt. The 20% of persons in the latter group, who receive about 2% of pretransfer money income, receive about 10% of total income (total income defined to include all SWE).[5]

These numbers about the pretransfer-poor incidence of benefits should be taken with a grain of salt. There is what we may call a secondary beneficiary in many cases, that is, a person who would have made a private payment to the poor beneficiary if the public program did not exist. For example, an elderly person might have been supported by his adult children, who may or may not be poor. The calculations above use as the counterfactual a world with no private transfers and thus show more redistribution toward the poor than may be credible.

A critic may ask: Are we sure that the number of posttransfer poor is less than it would be if SWE were only half as great, that is $1,500 per pretransfer poor person instead of the present $3,000? That question is not easy to answer because it requires assumptions about behavioral responses to the availability of SWE benefits and to the "poverty trap," or high benefit-reduction rates (which are particularly severe for the poor) associated with those benefits.

One of the longstanding debates in this field is whether people can be "helped" out of poverty, or whether they must be induced or coerced out of the "culture of poverty" by what Sidney and Beatrice Webb called "the exercise of plastic power." There can be no doubt that the coercive approach to poverty is still followed to some degree, but it is less popular than it once was.

We now move to the fourth immediate goal of the SWE system, namely, sharing the tax burden fairly. Inductive inquiry into the goals of the American tax system indicates the desire for a set of combined tax rates that are roughly proportional throughout most of the posttransfer income range. Progressivity does not begin short of the top 5% or so of income receivers, according to the consensus view of tax incidence. (However, if one holds, with a minority of economists, that property taxes, sales taxes, and payroll taxes are progressive, then one would conclude that our tax system is progressive throughout.) Although the level of taxes is higher than it was, the pattern across income ranges has changed very little in the last several decades.

We apparently want our income taxes to recognize family size, to offset extraordinary medical expenses, to encourage private health and retirement insurance, and also to subsidize home ownership and child day care. Through exemptions, exclusions, deductions, and credits, income tax expenditures duplicate SWE's pursuit of the goals of offsetting income loss and helping people buy essentials. The idea of the NIT is to extend the income tax mentality to pursue the goal of reducing income poverty. One example of this in the current tax law is the earned income refundable credit for low-income families with children.

SOME BROADER GOALS

The four immediate goals of the SWE system relate to the secondary distribution of income. The primary distribution arises in the market-place, but it, too, is subject to social goals, the most important of which are high employment and positive growth in per capita production. Attainment of these goals, which may be aided by skillful application of fiscal, monetary, and other policies, will ease the problem of reaching the goals of the secondary distribution. Conversely, high unemployment and negative growth will place a heavy burden on SWE.

There is a school of thought that teaches that we can alter the primary distribution by tax incentives for employers to hire disadvantaged workers, by carefully targeted public job creation, and an egalitarian incomes policy — that is, without relying upon conventional SWE — and thereby increase the share of pretransfer income going to the poor. Some argue that such a shift could be engineered even at a time when unemployment is high and economic growth is slow. However, most would agree that such policies have a better chance of succeeding (though they might think such policies are then unnecessary) in a more favorable economic climate.

The four immediate goals for the secondary distribution and the two for the primary distribution are reflective of still deeper goals we hold for our society. These include individual freedom of choice and equality of opportunity. (Incidentally, inequality in the size distribution of income is not a good indicator of attainment of equality of opportunity; measures of intergroup, e.g., black-white, income differences may be more meaningful.) This complex of goals has some internal conflicts; pursuit of one goal may entail losses with respect to another goal. For example, high offsets to income loss may cause a reduction in employment and hence a slowing of economic growth. Or steps to reduce inequality of opportunity may infringe on some individuals' freedom of choice.

Similarly, there are problems of achieving an appropriate balance among efforts to achieve each of several goals. Here we confront an economist's paradox. There is such a thing as too much of a good thing — or less than the optimum amount of a bad thing, such as pollution or poverty — and that can be avoided only by balancing benefits and costs at the margin. For example, suppose we were considering adding $50 billion to SWE. Putting the whole amount into, say, helping people buy essentials might add less to social utility than putting part of it into reducing (money) income poverty. While there may be wide agreement that the goals enumerated above are the operative goals for policy choice, there is less agreement about the priorities among them.

WELFARE REFORM REVISITED

Let us return now to the question of welfare reform. Our review of the goals of SWE and of the broader goals for primary distribution may enable a better evaluation of the controversy among those who call themselves welfare reformers. That review turned up the following points:

- Most SWE benefits go to the nonpoor.
- The SWE benefits received by the poor far exceed the welfare benefits listed in Table 1.2.
- The recipients of welfare are mostly poor, but not all the poor receive welfare.
- Not all of the ways to reduce income poverty are listed in Table 1.2, nor even in Table 1.1 (tax reform and job creation are two that are left out).
- The goals for welfare, which is part of the SWE system, are the same as the goals for SWE.
- Pursuit of these goals presents harsher disincentives for the poor than for the nonpoor. This is because SWE are a larger part of total income for the poor than the nonpoor, and because benefit-reduction rates are higher for them.
- Pursuit of these goals differentially restricts freedom of choice for the poor. This is because a disproportionate part of their SWE

benefits take the form of goods and services (some of them designed especially for the poor) as opposed to money.

The challenge for welfare reformers is the same as that for SWE reformers, namely, to achieve, by recourse to reason and experience, a desirable balance among (1) the four goals of SWE and the taxes to pay for them, (2) the primary distribution goals of high employment and positive economic growth, and (3) the broader social goals of freedom of choice and equality of opportunity.

NOTES

1. A time series has also been developed on private social welfare expenditures. Such expenditures are not discussed in this paper.
2. The "explosion" that attracted the most attention was the rise in the number of AFDC recipients. This number went from 3.1 million in 1960 to 11.1 million in 1972 and has tended to decline since 1972, standing at 10.3 million in May of 1979.
3. This seems to be the way favored by the Reagan Administration in 1981.
4. One might characterize SWE designed to offset income loss as "helping people to buy leisure."
5. One may ask a question here as to whether some SWE, such as those for education, should be counted as capital transfers rather than as income transfers.

REFERENCES

McMillan, Alma. 1979. "Social Welfare Expenditures under Public Programs, Fiscal Year 1977." *Social Security Bulletin* (June):7.
U.S. Department of Health, Education, and Welfare, Social Security Administration, Office of Research and Statistics. 1980. *Research and Statistics Note No. 2* (14 February). Washington, D.C.: U.S. Government Printing Office.

2 WELFARE REFORM:
An Idea Whose Time Has Come and Gone
William P. Albrecht

The multibillion-dollar welfare system in the United States is hardly a system at all. It is a mélange of uncoordinated programs that have been created by a variety of legislative bodies and are administered by a variety of federal, state, and local agencies. As a result, welfare benefits vary widely from person to person and from state to state.

The many apparent shortcomings of our welfare system have, over the past decade, led to persistent demands for welfare reform. These demands continue to be heard from presidents, governors, legislators, taxpayers, welfare recipients, and participants in conferences on welfare reform. Such demands, however, are both futile and unwarranted. They are unwarranted, because today's welfare system, despite its shortcomings, is a relatively good one. These demands are futile, because welfare reform is dead politically.

THE POLITICS OF WELFARE REFORM

The reason for asserting that welfare reform is dead is a simple one: *welfare reform will not be enacted by Congress; it is politically impos-*

15

sible. This statement applies equally to comprehensive or incremental reform. It applies whether by *reform* one means the development of a rational, coordinated federal system, or a return of the welfare system to the states; a substantial reduction in benefit levels, or a substantial reduction in the number of people receiving welfare benefits.

In *Slaughterhouse Five*, Kurt Vonnegut likens writing an antiwar book to writing an antiglacier book, because it is futile to oppose both war and glaciers. Welfare reform, like tax reform, will continue to be talked about; but both have about as much chance in the U.S. Congress as would a campaign to eliminate glaciers.

The experience with President Nixon's welfare reform proposals in 1970 and President Carter's proposals in 1978 provide empirical support for this political judgment (Weil 1978).[1] As an example, consider the fate of Carter's attempt to create 1.4 million public service jobs. Under Carter's proposal many people would be classified as "expected to work." Since experience suggested that there would not be private sector jobs available for all those expected to work, a jobs program was an important element in the president's approach to welfare reform. Despite widespread agreement that a good welfare system would encourage people to work, not everyone agreed that a jobs program was desirable. Many were opposed to additional federal spending. Others, while not opposed to expansion of the government sector in general, wondered about the effectiveness of such a massive jobs program. Supporting the idea of a jobs program were many of those belonging to the natural constituency for welfare reform. Their support was critical to enactment of a jobs program, but they could not agree with others or the president over the details of the program. Some of them, such as the National Association of Social Workers (NASW) criticized the plan for not providing enough jobs. The real stumbling block, however, seemed to be the wage rate.

The Carter Administration proposed a low wage for a variety of reasons — not the least of which was the laudable goal of encouraging workers to take jobs elsewhere as they developed skills and as jobs became available. Organized labor, however, objected strenuously. It was concerned that public employees would be displaced by the lower-priced workers in the jobs program. Labor, therefore, demanded job guarantees for those currently employed in the public sector. NASW, the American Public Welfare Association, and the Urban League joined in the attack on the low wage rate, claiming that it and other features of the program would create a secondary work force that would be exploited by its employers. In essence, Carter was attacked on one side for spending too much money and on the other for not creating a full-scale, high-wage, full-employment program regardless of the economic or political difficulties involved.

The moral of this little episode is clear. There will be no jobs program that provides adequate job opportunities for unskilled, low-income people who cannot obtain employment in the private sector. If there is a jobs program, most of the jobs will pay more than the minimum wage, thereby making the program so expensive that there will be fewer jobs created than are needed. Additionally, the high wage rate will make the jobs attractive to relatively skilled workers, and the low-skill individuals for whom the program was proposed will not get the jobs.

Similar stories can be told concerning almost every feature of Carter's Program for Better Jobs and Income (PBJI) or Nixon's Family Assistance Plan (FAP). Too many people have vested interests in existing welfare programs to permit reform to occur. The only way in which change can occur is to placate the relevant interest groups by giving each one something it wants. Accordingly, the only changes in the welfare system that are likely to occur are incremental changes in benefit levels and in the number of people on the welfare rolls. In most previous attempts at welfare reform, the main accomplishment has been to *increase* both benefit levels and the number of recipients. The Reagan Administration is clearly determined to reverse this trend, but significant reductions are most unlikely. Indeed, the reductions proposed in 1981 were quite modest. They would merely slow the rate of growth of welfare expenditures. The modesty of this approach suggests that President Reagan has already learned the major lesson of welfare reform. As more and more people develop a stake in the existing system and as the process of incrementally increasing the welfare budget continues, movement toward a significantly different system becomes increasingly unlikely.

The realization that welfare reform is dead should help us focus attention on the real political issue concerning welfare — the amount of money going into the system. Indeed, for many of the participants in the welfare reform debate, this has always been the real issue. Some have stressed the reform side of their proposals for changing the system as a way of disguising their attempts to increase the welfare budget. Others have seized on reform as the only possible means of reducing welfare rolls, or at least reducing their rate of growth. Most political struggles are exactly of this sort. There are battles over the distribution of income in which each participant has a ''public interest'' argument to justify his request for a larger share of national income. It is not, therefore, terribly surprising that welfare reform is essentially the same kind of struggle and that it will be resolved on the basis of its political rather than economic merits (Stigler 1971).[2]

CHARACTERISTICS OF A GOOD WELFARE SYSTEM

Many proposals for welfare reform are floating around. Some would return welfare to the states; others would replace the existing program with non–income-conditioned programs, such as a children's allowance (see, e.g., Danziger, Garfinkel, and Haveman 1979). The most common proposal for welfare reform, however, is a comprehensive, unified negative income tax. None of these proposals is likely to replace what we have, but the impossibility of welfare reform does not mean that we are doomed to live with a terrible system. On the contrary, the existing system has a number of the features that many believe should be found in a good welfare system. Furthermore, it is not at all clear that any existing proposals for reform (were they miraculously enacted) would unambiguously improve the system.

There appears to be general agreement that a good welfare system will have the following characteristics: (1) adequate benefits, (2) vertical equity, (3) horizontal equity, (4) target efficiency, (5) administrative efficiency, (6) adequate work incentives, (7) adequate work opportunities, and (8) responsiveness to individual needs. Agreeing on the desirability of these characteristics, however, still leaves considerable room for disagreement. One source of disagreement is over the specifics of each of these features. As these terms are defined or discussed below, some of the problems involved in determining specific program characteristics become apparent:

1. *Adequate benefits.* The chief purpose of any welfare program is to provide some people with a better standard of living. But how much better? What is adequate? Is it poverty line income? 65% of poverty line income? 150%? And who should receive these adequate benefits? All people with low incomes? Only those "unable to work" or "not expected to work"?

2. *Vertical equity.* Families with higher pretransfer incomes should have higher posttransfer incomes, but how much higher? By the full differences in the pretransfer incomes? Or by some percentage? What percentage?

3. *Horizontal equity.* Families in similar circumstances should receive similar benefits. But what factors determine similar circumstances? How similar are the circumstances of a low-income family with two adults present to those of a family of the same size with only one adult present? How similar is a family with educated, skilled adults to a family with uneducated, unskilled adults?

4. *Target efficiency.* Benefits should be concentrated on those most in need, and the most assistance possible should be provided to the needy for each dollar of benefits delivered. But what is the best way to give assistance? Are cash payments or in-kind payments more efficient?

5. *Adequate work incentives.* For most economists, work incentives must be maintained by a low income guarantee and a low marginal tax rate (benefit-reduction rate).[3] Benefits must be reduced by less than one dollar for each dollar of earned income. But by how much? Does a marginal tax rate of 30% provide adequate incentives? Does 40%?

6. *Adequate work opportunities.* A desire to work is not enough; jobs must be available. This means that high aggregate demand is a necessary condition for a successful welfare program. But is it a sufficient condition? Or should government help create specific jobs for welfare recipients? Can this be done through private employers? Or are public sector jobs also required? If so, at what wage rates?

7. *Administrative efficiency.* The welfare system should deliver a given level of benefits at the lowest possible cost. This is a fairly straightforward proposition, but it is impossible to determine whether this goal has been achieved. Some people will always argue that there are too many bureaucrats employed by the system, while others will argue for hiring more people to reduce fraud or to provide more individual attention for people with special needs.

8. *Responsiveness to individual needs.* A good welfare system must be more than a computerized operation run from a central location. Welfare recipients have financial and other emergencies that require special or immediate assistance. Needs may vary regionally or seasonally. The critical question is: How many resources should be devoted to this feature of the welfare system?

The preceding discussion of the specifics of a welfare system may seem to belabor the obvious, but it does raise important issues that are often overlooked by critics of the existing system. Furthermore, the difficulty of giving specific content to each of the eight characteristics is increased by the fact that many of them, however specified, are incompatible with one another.

These incompatibilities are well known and do not require lengthy discussion. Most economists would argue that the most serious problem concerns the trade-off among benefit adequacy, target efficiency, horizontal equity, and adequate work incentives. If there is a uniform system of benefits (horizontal equity, according to some), and if benefits are adequate and go only to those who need them (target efficiency), then the marginal tax rate is high and work incentives are low. If such a system is target efficient and the income guarantee and the marginal tax rate are low enough to provide adequate work incentives, benefits for many people will be inadequate. If such a system provides adequate benefits to all in need and has a low enough tax rate to provide adequate work incentives, it will not be target efficient. Benefits will go to those not in need and the system will be rather expensive. Or a high income guarantee may reduce work incentives so much that even a zero marginal tax rate will not overcome the problem of inadequate work incentives.

These problems, which are inescapable with a uniform negative income tax (a single-track system), lead us to contemplate a system with two or more tracks. Such a system tries to maintain a better balance among benefit adequacy, work incentives, and target efficiency by establishing different categories of people. It provides high guaranteed benefits and high marginal tax rates for those who are unemployable or for those whose unemployment society is willing to subsidize (e.g., the elderly or single parents with young children). It provides lower guaranteed benefits and lower marginal tax rates for those who are considered employable. This approach raises the issue of horizontal equity; many believe that a two- (or more) track system violates the standard of similar treatment for those with similar needs. A further disadvantage of this approach is that administrative costs rise as the number of tracks increases. The United States, of course, suffers the above disadvantages of a multitrack system, and more. Not only are there a number of tracks, but they are not well coordinated. We have added track after track with apparently little thought to what each addition does to the *system*. But the result, for whatever reason, is something that seems to represent a reasonable compromise among our eight characteristics. Let us now go through each of them once again to see how this assertion can be supported.

WELFARE IN THE UNITED STATES

Adequate Benefits.   The most reasonable and most accepted definition of benefit adequacy is that benefits be high enough to eliminate poverty. In the United States, this goal has almost been reached, despite the relatively high Census Bureau or "official" estimates of the incidence of poverty. Although the census estimate of this incidence for 1979 is 11.3%, this figure is misleading. Census does not include the value of in-kind transfer payments when calculating the income of a household. Additionally, the census figures suffer from a substantial underreporting of cash income. Because of these two factors the Census Bureau substantially overstates the incidence of poverty in the United States, a fact that has been well demonstrated in a number of recent studies, including those by Smeeding (1977), the Congressional Budget Office (1977), and (in the present volume — chs. 5, 4, and 3, respectively) Paglin, Hoagland, and Danziger and Plotnick. The lowest estimate emerging from these studies is Paglin's 3.6% for 1976; the highest is Smeeding's 6.6% for 1972. Hoagland uses Smeeding's technique to come up with a 1980 forecast of 4.1%. Since it is based on the Congressional Budget Office's January 1980 economic forecasts, Hoagland's figure is probably lower than the same technique would produce using actual 1980 economic conditions. Paglin's method, however, would undoubtedly lead to a 1980 estimate of less than 3%, since it includes some in-kind transfers omitted by Smeeding and Hoagland, and uses the market value of in-kind transfers, whereas Smeeding and Hoagland deflate market value to their cash-equivalent values.

There remains the issue of whether the value of in-kind medical transfers should be included in a household's income. A good case can be made that at least part of these payments should be excluded. Hoagland's estimates of the 1980 incidence of poverty, when medical transfers are excluded, is 6.1%. Thus, without arguing over the relative merits of how in-kind transfers should be valued, one can reasonably estimate that the incidence of poverty in the United States is between 3% and 6%. It has fallen so low that one is tempted to claim that the war on poverty has almost been won. Accordingly, on the most important of all eight criteria — benefit adequacy — the current welfare system must receive a passing grade.

There is, however, one important qualification to this conclusion about benefit adequacy. Because the incidence of poverty in the South is approximately twice as high as in the North (Smeeding 1977; Congressional Budget Office 1977), it is difficult to argue that benefits in the former region are adequate. This situation would have been greatly improved by enactment of the Social Welfare Reform Amendments of 1979 (SWRA). This bill, which passed the House of Representatives in 1979, called for two major changes in the AFDC program. It required all states to provide AFDC–Unemployed Parents (making two-parent families eligible for AFDC), and it mandated a minimum benefit level of AFDC plus food stamps equal to 65% of poverty line income by 1981. Of the 15 states in which AFDC plus food stamp benefits were less than 65% of poverty income in 1979, 13 were in the South. Of the 24 states without AFDC–UP, 12 were in the South. Thus SWRA would have greatly reduced the grounds for qualifying the conclusion that benefits are adequate. But SWRA is dead, and there is little likelihood of similar legislation emerging from the 97th Congress. Any major reduction in poverty in the South in the early 1980s will have to come from earned income, not from transfer payments.

Vertical Equity.   Our welfare system falls short in terms of vertical equity, since it is possible for families on welfare to receive more income than families in which a member is working full-time. This can be true within a state, where some families are eligible for AFDC and others are not, and it is certainly true among states. A welfare family in a high-benefit state may well have a higher income than a working family in a low-benefit state (where wages as well as benefits tend to be low).

Nevertheless, it is not clear that such inequities should be eliminated. The costs of eliminating them may be too high, not necessarily in dollar costs, but in terms of other goals that must be sacrificed to achieve vertical equity. There are three main sources of vertical inequity: (1) some programs (primarily AFDC, Medicaid, and SSI) vary by state; (2) there is a multitrack system (some classes of people are eligible for more benefits than others); and (3) marginal tax rates are less than 100%. The first two items affect horizontal equity also and will be discussed later. Marginal tax rates of less than 100% mean that families can continue receiving benefits after their income rises above the level that made them eligible for a program. Raising marginal tax rates might raise the degree of vertical equity, but it would presumably lower work incentives.

Another remedy for the vertical inequity problem would be to make it easier for working families to receive benefits. This, of course, would lower target efficiency and perhaps work incentives. A partial remedy that has been implemented is the earned income tax credit (EITC). The EITC does add another program to the system, but its administrative cost should be fairly low. And in addition to increasing the degree of vertical equity, it increases work incentives, since it establishes a lower marginal tax rate on earned income than on unearned income.[4]

Horizontal Equity.   To many observers, the high degree of horizontal inequity is the worst feature of the existing welfare system. As in the case of vertical inequity, horizontal inequity is attributed largely to differences among states and the multitrack system.

Consider first the interstate differences. Some states have much higher AFDC benefits than others, and in some states two-parent families are eligible for AFDC, while in others only one-parent families are eligible. In some states only AFDC families are eligible for Medicaid, while elsewhere other low-income families and individuals may receive Medicaid benefits. It is difficult to justify these differences using any of our eight criteria for a welfare system. Nevertheless, it is highly unlikely that all interstate differences will ever be eliminated; nor should they be. Given the uncertainty about how welfare affects behavior, some diversity among state systems might be worth encouraging. Furthermore, if a state wants to provide higher benefits than other states or more than Congress is willing to appropriate, it is difficult to argue that it should not be allowed to do so. The issue, then, really becomes one of benefit adequacy rather than uniform national benefits (more on this subject shortly).

The main sources of intrastate inequality are also AFDC and Medicaid. Only families (in some states, only single-parent families) with dependent children are eligible for AFDC, and in some states only those families receiving AFDC benefits are eligible for Medicaid. Thus, in some states, low-income single individuals and couples (with or without children) can receive neither AFDC nor Medicaid, and, unless they are elderly, blind, or disabled, public assistance for them is limited essentially to food stamps. This is indeed inequality, but how deplorable is it? A multitrack system appears to be both inevitable and desirable. It is the only way of achieving reasonably low marginal tax rates on earned income without sacrificing too much in the way of target efficiency. The current system is a multitrack one, with the general qualities that one would hope to have in such a system — greater guaranteed benefits and higher marginal tax rates for those not expected to work. The critical question as to the acceptability of this system is whether the guaranteed income for those expected to work is so low that the system is unacceptable.

In answering this question, let us refer back to the discussion of benefit adequacy. If poverty in the United States has been virtually eradicated, then the benefits, however unequal, are adequate. Given the very low benefit levels in some states, there may be readers who continue to resist this conclusion. One must, however, admit that the end result is better than one might judge by looking solely at guaranteed benefit levels.

Target Efficiency.   The system is not target efficient, but certainly no one expects 100% efficiency. Furthermore, it is difficult to find suggestions that would be likely to improve target efficiency significantly (unless one believes there is a tremendous amount of welfare fraud) without sacrificing benefit adequacy or increasing marginal tax rates (and reducing work incentives).[5] A possible exception would be to replace in-kind benefits with cash payments, but not everyone agrees that all benefits should be in cash.

Adequate Work Incentives.   The impact of welfare on work incentives has been debated for years and continues to be debated. The more papers this economist reads on this subject, however, the more he feels inclined to return to the old intuition or theory that, *ceteris paribus,* the higher the marginal tax rate, the lower the incentive to work. Much of the recent work in this area suggests that a high income guarantee reduces work incentives more than does a high marginal tax rate (see Moffitt, present volume, ch. 11). If work incentives are significantly affected by income guarantees or marginal tax rates, one is led to the conclusion that a multitrack system is the only reasonably target efficient (and politically feasible) method of achieving adequate benefits. In general, in the United States, the less likely a family head is to work or the less reason there is to encourage that person to work, the more welfare programs the person is eligible for, the higher the benefits, and the higher the marginal tax rate. (The marginal tax rate rises as the number of income-conditioned programs one is participating in rises.) The system, in effect, has a sliding scale of marginal tax rates. Similarly, it has a sliding scale of guaranteed incomes. A person's placement at a particular point on each of those sliding scales is not dependent upon an official determination of the degree to which that person is expected to work. But roughly speaking, these points on the scale are determined by society's level of expectation that the person work: the lower those expectations, the more programs one is eligible for, the more benefits one receives, and the higher the marginal tax rate. It is not entirely inconceivable that this system is more efficient and more humane than a uniform negative income tax or a system such as Carter's PBJI, in which an individual is officially categorized as either expected to work or not expected to work.

Adequate Work Opportunities.   The work opportunities aspect of the welfare problem has received increased emphasis recently. In part, this is due to the growing realization that further expansion of transfer programs is a very expensive way to get at the relatively small number of people still living in poverty. Additionally, for those people who are expected to work, continued reliance on transfer programs is not a very satisfactory solution to the problem of low income. Most of them would be better off if they were working, and certainly society as a whole would much prefer that they worked. Thus, for some observers, the existing welfare system (and the entire economy) falls short of meeting the criterion of adequate work opportunities.

There is no doubt that it is difficult for poorly educated, unskilled workers to find decent jobs. Table 2.1, however, suggests that the inability to find work is not currently the major cause of poverty in the United States.[6] Given this information in Table 2.1, the high employment rate in recent years, and the low incidence of poverty in this country, this observer is willing to give the system a passing grade in the category of work opportunities.

Administrative Efficiency.   Measuring efficiency, especially efficiency in government, is always a difficult task and will not be attempted here. The plethora of welfare programs and program overlap in the United States undoubtedly causes more resources to be devoted to administration than would be the case in an ideal system. This paper has argued that a multitrack system is desirable, but not necessarily that we must have a multiprogram system. The political reality of the situation, however, holds little promise for program consolidation. The possible cashing out of food stamps for SSI recipients is one small step in this direction,

Table 2.1.   Reasons for Not Working, or Working Less than 50 Weeks, for Poor Unrelated Individuals and Heads of Poor Families, 1977

| | *Percentage of All* | | | |
Reason for Not Working, or Working Less than 50 Weeks	*Poor Unrelated Individuals*	*Poor Families*	*Poor Families with Head Aged 22–64*	*Poor Families with Children 18 and Under*
Unable to find work	11.1	15.2	17.1	17.6
Ill or disabled	24.9	18.1	17.5	14.8
Keeping house	21.5	29.7	31.2	35.6
Going to school	12.2	3.7	3.3	4.0
Retired	12.5	7.7	1.7	1.8
Other	8.4	4.0	5.6	4.7
Total[a]	90.6	78.4	76.4	78.5

SOURCE: U.S. Bureau of the Census.

[a]The difference between this number and 100.0 is the percentage that worked 50 weeks or more.

but even this approach is not without its perils, as Giertz and Sullivan show later in this book.

Responsiveness to Individual Needs.   A welfare system should be more than a mechanism that treats everyone in exactly the same way. In discussing work incentives, it was suggested that the variety of programs in the United States serves a useful purpose. It permits a sliding scale of guaranteed incomes and marginal tax rates that apply to persons more or less in accordance with their needs.

A welfare system should also be more than a device for transferring income from one group of people to another. People often require personal assistance for their own special problems. The hard and fast eligibility requirements concerning assets and income can be helpfully interpreted and modified by a sympathetic administrator. Certainly some discretion by local authorities who administer some programs seems desirable.

It is difficult to evaluate how well the system responds to individual needs or even to specify what would be the optimal degree of responsiveness. The main point of the above discussion is to remind the reader that there is some responsiveness in the existing system and that welfare reform does not (or should not) entail abolition of all local control and discretion in administering welfare programs.

CONCLUSION

This paper has set forth two basic reasons why welfare reform's time has come and gone. The first is that reform, or a significant change in the structure of this system, is no longer (if it ever was) politically possible. Too many people have a stake in the existing system to permit changes that are significant enough to be labeled reform. Those with a stake in the existing system include more than welfare recipients and those responsible for administering the systems. For example, organized labor strongly opposes two proposals that many people consider essential to welfare reform — low-wage public sector jobs and a lower minimum wage.

The second reason for suggesting that we forget about welfare reform is that the existing system is reasonably satisfactory. Certainly, the strong opposition to reform suggests that it is reasonably satisfactory to many people, but the argument is stronger than that (not merely that reform would reduce the incomes of a number of people and should, therefore, be avoided). Basically, the existing system represents a relatively satisfactory mixture of the features we would like to see in a welfare system. Furthermore, movement toward a more unified federal system would not necessarily improve the system, since for every benefit generated by reforms, there will also be a cost. On balance, it is not entirely obvious that the net benefits would be positive.

Much of the argument over welfare reform avoids getting into the specifics of a welfare system, particularly concerning the trade-offs among the various goals. Some of the debate over welfare reform, therefore, is based on ignorance or unwillingness to get bogged down in specifics. One suspects, however, that most of the pressures for changes in the system stem from unhappiness with the amount of money going into the system: some want more; some want less. Or perhaps it would be more accurate to say that some want to increase the rate of growth of welfare payments, while others want to decrease it. Fundamentally, that is what the battle over welfare reform is all about: How much money will go into the welfare system?

Welfare reform is dead; the issue is now (as it always really has been) the size of the welfare budget. Some of the traditional welfare reform issues, however, remain pertinent to the debate over the size of the welfare budget. Benefit adequacy remains the primary criterion, but if poverty in the United States has been virtually eliminated, then benefit adequacy is no longer the major issue. One may indeed wish to increase benefits beyond the poverty line, but increasing attention must now be paid to the other aspects of the welfare system.

The issue of work incentives appears to be especially important. Given the existing set of programs, benefit increases mean higher guaranteed incomes and higher marginal tax rates. Any increases in benefits that are likely to occur are likely to reduce work incentives, especially for those most likely to be employable or expected to work. Further increases in benefits may also have significant macroeconomic consequences. What are the implications for unemployment, inflation, and productivity of devoting a rising share of GNP to welfare programs? And what are the possible effects of the higher taxes needed to support the higher welfare payments? Clearly, the Reagan Administration believes that the supply-side consequence of high taxes is to keep the economy from growing. This means, according to the Administration, fewer jobs and less opportunity for people to work their way out of poverty.

It appears, therefore, that the major welfare issue has become something other than welfare reform. The basic question today is whether we should continue to increase welfare benefits when doing so may have a significant impact on the size and rate of growth of national income, and not just an impact on its distribution. This, not welfare reform, is the welfare issue of the 1980s.

NOTES

1. Weil's account is an excellent description of the political obstacles to welfare reform encountered in the struggle to enact Carter's Program for Better Jobs and Income in 1978.

2. Stigler's theory of economic regulation applies to welfare reform as well as to regulation. This theory views regulation (or any economic legislation) as a means of transferring wealth and treats it as a product to be allocated in accordance with the principles of supply and demand. It is, therefore, allocated to those with the highest effective demand. Stigler shows that the groups with the highest effective demand will usually be relatively small. Thus, when wealth is transferred there are more losers than winners, but the gain per winner will exceed the loss per loser.

3. The marginal tax rate is the rate at which benefits are reduced when additional income is earned. For example, a marginal tax rate of .50 means that welfare payments are reduced by 50 cents for every dollar earned.

4. SWRA would have increased the EITC.

5. Danziger and Plotnick (present volume, ch. 3) state that a proportional increase in existing transfer programs would be only 5% target efficient in reducing poverty.

6. The figures in Table 2.1 would be different if the Smeeding (et al.) approach to estimating poverty were used. However, the total number of poor family heads or unrelated individuals would still likely be a small fraction of the total number of family heads and unrelated individuals.

REFERENCES

Congressional Budget Office, U.S. Congress. 1977. *Poverty Status of Families under Alternative Definitions of Income.* Washington, D.C.: U.S. Government Printing Office.

Danziger, Sheldon; Garfinkel, Irwin; and Haveman, Robert H. 1979. "Poverty, Welfare, and Earnings: A New Approach." *Challenge* 22 (September-October):28–34.

Smeeding, Timothy M. 1977. "The Antipoverty Effectiveness of In-Kind Transfers." *Journal of Human Resources* 12 (Summer):360–78.

Stigler, George. 1971. "The Theory of Economic Regulation." *Bell Journal of Economics and Management Science* 2 (Spring):3–21.

Weil, Gordon. 1978. *The Welfare Debate of 1978.* White Plains, N.Y.: Institute for Socioeconomic Studies.

II BENCHMARKS

It is possible to gain considerable insight into the questions of where we are and what is ahead in the war on poverty by refining our measures of the poor. The effectiveness of our antipoverty effort thus far and the current dimension of the problem depend in large part on how we define poverty. Unfortunately, there has been much confusion in the evaluation of present welfare policies owing to the various measures of income used. The difference in viewpoints presented in part II depends largely on how income is measured.

Sheldon Danziger and Robert Plotnick define two types of thresholds — absolute and relative — and four major income concepts — pretransfer, prewelfare, posttransfer, and adjusted. When, for example, official census data are adjusted for underreporting of incomes, payment of federal income and Social Security taxes, and receipt of in-kind transfers, the authors show that the incidence of poverty since 1965 has been dramatically reduced. Yet, when we look at income derived only from market sources or what the authors call *pretransfer income* (e.g., wages and property income), no decline in the incidence of poverty is revealed. The trend in relative poverty, regardless of the income concept chosen, also provides a less optimistic view: no downward trend. Above all else, the main merit of the empirical work by Danziger and Plotnick is that it demonstrates why divergent views regarding the outcome of the war on poverty are held by various analysts. According to some measures, welfare programs have done much to reduce measured poverty; according to others, they have not.

The paper by G. William Hoagland examines the effectiveness of government assistance programs in reducing the incidence of poverty between 1976 and 1980. Like Danziger and Plotnick, he, too, appeals to various income concepts and types of poverty threshold. The brief discussion of the connection between welfare politics and anti-inflation concerns is both useful and timely. The explanation of the simulation model, although more technical than the material or methods in the other papers, provides the reader with a good picture of how estimates of the poor are generated. The new generation of budget-cutters may find some comfort in Hoagland's conclusion that the recent decline in the growth rate of social welfare expenditures since 1975 has not seriously reduced the effectiveness of the current transfer system.

The data series on adjusted income poverty has led some analysts, notably Morton Paglin, to conclude that the war on poverty has almost been won. The 3% of Americans at or below the poverty threshold are resistant to transfer programs because, argues Paglin, they are "phantom poor," statistical anomalies rather than truly needy. His review of alternate poverty estimates and the conceptual differences between his and other studies of the poor result in a paper that complements the Danziger-Plotnick paper very well.

3 THE WAR ON INCOME POVERTY:
Achievements and Failures
Sheldon Danziger and Robert Plotnick

The history of antipoverty policy since the war on poverty began is one of significant policy changes. New programs were introduced and old programs were expanded; the emphasis of the federal budget shifted from military spending toward social welfare spending; the Office of Economic Opportunity was created and then dismantled; and all domestic policies came to be asked the question What Does It Do for the Poor? (Lampman 1974). The prevailing view at the outset of the war on poverty, expressed not only in President Johnson's speeches, but in academic journals as well, was optimistic — government actions could solve the poverty problem if enough resources were focused on the task, and if the economy experienced stable economic growth.

This research was supported in part by funds granted to the Institute for Research on Poverty at the University of Wisconsin (Madison) by the U.S. Department of Health, Education, and Welfare pursuant to the Economic Opportunity Act of 1964. The authors wish to thank G. William Hoagland and Timothy Smeeding for provision of the data on adjusted incomes, and Peter Gottschalk, George Jakubson, Robert Lampman, and Eugene Smolensky for helpful comments on a previous draft.

This optimism soured by the late 1960s, as the war in Vietnam replaced the war on poverty in the headlines and helped destroy faith in the government's ability to solve any problem. The arguments that problems could not be solved by "throwing money" at them and that the antipoverty attempts had failed were increasingly heard. In this pessimistic view of the early 1970s, the programs of the war on poverty were "poorly planned, passed in haste, inadequately funded" and hence programs that accomplished little (Aaron 1978). A radical expression of this view is exemplified by a book that appeared in 1973 — *How We Lost the War on Poverty* (Pilisuk and Pilisuk) — and also by Grönbjerg, Street, and Suttles (1978), who argue:

> The dramatic failure of the antipoverty program of the 1960s must be understood not simply as a whistling of reform against the wind of laissez-faire, but also as a prime example of the weakness of the American conception of reform. (P. 160)

In the late 1970s, a revisionist view gained credence. Its boldest expression asserts that rather than having been lost, the war on poverty has been won. Martin Anderson (1978), now domestic policy adviser to the Reagan Administration, concludes:

> The "war on poverty" that began in 1964 has been won. The growth of jobs and income in the private economy, combined with an explosive increase in government spending for welfare and income transfer programs, has virtually eliminated poverty in the United States. (P. 37)

Of course, not everyone subscribes to one of these two polar positions; many analysts would place themselves at various points in between.

These conflicting views of the results of the war on poverty influence not only the evaluation of the past fifteen years of antipoverty policy, but also guide prescriptions for the future. The view that the war on poverty was a dramatic failure gives rise to the conclusion that nothing can be done, that government antipoverty policy cannot alter the structure of economic opportunity or economic rewards. The view that the war on poverty has been won, which seems to have been adopted by the Reagan Administration, implies that no more *need* be done, that the problem has been solved, and that no new initiatives are in order.

This paper presents an evaluation of the war on poverty that lends some support to each of these opposing views. The contradictory evaluations arise because of differences over the goals of the war on poverty and the definition of poverty itself. We suggest that the answer to Has the War on Poverty Been Won? is neither a simple yes nor a simple no.

We derive our answer in the sections that follow. First, we review the background and goals of the war on poverty, and then analyze the trend in poverty, using a range of measures. We conclude that progress against poverty has been made, but if it is to be further reduced — if the war on poverty is to be won — antipoverty policy must shift away from the current reliance on income transfers. We advocate a redirection of policies toward one of the original goals of the war on poverty — the elimination of poverty for those who can work, through the enhancement of earned incomes.

THE WAR ON POVERTY

In the early 1960s, there were no official estimates of the nature or extent of poverty in the United States. The term *poverty* did not appear in government studies or programs, and a comprehensive bibliography of available research on the subject ran only a few pages. Since the Great Depression of the 1930s, little attention had been paid to poverty as a societal problem. Few legislative initiatives explicitly designed to aid the poor had been proposed. Economic policymakers in the post–World War II period had focused instead on full employment and economic growth. The conventional wisdom held that as the economy prospered, living standards would increase for all and poverty would wither away.[1]

Two influential books — *The Affluent Society,* by John Kenneth Galbraith (1958), and *The Other America,* by Michael Harrington (1962) — challenged this conventional view. Galbraith and Harrington spoke of the "forgotten" and "invisible" poor and advocated direct government action against poverty. More important than the details of their arguments was their success in calling public attention to the plight of the poor.

President Kennedy is said to have been influenced by the poverty he had observed while campaigning in West Virginia during the 1960 presidential primary, and by Harrington's book. In 1963, he asked Walter Heller, Chairman of the Council of Economic Advisers, for background information on the poverty problem. An analysis by Robert Lampman, a member of the Council's staff, concluded that although poverty had been declining since 1947, the rate of decline had slowed since 1956. Lampman's analysis supported the view that high levels of employment and economic growth, while necessary, would not prove sufficient for a high rate of poverty reduction.

After Kennedy's assassination, President Johnson pushed forward with the planning and analysis of various proposals to aid those with low incomes. In his first State of the Union speech in January 1964, he declared the War on Poverty and, shortly thereafter, transmitted to Congress the 1964 *Economic Report of the President,* which contained the first official analysis of poverty. This important document presented the conceptual foundation on which the war on poverty was based, provided an official definition of poverty (although this definition was later revised), analyzed the extent of poverty, and outlined a set of antipoverty initiatives.

The report listed a broad range of policy instruments: maintaining high employment, accelerating economic growth, fighting discrimination, improving regional economies, rehabilitating urban and rural communities, improving labor markets, expanding educational opportunities, enlarging job opportunities for youth, improving health, promoting adult education and training, and assisting the aged and disabled. It was expected that the achievement of some of these goals would directly reduce poverty, while the achievement of others would do so indirectly. The report recognized the complexity of the poverty problem and cautioned that no single program could meet the needs of all the poor.

The comprehensiveness of the strategies listed by the Council of Economic Advisers signaled a reorientation of all domestic policies toward a concern with poverty. Robert Lampman has argued that the very declaration of the war on poverty had an almost immediate and lasting effect — it required all existing programs and proposals for policy changes to address the question What Does It Do for the Poor?

In the months following the declaration, a wide variety of initiatives was proposed by the Johnson Administration and enacted by Congress. One of these, the cornerstone of the war on poverty, was the Economic Opportunity Act. The act created the Office of Economic Opportunity (OEO), the agency responsible for directing and coordinating the antipoverty effort, several programs designed to train young people (e.g., Job Corps, Neighborhood Youth Corps), the Community Action Program, several rural assistance programs, the Work Experience Program for welfare recipients, and VISTA, the domestic counterpart of the Peace Corps.

The primary focus of the direct OEO attack on poverty was to help the young achieve better employment opportunities and higher wages. The first year appropriations for all the titles of the Economic Opportunity Act, about $1 billion, were substantially smaller than the $20 billion of income transfers from existing government programs received by the poor in 1965. However, the indirect effects generated by OEO and the war on poverty were to become large and reach most of the poor, particularly the aged.

Neither the report of the Council nor the Economic Opportunity Act proposed either a public jobs program or an increase in cash assistance (except for the aged and disabled), although these were advocated by several policymakers at the time. Such approaches were not proposed because they were inconsistent with the prevailing view of the causes of poverty.

This view was apparently based on the assumptions that (1) a sufficient number of jobs existed in the private economy or could be generated through Keynesian policies to bolster aggregate demand (such as the 1964 tax cut); (2) at the core of the poverty problem were the inadequate levels of education and training of poor individuals; and (3) the antipoverty strategy had to be consistent with the American work ethic. Given these assumptions, an antipoverty strategy that stressed the delivery of services to the poor, rather than proposing major changes in the labor market or a guaranteed income, was in order. The view that poverty could be eliminated by "adapting and enriching" the poor was consistent with both the "culture of poverty" perspective and the human capital model and, thus, was widely held. Moreover, the American work ethic — "If you work hard, you will get ahead" — called for programs that provided an opportunity to escape poverty by one's own efforts, rather than programs that provided cash assistance. It was recognized, of course, that this approach would only work for those who could participate in the labor force, especially those who were able-bodied and nonaged.

There were recognized flaws that impeded the smooth functioning of labor markets — discrimination, inadequate labor market information — but these could be remedied by government actions (e.g., antidiscrimination legislation, the Employment Service) that did not require public provision of jobs. Policies to foster high employment and economic growth could increase demand for the labor of the poor, while education and training programs could increase the quantity and quality of the labor the poor supplied. The poor could then escape poverty in the same manner as the nonpoor — through the private labor market.

This emphasis on the provision of opportunity rather than on the direct provision of jobs or income maintenance was reflected in Johnson's remarks of 20 August 1964 when he signed the Economic Opportunity Act:

> We are not content to accept the endless growth of relief rolls or welfare rolls. We want to offer the forgotten fifth of our people opportunity and not doles.
>
> That is what this measure does for our times.
>
> Our American answer to poverty is not to make the poor more secure in their poverty, but to reach down and to help them lift themselves out of the

ruts of poverty and move with the large majority along the high road of hope
and prosperity.

The days of the dole in this country are numbered.

Perhaps as important as the antidole philosophy was the expectation that
either a jobs program or an income maintenance program (or both) would
be very expensive, and could not be financed without a tax increase.

Closely connected to the war on poverty were the larger goals of the
Great Society. While the war on poverty attempted to increase the resources available to the poorest citizens, the goals of the Great Society
were broader and included, according to the 1965 *Economic Report of
the President,* meeting the challenge of urbanization, educating citizens,
raising health standards, reducing poverty, and assuring equality of opportunity. The central focus was the reduction of discrimination against
and the enhancement of opportunity for the disadvantaged, but improvements in the physical and social environment were expected to benefit
all citizens.

The banner of the Great Society stretched beyond the goals of eliminating poverty and providing equal opportunity to the transformation of
a wide range of societal institutions. Changes in the political and legal
context had to be concomitant with those in the economic arena. Thus,
the Community Action Program was to foster citizen participation and
power, the Legal Services Program to give the poor an equal chance in
the courtrooms, and the Model Cities Program to revitalize urban centers.
Legislation during this period was influenced not only by the concepts of
the Great Society and the War on Poverty, but also by the goals of the
Civil Rights Movement. Unprecedented social legislation expanded the
scope of the American social welfare system and brought the federal
government into areas previously reserved for state and local governments or the private sector.

This brief history of the War on Poverty foreshadows the sources of
the divergent views regarding the outcome of the war that came to be
held by various analysts in the late 1970s. Poverty emerged during the
1960s as a "paradox in the midst of plenty," at a time when there was
little experience on which to draw, few experts who could be called upon
for advice, and no detailed plan of action awaiting implementation. What
emerges from the report of the Council of Economic Advisers and from
Johnson's speeches is a commitment to an attack on poverty based on
the view that the poor could be changed and/or given an opportunity to
work their way out of poverty.

Nonetheless, there was no agreement on the nature or definition of poverty or on the specific means for attack. Enthusiasm for the effort encouraged rhetorical excesses, such as Johnson's promise of "total victory." These raised expectations so high that progress, if short of the total elimination of poverty, has been judged a failure by some critics. Other observers have pointed out the achievement of the national goal, citing as evidence a large decline in measured poverty. But they have not addressed the means by which the reduction in poverty was achieved.

We now turn to an examination of the central goal of the war on poverty — the elimination of income poverty. We discuss not only the progress that has been made, but also the process by which change has occurred.[2]

THE TREND IN POVERTY: THE EVIDENCE

An analysis of income poverty requires the specification of both a poverty threshold and an income concept. A household is considered poor if its income falls below the poverty threshold. Different poverty thresholds and income concepts convey different information about the nature and magnitude of the poverty problem. Rather than select a single measure of poverty, our analysis is based on a set of measures derived from two types of thresholds — absolute and relative — and four income concepts — pretransfer, prewelfare, posttransfer, and adjusted income. We begin by describing the official definition of poverty. Then we introduce the other measures and evaluate the trend in poverty since 1965.

The federal government's official measure of poverty provides a set of income cutoffs adjusted for inflation, family size, age and sex of family head, number of children under age 18, and farm-nonfarm residence. The cutoffs provide an *absolute poverty threshold,* which specifies in dollar terms minimally decent levels of consumption possibilities for families of different types. For 1978, the official poverty thresholds range from $2,650 for a single aged female living on a farm to $11,038 for a two-parent family of seven or more persons not living on a farm. The archtypical nonfarm family of four had a cutoff of $6,665.

The official income concept is current money income received during the calendar year.[3] Current money income does not include government or private benefits in-kind (e.g., Food Stamps, Medicare benefits, employer-provided health insurance), nor does it subtract taxes, although these factors affect a household's command over resources. We refer to the official income concept as *posttransfer* income.

Some writers have argued that absolute poverty thresholds, such as the official ones, fail to measure adequately changes in poverty in a society with an increasing standard of living. They conclude that persons whose incomes fall well below the prevailing average in their society are regarded as poor by that society, no matter what their absolute incomes may be. Thus, they advocate relative poverty thresholds that vary directly with average income.

To reflect this concern about income inequality, we use *relative poverty thresholds* in addition to the official ones. In 1965, the first year for which we present detailed data, we set the relative poverty lines equal to the official absolute ones. (In 1965, the official lines were equal to about 45% of the median income.) In succeeding years the relative lines are changed at the same rate as the median income.[4] With this approach, trends in absolute and relative poverty are easily compared because they begin with the same base-year value. In applying the relative thresholds, we use the posttransfer income concept employed by the official measure.

We can apply the absolute and relative lines to three income concepts in addition to posttransfer income. Posttransfer income does not distinguish between income derived from market sources (e.g., wages, property income) and income derived from government sources (e.g., Social Security, Public Assistance). As such, it fails to separate the market's antipoverty performance from the performance of government cash transfer programs. Our second income concept, *pretransfer income,* makes this distinction. Families and unrelated individuals who do not receive enough money income from market sources to raise themselves over the poverty lines constitute the pretransfer poor (a more exact title would be *pre–government-transfer poor*). Because pretransfer income is always less than or equal to posttransfer income, this concept suggests a larger poverty population.

A related measure of income is *prewelfare income.* While pretransfer income does not count any money income from government programs, prewelfare income excludes only income from public assistance (i.e., welfare) programs. Social insurance benefits (e.g., Social Security, unemployment insurance) are included in prewelfare income because they do not depend on the current income of the recipient. They are based on the individual's (or sometimes, spouse's) past earnings and contributions, and are received because of retirement, disability, unemployment, work injury, or death. Thus, social insurance benefits are generally perceived by the public as earned. For many, the "real" poverty population, the one to whom antipoverty policy should be addressed, is the prewelfare poor.

Our fourth concept, *adjusted income,* corrects three flaws in the data used to measure poverty that bias estimates of the poverty population. First, posttransfer income does not include in-kind income provided by government sources. Since these benefits increase a family's command over resources, their exclusion leads to an overestimate of the poverty population. Second, many persons misreport (underreport) their incomes. The official statistics make only a partial correction for underreporting; so this defect also overestimates the number of low-income persons. Third, direct taxes are ignored, and so the amount of income available for household consumption spending is overstated. Because the official lines represent the cost of minimally decent levels of consumption, not adjusting for taxes underestimates the size of the poverty population.

The adjusted income concept confronts these three problems. We use data that have been corrected for income underreporting, and to which the amount of in-kind income each living unit receives from the largest government in-kind programs has been added, and from which federal income and Social Security tax liabilities have been subtracted. These corrections yield a better measure of the income actually available to each household for consumption spending than does the official approach.

We now present our analysis of the trends in poverty using these four income concepts and these two types of poverty threshold.[5] Explanations for these trends are offered in the next section. The different measures of poverty lead to divergent conclusions about how much progress against poverty has been made since 1965. While absolute pretransfer poverty has remained constant throughout this period, adjusted income poverty has been dramatically reduced. The trends in relative poverty for each of the income concepts show a less favorable trend.

Table 3.1 presents the trend in the incidence of poverty among persons for each poverty measure. We first discuss the trends in absolute poverty, shown in the top panel, then briefly consider the relative data, shown in the lower panel.

Pretransfer Poverty.   The size of the pretransfer poverty population has received little attention, primarily because such data are not published by the Census Bureau. This information is essential for policy analysis. For example, a goal of the war on poverty was to provide an opportunity for poor persons to earn their way out of poverty. The pretransfer poverty statistics suggest how many and what kinds of persons need skill training, job placement assistance, and, perhaps, public employment.

A striking pattern emerges from column 1. The level of absolute pretransfer poverty was nearly stagnant during the period. In 1965, 21% of all persons were pretransfer poor. The incidence declined from 1965

Table 3.1.   Trends in the Incidence of Poverty among Persons

Poverty Measure, Year	Income Concept			
	Pretransfer Income	Prewelfare Income	Posttransfer Income	Adjusted Income[a]
Absolute				
1965	21.3%	16.3%	15.6%	12.1%
1968	18.2	13.6	12.8	10.1
1970	18.8	—	12.6	9.4
1972	19.2	13.1	11.9	6.2
1974	20.3	13.1	11.6	7.8
1976	21.0	13.1	11.8	5.9
1978	20.2	12.6	11.4	—
1980	—	—	—	4.1
% change, 1965–1978[b]	− 5.2	−22.7	−26.9	−66.1
Relative				
1965	21.3%	16.3%	15.6%	
1968	19.7	15.3	14.6	
1970	20.8	—	15.1	
1972	22.2	—	15.7	
1974	22.9	16.1	14.9	
1976	24.1	16.3	15.4	
1978	23.9	16.5	15.5	
% change, 1965–1978[b]	+12.2	+ 1.2	− 0.6	

SOURCE: Unless noted otherwise, the data are computations by the authors from the Survey of Economic Opportunity (for 1965) and various March Current Population Surveys (for other years).

[a]Adjusted income for 1968–1972 is taken from Smeeding 1975. For 1965, it is extrapolated from Smeeding's 1968 result. For 1974, it is computed according to methods developed by Smeeding. For 1976 and 1980, see chapter 4, present volume, by G. William Hoagland. Hoagland's data are for fiscal years and are only roughly comparable with earlier years because of methodological differences. All adjusted estimates for 1965–1980 include benefits from Food Stamps, Medicare, and Medicaid. The 1972, 1976, and 1980 estimates also include public housing; the latter two also include school lunch benefits.

[b]Percentage change for adjusted income poverty is for 1965–1980, not 1965–1978.

to 1968, but returned to over 20% by 1974, and has remained at that level.

Prewelfare Poverty.   Prewelfare poverty data have also not received much attention and are also not published, even though this concept is relevant for welfare reform debates. In 1965, 16.3% of all persons were prewelfare poor (column 2). Owing partly to a strong labor market and partly to increased social insurance transfers, prewelfare poverty declined to 13.6% in 1968. Since 1968, despite a substantial increase in real social insurance benefits, prewelfare poverty has barely declined; it was 12.6% in 1978.

Posttransfer Poverty.   The incidence of posttransfer poverty (the official measure) declined by about 27% between 1965 and 1978. Again, most of the decline occurred before the 1970s. Poverty in 1978, 11.4%, was only 1.4 percentage points below the 1968 value.

Adjusted Poverty.   When census data are adjusted for underreporting of incomes, payment of federal income and payroll taxes, and receipt of in-kind transfers, a major decline in the incidence of poverty is revealed (column 4). While 12.1% were poor in 1965, adjusted poverty was cut by two-thirds. Only 4.1% were poor in 1980.[6]
    The adjusted poverty data have led some analysts to conclude that the war on poverty has been won. Yet, an incidence of 4.1% for the entire population means that about 9 million persons remain poor. And among some subgroups, even adjusted levels of poverty remain quite high. For example, in 1976 about $1/5$ of persons living in households headed by nonaged black females, $1/9$ living with white females, and $1/10$ living with black males remained poor. While the adjusted data do suggest that substantial progress against poverty has been made, they should not deflect concern away from the problem that remains.

Relative Poverty.   For the three income concepts shown, the relative measure provides a less optimistic view — a higher level of poverty in each year and no downward trend. Relative pretransfer poverty, 23.9% in 1978, was 12.2% higher than its 1965 level. Relative prewelfare and posttransfer poverty have fluctuated only slightly during the period, and remain at about 16% and 15%, respectively.

Poverty Gap.   The incidence of poverty, as shown in Table 3.1, reveals the percentage of persons whose incomes fall below the poverty threshold, but does not distinguish the degree of poverty. The *poverty gap,* which measures the total amount of income required to bring every poor person up to the poverty threshold, does distinguish between poor persons who are very close to being nonpoor and those who are farther away from the thresholds. The data on the magnitude of the poverty gap (table not shown), computed for each of our poverty thresholds and income concepts, conform to our conclusions on the incidence. Greater progress against poverty is shown for the absolute rather than the relative thresholds, and the adjusted rather than pretransfer income concepts. In 1978, the absolute poverty gaps range between $20.4 billion for posttransfer poverty and $62.7 billion for pretransfer. The official gap, $20.4 billion, represents about 1% of the gross national product. The adjusted income gap was $9.6 billion in 1980. All relative poverty gaps increased since 1965; in 1978, the relative posttransfer gap was $31.9 billion.[7]

Summary.   Our review of the data gives a contradictory impression about the trend in poverty and the current dimension of the problem. The facts do not speak for themselves. Absolute poverty has diminished, and the needs of the poor are being better met, but the level of pretransfer poverty has not declined. Relative poverty has not declined; so the incomes received by those at the bottom have not increased relative to the average. These facts do not lead us to conclude either that the war on poverty has been won or that government policy has been ineffectual. The income poverty problem is multidimensional, and our diverse set of measures emphasizes its complexity. We are concerned not only with the absolute well-being of the poor, but with the process by which that well-being is achieved, and with how their level of well-being compares to that of the rest of society. In the next section, we discuss some explanations for these trends.

THE TREND IN POVERTY: EXPLANATIONS

At an elementary level, the trends in posttransfer and adjusted poverty can be readily explained. Because absolute pretransfer poverty did not fall, but posttransfer and adjusted poverty did, government transfer must have grown and/or become increasingly effective. Also, increased transfers helped maintain a constant level of relative posttransfer poverty despite an increase in relative pretransfer poverty. In this section we consider several reasons for the failure of pretransfer poverty to decline, then assess the antipoverty impact of cash and in-kind income support.

Pretransfer Poverty.   We explore three main hypotheses for the failure of pretransfer poverty to decline — (1) demographic change, (2) decreased earnings in response to improved transfer benefits, and (3) a stagnant national economy. We focus on absolute poverty statistics for convenience; analysis of relative data yields similar conclusions.

The proportion of persons in households headed by females steadily rose over the period. Over half of this group remains pretransfer poor because of low rates of labor force participation and low wage rates, caused by sex discrimination and relatively low job skills. Hence, increases in the percentage of households headed by females raise the overall incidence of pretransfer poverty. An increase in the fraction of persons in households headed by aged males has had a similar, but quantitatively smaller effect. In the absence of such demographic changes, pretransfer poverty would have been 17.0% in 1978 (instead of the observed 20.2%), or 4.3 percentage points below the 1965 level.[8] Thus, declines in the incidence of pretransfer poverty among certain demographic groups were offset by population shifts toward groups with higher than average rates of pretransfer poverty.

The incidence of pretransfer poverty is also affected by income transfer programs. Recipients of transfers are induced to work less than they otherwise would, and these declines in earnings cause some persons to become pretransfer poor who would otherwise not have been poor. As more people receive transfers and as benefit levels rise, pretransfer poverty could increase, *ceteris paribus*. Some analysts have suggested that the lack of progress against pretransfer poverty may have been caused by a reduction in work effort induced by the recent expansion of transfers.

To assess this hypothesis, we simulated the labor supply and earnings effects of major cash transfer programs for 1967 and 1974, and used the results to determine what the level of pretransfer poverty would have been in the absence of transfers (see Plotnick 1980). The major results are summarized in Table 3.2. The population in the simulation includes persons in families with a head between the ages of 20 and 59. Thus, the numbers in this table cannot be directly compared to those in Table 3.1.

Column 1 shows an observed rise in pretransfer poverty from 12.5% to 13.9%. As expected, column 2 reveals that without transfers, the extent of pretransfer poverty would have been lower in both years. Nonetheless, even if transfers had not increased, pretransfer poverty would still have risen over time. This simulated increase from 11.9% to 12.4% would have been smaller than what was actually observed. Hence,

Table 3.2. Actual and Simulated Trends in Pretransfer Poverty among Persons, and the Antipoverty Impact of Transfers, 1967 and 1974

Incidence of Poverty	Observed	Simulated
Pretransfer		
1967	12.5%	11.9%
1974	13.9	12.4
% Change	+11.2	+ 4.2
Posttransfer[a]		
1967	11.2%	11.2%
1974	11.4	11.4
Reduced by transfers[b]		
1967	10%	6%
1974	18	8

SOURCE: Various March Current Population Surveys.
NOTE: Sample includes all persons living in families headed by persons between the ages of 20 and 59 and not in the armed services.
[a]The incidences of posttransfer poverty in both columns are the observed rates.
[b]Defined as [(pretransfer incidence − posttransfer incidence)/ pretransfer incidence] × 100. For example, for 1974 observed data, $((13.9 - 11.4)/13.9) \times 100 = 18\%$.

one may conclude that transfers are responsible for a *poverty inducement effect,* but it does not seem very large.

The stagnant economy of the 1970s is the third and probably the major reason for the persistence of pretransfer poverty. Between 1965 and 1968, real pretransfer income per household grew 7.1%. The "trickle down" effect of this growth is evident in the decline in pretransfer poverty over this period (see Table 3.1). Between 1968 and 1972 real pretransfer income per household only rose 1.4%,[9] and pretransfer poverty began to increase. During 1972–1978, real pretransfer income per household actually *dropped* 1.3%. This decline is probably the major cause of the increase in pretransfer poverty after 1972.

The Antipoverty Effectiveness of Transfers.   Between 1965 and 1978 the growth in real expenditures on cash and in-kind transfer per recipient household far exceeded the real increase in per household income. This

growth, a major development in American social welfare policy, accounts
for much of the observed declines in absolute poverty.

Table 3.3 measures the antipoverty effectiveness of transfers by the
percentage of the pretransfer poor removed from poverty by transfers.[10]
The table divides all government transfers into social insurance transfers,
public assistance transfers, and in-kind transfers (whether social insurance or public assistance).

For each type of transfer and for each measure of poverty, public
transfers became increasingly effective since 1965. The fraction of absolute pretransfer poor households receiving a cash transfer payment
rose from less than 70% in 1965 to over 80% in 1978, and the real value
of the typical household's transfer also increased. As a result, transfers
removed about 43% of the pretransfer poor from absolute poverty in
1965, and over 70% in 1976. The larger effect was due both to the increase
in average benefit level and to the increasing recipiency rate among the
pretransfer poor.

Cash social insurance transfers removed more persons from poverty
in both years and for both measures than did cash public assistance
transfers, because a greater portion of the pretransfer poor received

Table 3.3. The Antipoverty Effectiveness of Transfers

Poverty Measure	Percentage of the Pretransfer Poor Removed from Poverty by Means of			
	Cash Social Insurance Transfers[a]	Cash Public Assistance Transfers[b]	In-Kind Transfers[c]	All Transfers
Absolute				
1965	23.5	3.3	16.4	43.2
1976	37.6	6.2	28.1	71.9
1978	37.6	5.9	—	—
Relative				
1965	23.5	3.3	—	—
1976	32.4	3.7	—	—

SOURCE: Various March Current Population Surveys.

[a]Cash social insurance transfers include Social Security, Railroad Retirement, unemployment
compensation, workmen's compensation, government employee pensions, and veterans' pensions and compensation.

[b]Cash public assistance transfers include AFDC, SSI (OAA, APTD and AB in 1965), and
General Assistance.

[c]In-kind transfers include Medicare, Medicaid, food stamps, and, for 1976, school lunch and
public housing; this figure also adjusts for direct taxes and the underreporting of cash transfers.

them, and because the average social insurance benefit was higher. In-kind transfers — which include benefits from both social insurance and public assistance programs — had a smaller antipoverty impact than cash social insurance and a larger impact than cash public assistance transfers.

The figures of Table 3.3 overstate the net antipoverty impact of trans-fers because of the induced work reductions mentioned above, and be-cause transfers may have induced changes in living arrangements. For example, rising levels of Social Security have been accompanied by an increase in the percentage of elderly couples who maintain separate households. Some of those now choosing to live alone are pretransfer poor, but receive enough Social Security to avoid posttransfer poverty. Without Social Security, or with smaller benefits, some of them might have lived with children earning nonpoverty incomes. If this were the case, pretransfer poverty, as it is conventionally measured, would have been lower. Hence, some of the pretransfer poverty that is observed to be eliminated by transfers might in fact have been created by the labor supply and living arrangement choices induced by these programs.

How serious is the overstatement stemming from these two behavioral responses to transfers? Current estimates suggest that the impact of public assistance transfers on living arrangements and the resulting effect on poverty are rather small (Danziger et al. 1980). The simulation results in the bottom panel of Table 3.2 show that after adjusting for the negative labor supply responses, the net decline in pretransfer poverty due to transfers would have been 8%, rather than the observed 18% in 1974. However, both the simulated and observed data suggest that the anti-poverty effectiveness of transfers increased between 1967 and 1974.

Summary.   We have shown that the observed trend in posttransfer poverty is influenced by three distinct components: the trend in pretrans-fer poverty, changes in the transfer system's antipoverty effectiveness, and demographic change in the composition of households. A simple statistical decomposition confirms the importance of each of these fac-tors.[11] We compute what the level of posttransfer poverty would have been in 1978 if one of the three components had remained at its 1965 level, while the other two components had been at their 1978 levels. Then we compare this hypothetical incidence with the actual 1978 inci-dence. If the hypothetical incidence exceeds the actual level, the change in the component between 1965 and 1978 contributed to a reduction in posttransfer poverty.

Between 1965 and 1978, observed posttransfer poverty as officially measured declined from 15.6% to 11.4%. If the incidence of pretransfer poverty for each demographic group had been constant at the 1965 levels, but if the antipoverty effectiveness of transfers and the distribution of the population among demographic groups had been at their 1976 levels, then posttransfer poverty would have been 14.2% instead of 11.4%. Thus, as noted earlier, there was a decline in pretransfer poverty for some demographic groups. Similarly, posttransfer poverty would have been 14.4% if the antipoverty effectiveness of the transfer system had not improved. Because this simulated value is higher, we can conclude that the increased antipoverty impacts of transfers were more important than declines in pretransfer poverty. Demographic changes, however, contributed to an increase in posttransfer poverty. If the composition of households across demographic groups had remained at 1965 proportions, poverty would have been only 9.3%.

TOWARD A NEW WAR ON POVERTY

The data discussed above lend some support to the divergent views on the future of antipoverty policy. Some, looking at the adjusted data, have claimed that income poverty is now all but erased, and that the undesirable side effects of antipoverty policies have grown large. They claim that work and savings incentives have been eroded — for both the poor and the rich — and as a result, economic growth has been impeded and productivity retarded. Some taking this position argue that the growth of these programs should be curtailed; others want the programs scaled back or eliminated.

We offer a quite different evaluation. In our view, the evidence does not sustain the claim that retrenchment is in order, even though all is not as it should be. (For a complete review of the equity and efficiency effects of the income support system, see Danziger, Haveman, and Plotnick 1981.) Critics have overstated both the gains against poverty and the negative efficiency effects of the existing income support system. Although progress has been made by the standard of adjusted poverty, pretransfer poverty and relative poverty have not declined. And while the growth of income transfers has increased work disincentives, their magnitude poses no serious threat to the efficiency of the economy. From our reading of the evidence, neither the drastic fiscal retrenchment proposed by President Reagan nor continued expansion of current programs is the appropriate policy response. Retrenchment might promote efficiency, but it will also increase poverty. While current transfer programs have been effective in reducing poverty, their expansion is not likely to produce a noticeable reduction in the number of poor people because most of the additional transfers would go to recipients who are already above the poverty line (Plotnick and Smeeding 1979). However, such an expansion would cause further erosion of work effort.

We envision a reorientation of income support policy that emphasizes work opportunities rather than cash support and focuses on the distinction between those who are not expected to work — those who are aged, disabled, or in school, or who have to care for young children — and those who are expected to work. (For a more complete reform proposal, see Danziger, Garfinkel, and Haveman 1979.) Real levels of income transfers should be maintained for those not expected to work. Most, but not all, of these households currently receive transfers, and their declines in poverty since 1965 are mainly due to increasing transfers. Because the official poverty lines are adjusted for cost-of-living increases, transfers to these groups must increase or poverty will increase. Yet, the prospects for such increases are not favorable. Benefit levels are not likely to be increased in programs where they are not already indexed because of taxpayer complaints about high tax burdens. Indeed, there have been proposals for de-indexing some benefits and for restructuring others.

Antipoverty policy must especially confront the financial needs of female-headed families. A large proportion of these households remain poor even though about 40% receive transfers, and about three-quarters already work at least part-time. Members of this group cannot now be easily classified as expected to or not expected to work. The past consensus that a woman without a husband should remain at home to care for her children has been eroded by the growth of labor force participation by mothers in two-parent families. If single parents do not increase their work effort, and if, as we have argued, benefits in existing programs are not likely to be greatly increased, then the standard of living of single-parent families will remain low.

About a third of all pretransfer poor household heads are in our expected-to-work target group. Members of this group — especially males heading households and single males and females — are less likely to receive income support from current programs than are the rest of the poor. Policies to enhance employment and earnings for these persons warrant attention for two major reasons. First, reductions in work induced by the current system are its most significant negative efficiency effect. These reductions entail real economic losses and generate vociferous public dissatisfaction. Second, the major lesson that we draw from the reform debates of the past decade is that a welfare reform of the negative income tax variety that does not promote independence from support payments cannot solve the "welfare mess" (Danziger and Plot-nick 1979). To do so requires that we reduce poverty, not by providing more income support payments to those who are expected to work, but by providing more job opportunities and higher earnings.

The Reagan Administration seems to have adopted the pre–war on poverty view that a growing economy is a sufficient antipoverty policy. However, the experience of the recent past suggests that a jobs-oriented approach for aiding the poor is necessary even when the economy is operating at high levels of employment. (For a discussion of the types of proposals we envision, see Haveman, present volume, ch. 10).

As we enter the 1980s, a reorientation of antipoverty policy toward increasing the demand for low-productivity workers offers the potential for reducing both poverty and dependence on government payments. More importantly, such an emphasis returns us to one of the major goals of the war on poverty. The war on poverty marks an important turning point in the evolution of American social welfare policy. Significant gains have been made; yet further initiatives are needed. The War on Poverty of the 1960s has run its course. Now is the time to declare a new war on pretransfer poverty for those who can work, and to continue transfer programs that reduce poverty among the rest of the poor.

NOTES

1. This section draws from several histories of the war on poverty. In particular, see Aaron (1978); Kershaw (1970); Levitan (1969); Sundquist (1969); Tobin (1968); Lampman (1971); Haveman (1977); Friedman (1977); and Levitan and Taggart (1976).

2. As mentioned above, there were other goals of the period and other (nonincome) dimensions of poverty that were to be attacked. An examination of these other goals and dimensions is beyond the scope of this paper.

3. This is measured by the Census Bureau as the sum of money wages and salaries, net income from self-employment, Social Security income and cash transfers from other government programs, property income (e.g., interest, dividends, net rental income), and other forms of cash income (e.g., private pensions, alimony).

4. This threshold differs from the half-the-median standard offered by Victor Fuchs. The specifics of this measure are as follows. We divide each family's current money income by its official poverty line. This yields a *welfare ratio* that indicates the fraction by which the family's income exceeds or falls below the official poverty line. Families with the same welfare ratio are assumed to be equally well-off. We define the relative poor as those families with welfare ratios below .44 of the median ratio.

The fraction .44 was not an arbitrary choice. In 1965, the base year for our analysis of changes in poverty, the median welfare ratio was 2.25. All living units with incomes below the official poverty lines had, of course, welfare ratios less than one. Thus, any household that in 1965 was poor under the official definition necessarily had a welfare ratio less than

1.00/2.25 of the median. Defining the relative poor as those with welfare ratios below 1.00/2.25 = .44 of the median yielded, in 1965, the same group of households as were poor from the absolute perspective.

5. We do not combine the adjusted income data with a relative poverty line. Estimating in-kind income from private sources (e.g., fringe benefits) and taxes paid by the nonpoor poses such severe problems that we could not accurately determine their level of adjusted income. Thus, we could not compute a relative measure based upon the median adjusted income.

6. Hoagland's 4.1% figure is based on a 1978 data base that is statistically aged to 1980 using macroeconomic assumptions more favorable than the 1980 reality. Adjusting for this discrepancy would yield an estimate of poverty after the receipt of cash and in-kind transfers of about 6%.

Paglin's paper in the present volume (ch. 5) shows an even lower incidence of adjusted income poverty. However, his estimates rest on questionable assumptions for distributing some in-kind transfers, are not derived from microeconomic data (and thus fail to distinguish households with a given income that are eligible from those that are not eligible for benefits), and do not account for taxes paid. Each of these points leads to an underestimate of the number of poor persons.

Nevertheless, estimates of poverty from all of the studies that account for in-kind transfers are closer to each other than they are to the estimates of studies using census data excluding in-kind transfers.

7. All poverty gap data are expressed in 1978 dollars. One cannot conclude that an increase of only $20.4 billion in transfers could have eliminated poverty. This figure is clearly a lower bound. Any current transfer program that would bring everyone up to the poverty line would aid many with incomes already above the line. Also, increases in transfers would lead some recipients to work less, increasing their poverty gaps and the transfers needed to bring them out of poverty.

The posttransfer relative gap was 1.9% of personal income in both 1965 and 1978. To the extent that relative poverty is concerned with the share of income going to the least affluent, one might argue that the relative poverty gap remained constant during this period. However, data on the average posttransfer poverty gap per person increased for both the absolute and relative measure, indicating that the poor in 1976 were somewhat farther from the poverty thresholds than the poor in 1965.

8. To control for demographic change, we assumed the proportion of persons in each of sixteen major demographic groups remained constant between 1965 and 1978, but that the incidence of pretransfer poverty within each group changed as observed. By multiplying the 1965 proportions by the 1978 incidence values and summing, we obtain the hypothetical level of pretransfer poverty that would have existed in 1978 if no demographic shifts had occurred. The sixteen groups are listed in note 11.

9. During 1968–1972, real pretransfer income *per person* rose 7.1%. The demographic shift toward smaller living units during these years caused the number of households to grow faster than the number of people. Because poverty is measured by household income, it is appropriate to focus on household data. (For a critique of the "trickle down" view, see Gottschalk 1981.)

10. The antipoverty impacts of seven cash and three in-kind transfer programs are assessed here. They are (1) Social Security and Railroad Retirement, (2) Medicare, (3) federal, state, and local government employee pensions, (4) unemployment insurance, (5) workers' compensation, (6) veterans' compensation and pensions, (7) Supplemental Security Income, (8) public assistance (AFDC, AFDC–UP, General Assistance, and prior to

1974, OAA, APTD, and AB), (9) Food Stamps, and (10) Medicaid. While several in-kind transfer programs and all expenditures on public education have been omitted, Food Stamps, Medicare, and Medicaid alone account for over 80% of all federal in-kind transfers. For 1976, school lunch and public housing benefits are also included.

11. Simple algebra shows how these three factors are related. For demographic group i, the incidence of posttransfer poverty, p_i, equals $pr_i t_i$, where pr_i is the incidence of pretransfer poverty and t_i is the fraction of the pretransfer poor not taken out of poverty by transfer $(1 - t_i$, therefore, is a measure of the amount of poverty relieved by public transfers). The overall incidence of posttransfer poverty, P, equals $\Sigma_{i=1}^{N} c_i p_i$, where c_i is the fraction of the total population found in group i and $\Sigma_{i=1}^{N} c_i = 1$. Substituting for p_i, we find $P = \Sigma_{i=1}^{N} c_i pr_i t_i$. To assess the effect of change in any one of these variables on P, we can, for example, hold pr_i and t_i constant at their values in the first year and let c_i vary as observed. The resulting value for P indicates the impact of demographic change on the level of poverty. This statistical decomposition is based on the assumption that the three factors — pretransfer poverty, transfers, and demographic composition — are independent of each other. As we stated earlier, demographic change also affects pretransfer poverty, and transfers affect both demographic composition and pretransfer poverty. As a result, this decomposition should be viewed as an approximation.

The population was divided into sixteen groups based on the age of head (over 65, under 65), race (white, nonwhite), sex of head, and household type (family, unrelated individual).

REFERENCES

Aaron, Henry J. 1978. *Politics and the Professors*. Washington, D.C.: Brookings Institution.

Anderson, Martin. 1978. *Welfare*. Stanford, Calif.: Hoover Institution Press.

Danziger, Sheldon; Garfinkel, Irwin; and Haveman, Robert H. 1979. "Poverty, Welfare, and Earnings: A New Approach." *Challenge* 22 (September-October):28–34.

Danziger, Sheldon; Haveman, Robert H.; and Plotnick, Robert. 1981. "How Income Transfer Programs Affect Work, Savings, and the Income Distribution: A Critical Review." *Journal of Economic Literature* 29, no. 3 (September):975–1028.

Danziger, Sheldon; Jakubson, George; Schwartz, Saul; and Smolensky, Eugene. 1980. "The Welfare System as a Determinant of Female Household Headship." Mimeographed discussion paper. Institute for Research on Poverty, University of Wisconsin (Madison).

Danziger, Sheldon, and Plotnick, Robert. 1979. "Can Welfare Reform Eliminate Poverty?" *Social Service Review* 53 (June):244–60.

Friedman, Lawrence. 1977. "The Social and Political Context of the War on Poverty." In *A Decade of Federal Antipoverty Programs,* edited by Robert H. Haveman. New York: Academic Press.

Galbraith, John Kenneth. 1958. *The Affluent Society*. New York: New American Library.

Gottschalk, Peter. 1981. "Transfer Scenarios and Projections of Poverty into the 1980's." *Journal of Human Resources* 16 (Winter):41–60.

Grönbjerg, Kirsten; Street, David; and Suttles, Gerald. 1978. *Poverty and Social Change*. Chicago: University of Chicago Press.

Harrington, Michael. 1962. *The Other America*. New York: Macmillan.

Haveman, Robert H. 1977. "Poverty and Social Policy in the 1960's and 1970's." In *A Decade of Federal Antipoverty Programs*, edited by Robert H. Haveman. New York: Academic Press.

Kershaw, Joseph A. 1970. *Government against Poverty*. Washington, D.C.: Brookings Institution.

Lampman, Robert J. 1971. *Ends and Means of Reducing Income Poverty*. Chicago: Markham.

———. 1974. "What Does It Do for the Poor? A New Test for National Policy." *Public Interest*, no. 34 (Winter):66–82.

Levitan, Sar A. 1969. *The Great Society's Poor Law*. Baltimore: Johns Hopkins University Press.

Levitan, Sar A., and Taggart, Robert. 1976. *The Promise of Greatness*. Cambridge, Mass.: Harvard University Press.

Pilisuk, Marc, and Pilisuk, Phyllis, eds. 1973. *How We Lost the War on Poverty*. New Brunswick, N.J.: Transaction Books.

Plotnick, Robert. 1980. "The Redistributive Impact of Income Support Programs." Mimeographed discussion paper. Institute for Research on Poverty, University of Wisconsin (Madison).

Plotnick, Robert, and Smeeding, Timothy. 1979. "Poverty and Income Transfers: Past Trends and Future Prospects." *Public Policy* 27 (Summer):255–72.

Smeeding, Timothy. 1975. "Measuring the Economic Welfare of Low Income Households and the Anti-Poverty Effectiveness of Cash and Non-Cash Transfer Programs." Ph.D. dissertation, University of Wisconsin (Madison).

Sundquist, James, ed. 1969. *On Fighting Poverty*. New York: Basic Books.

Tobin, James. 1968. "Raising the Incomes of the Poor." In *Agenda for the Nation*, edited by Kermit Gorden. Washington, D.C.: Brookings Institution.

4 THE EFFECTIVENESS OF CURRENT TRANSFER PROGRAMS IN REDUCING POVERTY

G. William Hoagland

Social welfare expenditures grew rapidly throughout the early 1970s, but the rate of growth peaked in fiscal year 1975, measured in both current and constant prices. Since 1975, the growth rate for these expenditures has shown a considerable decline, dropping from an annual increase of 21.2% in 1975 to 9.1% in 1978. In constant prices, the drop was from an annual increase of 9.5% in 1975 to 2.5% in 1978. A major share of this relative decline can be attributed to the 1974–1975 downturn in the general economy, contrasted with a more stable economy in the latter part of the 1970s. In fiscal year 1978, social welfare expenditures (including education)[1] reached nearly $395 billion for all levels of government, or about 19% of the gross national product (U.S. Department of Health, Education, and Welfare 1980).

The economic, political, and social climate ushered in with the new decade of the eighties has included policies designed to moderate further

The views expressed in this paper are those of the author and are not necessarily those of the Congressional Budget Office or other staff. The author wishes to acknowledge the invaluable computer programming assistance provided by Lynn Paquette of the Congressional Budget Office.

53

the growth in social welfare expenditures. The Carter Administration's budget request, as well as the House and Senate Budget Committee's adopted recommendations for fiscal year 1981, would rescind, reduce, or defer action on a number of social welfare programs. For example, the implementation of major provisions in the welfare reform bill passed by the House of Representatives in November 1979 (H.R. 4904, the Social Welfare Reform Amendments of 1979) would have been delayed by one year.

Proponents of these reduction and deferral strategies argue that a moderation in government spending can be expected to reduce aggregate demand temporarily and thereby help curtail inflation. The argument proceeds: If inflation were not controlled, the poor would suffer more than other groups. Proponents argue further that existing government transfer programs have significantly reduced the incidence of poverty. Finally, because benefits in most of the programs are indexed to price changes, current recipients are insured against inflation, and program expansion to new recipients can only exacerbate overall inflation.

Opponents of reduction or moderation strategies argue that it is unfair to place the burden of reducing inflation on the very groups that are most hurt by spiraling prices, and that some low-income groups are left out of the government's minimal largess. These social critics also note that the poverty index itself is limited and that the food plan upon which the index was initially developed was designed for short-term use and was not intended to be a permanent plan that would cover family needs for an indefinite period. Others have argued that the original food plan developed in 1964 would not permit formulation of a nutritious diet in line with present food consumption patterns. More importantly, they argue that poverty should be measured in terms of relative income inequality, not absolute levels.[2]

This paper examines the effectiveness of government assistance programs in reducing the incidence of poverty between fiscal years 1976 and 1980. The paper was developed in the same tradition of a number of other recent studies in this area, updating the analysis to the current time period.[3] The major issue addressed is: What effect has the decline in the rate of growth of social welfare expenditures since 1975 had on the effectiveness of the current transfer system in combating poverty? The paper does not directly address the issue of whether or not the current official benchmark used to measure poverty is an adequate level of income.[4]

The paper consists of three sections: (1) an overview of the methods used to estimate the transfer system's poverty reduction impact; (2)

estimates of the incidence of poverty for fiscal years 1976 and 1980 and the relative effectiveness of different types of transfers; and (3) comparisons of the distribution of transfer benefits by quintiles and estimates of the changes in the poverty gap between fiscal years 1976 and 1980.

METHODS AND PROCEDURES

The development of economic assumptions and concomitant transfer program projections at the Congressional Budget Office (CBO) is an ongoing process. This process involves a number of steps and is crucial to the overall objective of developing a consistent Congressional Budget Resolution each year.

Early in 1979, a consistent set of economic and program projections was developed for the fiscal year 1980 Congressional Budget debates and used for the development of two aged micro-data files. (For a description of the basic procedure, see Congressional Budget Office 1977; Mathematica Policy Research 1977.)[5] Three major tasks were involved in this activity: (1) development of economic assumptions and modifying the assumptions to be consistent with Current Population Survey (CPS) income and population concepts; (2) adjustment of the March 1978 CPS to reflect changing demographics, economics, and tax and transfer program projections by fiscal year 1980; and (3) imputation of tax and transfer program benefits for individuals and households on the adjusted CPS file.

Economic Assumptions.   The January 1979 economic assumptions used to develop the 1980 data set are presented in Table 4.1. These assumptions are contrasted with more recent assumptions (January 1980). Despite the rapidly changing economic environment over the last few years, the assumptions developed in January 1979 are not significantly different from those currently being used by the CBO. The salient differences are that the 1980 assumptions show less unemployment, but more inflation than was projected a year ago.

The economic assumptions are generated on a national income accounts (NIA) basis. In order to produce economic assumptions that are consistent with the population covered in the census CPS, the NIA projections were adjusted. (For a detailed discussion of the issues involved in comparing CPS and NIA data, see Budd and Radner 1975.) For example, NIA projections for personal wages and salaries must be reduced by the earnings of decedents, civilians living overseas, military persons on posts and overseas, and the value of food and lodging pro-

Table 4.1. Comparison of Major Economic Assumptions for Fiscal Year
1980

| | *Fiscal Year 1980 Forecasts* | | |
Economic Assumption	*January 1979*	*January 1980*	*Percentage Difference*
Real GNP[a]	1,445.1	1,422.8	−1.5
Change from prior year	1.7%	−0.4%	−2.1
Nominal GNP[b]	2,515.1	2,507.3	−0.3
Change from prior year	9.7%	8.4%	−1.3
Unemployment rate	6.75%	6.49%	−0.3
Civilian labor force[c]	104,742	104,310	−0.4
Employment[c]	97,669	97,537	−0.1
Unemployment[c]	7,070	6,770	−4.2
Consumer Price Index[d]	224.4	236.5	+5.4
Change from prior year	8.0%	12.1%	+4.1
Taxable personal income[b]	1,726.0	1,732.9	+0.4
Wages and salaries[b]	1,312.0	1,307.0	−0.4

[a] In billions of 1972 dollars.
[b] In billions of dollars.
[c] In thousands.
[d] 1967 = 100.

vided directly to civilian employees. The NIA projections for wages and
salaries, nonfarm self-employment income, farm income, interest, dividends, and net rental were adjusted to reflect the CPS income and population concepts through a series of adjustments developed in
consultation with the Department of Commerce, Bureau of Economic
Analysis. (For a full discussion of these procedures, see Doyle et al.
1980.)

Demographic and Income Aging.   The demographic characteristics of
the population on the base March 1978 CPS were altered by reweighting
each observation on the file.[6] The adjusted weights result in a total
population reflecting independent Census Bureau projections for fiscal
year 1980 of households by type and age of head, and persons by age,
race, and sex (see U.S. Bureau of the Census 1977; 1979).

Income adjustments involved the application of multiplicative growth
rates to various sources of income reported on each person's record in
the base CPS file. The adjustment rates for wages, self-employed farm
income, self-employed nonfarm income, interest income, rents, and div-

idends were derived by comparing the independent projections described above to the totals for these sources reported in the March 1978 CPS. Similar procedures were used to adjust some entitlement transfer programs — Social Security, government and private pensions, unemployment compensation, workers' compensation, and veterans' benefits.

Since the March 1978 CPS was subject to both nonreporting and underreporting of certain types of incomes, nonreporting and underreporting continue in the 1980 file. Nonreporting and underreporting of unearned income were corrected by: (1) inflating reported incomes when sufficient recipients existed on the aged file, but incomes reported did not agree with the independent projections; or (2) imputing incomes to stochastically selected recipients when insufficient recipients and income existed, compared with the independent projections.

Tax and Transfer Programs. The major means-tested transfer programs — Aid to Families with Dependent Children (AFDC), Supplemental Security Income (SSI), Food Stamps, and General Assistance — were imputed to the 1980 file using microsimulation techniques. This procedure involved first calculating eligible units on the file and then selecting participants based on probabilities of participation derived from exogenously projected participant and benefit payments.[7]

The records of adults in the file were supplemented with estimates of their total federal personal income tax liabilities and their tax liabilities for three payroll tax programs — Social Security, Railroad Retirement, and federal civil service retirement. These tax liabilities were computed for each observation on the basis of tax rules in effect in 1980.

Average Medicaid insurance values were imputed for both the categorically needy and the medically needy populations on the file. Average medical insurance values for the categorically needy were defined as the projected Medicaid payments to the noninstitutionalized population divided by the estimated size of the eligible population. For the medically needy population, the 1976 Survey of Income and Education (SIE) was tabulated to find those persons reporting receipt of Medicaid benefits who would not have been categorically eligible for such benefits. Probabilities that members of different groups would incur medical expenditures large enough to qualify for the medically needy program were calculated from the SIE cross-tabulations. Insurance values were then calculated for all those deemed potentially eligible under the medically needy provisions. Similar procedures were used for the Medicare program, with an adjustment for the out-of-pocket premium payment.

Finally, child nutrition and housing benefits were imputed to the file based on a stochastic process, involving exogenously projected control totals for fiscal year 1980.

THE EFFECTIVENESS OF CURRENT TRANSFER PROGRAMS IN REDUCING POVERTY

Based on the most current published statistics, the number of persons in poverty dropped from about 25.9 million in 1975 (12.3% of the population) to 25.2 million in 1978 (11.6% of the population). These statistics are based on a pretax, post–money transfer income concept. When contrasted with the annual rate of decline in poverty experienced between the early 1960s and mid-1970s, these statistics suggest a moderation in the government effort to combat poverty. Just as the growth rate in government expenditures for social welfare expenditures peaked in the mid-1970s, according to the official measurement, the incidence of poverty appears to be relatively stable now at around 11% of the population.

The adjusted fiscal years 1976 and 1980 CPS files, however, show a different story. Correcting the published statistics for underreporting and nonreporting of survey income, and including the full value of nonmedical in-kind transfers and tax payments, shows a significant decline in the incidence of poverty over the last half of the 1970s. Table 4.2 contrasts the number of poor persons in fiscal years 1976 and 1980 under alternative income definitions. Also shown is the percentage reduction in poverty using the alternative income definitions.

Pretransfer Income.   Between fiscal years 1976 and 1980 pretransfer income (e.g., wages and salaries) grew about 38%, reaching nearly $1.5 trillion in 1980. Before any direct government intervention, however, little progress was made in reducing poverty as the result of aggregate income growth. This is partially due to the changing demographic shifts toward more elderly and single-parent families, which tend to have a higher incidence of pretransfer poverty. While the total population grew by about 3.3% between fiscal year 1976 and 1980, the population over the age of 64 grew by approximately 8%. Even more startling has been the continued increase in the population living in families headed by a female (primarily single-parent families); between 1976 and 1980, this population grew by nearly 17%. The reduction in poverty measured on a pretransfer basis was estimated to be less than 2% between 1976 and 1980. Nearly 41.8 million persons were estimated to be poor on this basis in 1976, 41.1 million in 1980.

Table 4.2. Persons in Poverty in Fiscal Years 1976 and 1980 under Alternative Income Definitions

Persons in Poverty	Pretransfer Income	Pretax, Post–Social Insurance Income	Pretax, Post–Money Transfer Income	Pretax, Post–In-Kind Transfer		Posttax, Post–Total Transfer	
				No Medical	With Medical	No Medical	With Medical
FY 1980							
Number in thousands	41,096	22,811	18,793	12,957	8,496	13,455	8,951
Incidence percentage	18.8	10.4	8.6	5.9	3.9	6.2	4.1
FY 1976							
Number in thousands	41,755	25,408	21,222	15,551	11,137	17,247	12,420
Incidence percentage	19.3	12.0	10.0	7.4	5.3	8.2	5.9
Percent Change in Poor Persons within							
FY 1980		−44.5	−17.6	−31.1	−34.4	+3.8	+5.5
FY 1976		−39.1	−16.5	−26.7	−28.4	+10.9	+11.5

NOTE: See Tables 4.A1 and 4.A2 for further details on persons in poverty in these fiscal years.

Social Insurance Programs.   Social insurance transfer benefits include Social Security, federal disability, unemployment compensation, workers' compensation, government pensions, and veterans' compensation. These grew by over 54% between 1976 and 1980, reaching nearly $186.8 billion in 1980. Poverty measured by a pretax, post–social insurance concept showed a decline from 25.4 million to 22.8 million persons between 1976 and 1980 — a 10.2% decline.

Social insurance benefits have the largest absolute and relative impact on reducing pretransfer poverty, both in 1976 and 1980, contrasted with other types of transfer benefits. Furthermore, the relative impact of social insurance benefits in reducing poverty compared with pretransfer measures appears to have increased between 1976 and 1980. Social insurance benefits reduced the size of the poverty population by 39.1% in 1976, and by 44.5% in 1980, compared with pretransfer measures. Given the increasing retirement age population, social insurance programs (primarily Social Security) will continue to grow in importance as the major transfer programs for combating poverty measured on a pretransfer basis.

Post–Money Transfer Programs.   Cash assistance transfers include categorical means-tested programs such as AFDC, SSI, and GA programs. They grew the slowest of any form of transfers over the period examined — about 22% between 1976 and 1980, reaching $21.4 billion in 1980. Poverty measured on a pretax, post–money transfer concept (the official census definition) showed a decline from 21.2 million to 18.8 million persons between 1976 and 1980 — an 11.4% decline. The relative impact of these programs was about the same in 1976 and 1980, however. Money transfers reduced the poverty measured on a post–social insurance basis by 16.5% and 17.6% in 1976 and 1980, respectively.

Post–In-Kind and Money Transfer Programs.   In-kind nonmedical transfers grew nearly as rapidly as social insurance benefits between fiscal years 1976 and 1980. In-kind nonmedical transfers reached nearly $14.2 billion in 1980, up 54% over their 1976 level.[8]

Poverty measured on a pretax, post–in-kind (not including medical) concept showed a decline from 15.6 million to 13.0 million persons between 1976 and 1980 — a 16.7% decline. The continued growth in in-kind recipients between the two years — particularly in Food Stamps and housing assistance — has resulted in these types of transfers having a greater relative impact on reducing poverty in 1980 than 1976. In-kind income transfers reduced the poverty population measured on a post–money transfer basis by 26.7% and 31.1% in 1976 and 1980, respectively.

Medical transfers increased to $42.7 billion in 1980, over 60% higher than the 1976 level. Medical transfers represent the most rapidly increasing form of any transfer benefits over this time period. Including the insurance value of medical transfers in the definition of income significantly reduces the measured size of the poverty population. The poverty population measured on a pretax, post–in-kind (including medical) basis was reduced to 8.5 million persons in 1980, or about 4% of the total population.

The continued rapid escalation in medical costs over this time period has resulted in a greater relative value for subsidized medical expenditures in 1980 than in 1976, a situation similar to that of food and housing subsidies. Since the official poverty threshold is indexed to overall price changes, inclusion of medical benefits in the definition of income results in a greater relative reduction in the size of the poverty population in 1980 than in 1976. Inclusion of medical transfers reduced the size of the poverty population from the pretax, post–in-kind (nonmedical) measure by 28.4% and 34.4% in 1976 and 1980, respectively.

Posttax, Post–Total Transfer Programs.   Personal taxes totaled about $298 billion in 1980, up 43% over the 1976 level. Personal taxes, it should be noted, grew faster than wages and salaries over this period, but poverty measured on a posttax, post–total transfer basis declined from 17.2 million in 1976 to 13.4 million in 1980 — a decline of over 22%. In 1980, according to this measurement of poverty, 6.2% of the population was poor, significantly less than the official statistic of 11% in 1978.

The tax system results in an increase in poverty primarily because of the regressive nature of the payroll taxes. But between 1976 and 1980, major changes in the federal income tax system (including expansion of the earned income tax credit, modifications in the zero bracket tax amount, reduced tax rates, and increased personal exemptions) have mitigated the effects of the payroll tax system. In 1976, including the effects of these tax systems in the measurement of the poverty population increased its size by nearly 11%. In 1980, the increase was less than 4%.

THE TARGETING OF TRANSFERS: CHANGES BETWEEN 1976 AND 1980

If the effectiveness of transfer systems were to be judged solely on the reduction in the incidence of poverty, the preceding section would suggest that advances have continued throughout the late 1970s, despite a slowing in the growth of direct social welfare expenditures. Poverty measured on a posttax, posttransfer basis (excluding medical transfers) affects about 13.4 million people, or 6.2% of the total population.

Constrained government budgets, combined with a desire to alleviate poverty for over 13 million citizens, will focus attention on targeting existing expenditures more carefully in the 1980s. This section briefly summarizes how transfer and nontransfer incomes are distributed, how the distribution changed over the late 1970s, and the relative position of different demographic groups in 1980. The paper concludes with estimates of the poverty gap for the total population.

Distribution of Incomes.   Many transfer programs are not designed to target benefits on the lowest income groups. This is particularly true for the major social insurance programs. Table 4.3 compares the distribution of various sources of income for family income quintiles measured by pretax, pretransfer values in fiscal years 1976 and 1980. Despite the relative nontargeting of the social insurance programs, a greater proportion of these benefits appears to be directed to the two lowest income quintiles in 1980 than in 1976. For the most part, however, the change in the relative distribution of incomes has been slight, and most changes shown by Table 4.3 could have resulted from measurement and simulation errors.

Nonetheless, some conclusions can be drawn from the data. The distribution of pretransfer income has not changed significantly. The lowest 20% of all families receive less than 1%, while the highest 20% receive nearly 50% of all pretransfer income. The estimated Gini coefficient for pretax, pretransfer income declined slightly from 0.583 in 1976 to 0.560 in 1980. Even after all transfers and taxes are included, the lowest income quintile (measured on a pretransfer basis) receives less than 8% of all forms of income, while the highest income quintile receives nearly 40%. The Gini coefficient on a posttax, post–total transfer basis declined from 0.484 in 1976 to 0.454 in 1980, suggesting a slight improvement in the relative degree of inequality between 1976 and 1980.

In general, it has not been the lowest income quintile, but the next to the lowest that has gained an increasing share of transfer income, particularly cash assistance and in-kind benefits. In part, this trend could reflect targeting of benefits on groups with some earnings in addition to those with no earnings. Finally, as discussed in the previous section, changes in the tax law between 1976 and 1980 have had an important effect on the incidence of poverty and on the distribution of income. The three lowest income quintiles experienced a modest reduction in their tax payments, while the two highest groups showed a slight increase in tax payments.

Table 4.3. Distribution of Types of Income and Tax Liabilities by Family Income Quintiles, Fiscal Years 1976 and 1980 (percentages)

Quintiles[a] (Pretax, Pretransfer Income)	Pretax, Pretransfer		Social Insurance		Cash Assistance		In-Kind (no medical)		In-Kind (with medical)		Taxes		Total Distribution	
	1976	1980	1976	1980	1976	1980	1976	1980	1976	1980	1976	1980	1976	1980
Lowest	0.6	0.6	34.9	33.0	64.1	63.5	52.0	50.6	51.5	46.8	0.5	0.4	6.4	6.5
Second	7.7	8.0	26.4	28.1	18.8	25.7	27.9	31.6	26.2	29.3	4.5	3.8	11.0	12.1
Third	16.5	16.4	15.8	15.3	8.7	7.6	11.1	10.6	11.3	11.9	13.4	12.8	16.9.	16.9
Fourth	26.2	26.7	11.7	12.8	4.7	2.8	5.5	4.3	6.0	6.8	24.6	25.0	24.1	24.6
Highest	49.1	48.2	11.4	10.8	3.7	0.4	3.4	2.8	5.0	5.2	56.9	58.1	41.7	39.8
Total	100.0	100.0	100.0	100.0	100.0	100.0	100.0	100.0	100.0	100.0	100.0	100.0	100.0	100.0
Gini co-efficient[b]	0.583	0.560	0.522	0.496	0.503	0.474	0.497	0.469					0.484	0.454

[a] The upper limits of the income quintiles for fiscal year 1976 are: lowest 20 percent, $2,366; second, $8,475; third, 14,460; and fourth, 22,091. For fiscal year 1980, they are: lowest, 2,807; second, 10,254; third, 17,845; and fourth, 27,624.
[b] Approximate estimates of the Gini coefficient were derived using the formula

$$\text{Gini} = 1 - \frac{2}{b^2} [b + e^{-b} - 1],$$

where

$$b = \frac{\Sigma(\ln \pi_i / \eta_i)(1 - \pi_i)}{\Sigma(1 - \pi_i)^2}$$

and π_i is the cumulative percentage distribution of all family units and η_i is the cumulative percentage of all income.

63

Poverty Gap.   The poverty gap measures the total amount of income required to raise the income of every low-income family to its poverty level. Measurements of the poverty gap provide an indication of the relative degree of poverty for those remaining in poverty. Table 4.4 summarizes the estimated poverty gap in 1976 and 1980 under alternative income definitions. The 1980 dollar figures are expressed in 1976 dollars to facilitate comparisons between the two years.

Measured on a pretax, pretransfer basis, the incomes of poor persons fell nearly $52 billion short of their poverty line in 1976. This measure declined by less than 4 percent in 1980, to $50 billion; that is, the average degree of poverty measured on a pretax, pretransfer income basis has changed only slightly. Similarly, the average amount of money required to raise every poor person's income to the poverty line was $1,244 per person in 1976, and $1,216 in 1980, a decline of 2.3%.

Measured by the traditional pretax, post–money transfer income concept, the poverty gap was $15.5 billion in 1976 and declined nearly 20%, to $12.4 billion, in 1980. In 1976, $731 would have been required to raise every person's pretax, post–money transfer income level to the poverty line; this declined by nearly 10%, to $658, in 1980.

After including in-kind transfers (except medical transfers) and adjusting for taxes, the poverty gap remained at $12.4 billion in 1976, but declined to $8.6 billion in 1980, or nearly a 30% drop. On a per-poor-person basis, the relative degree of poverty also declined from $720 in 1976 to $647 in 1980, a drop of 10%. Judged by this criterion, the transfer system may be improving its targeting on the lowest income groups.

Is Poverty Dead?   In general, then, the absolute level of poverty appears to have continued to decline over the last half of the 1970s. As measured by changes in the poverty gap over this period, the relative degree of poverty for those remaining behind has also been declining slowly. Judged by these various criteria, the moderation in social welfare expenditures since 1975 has not seriously reduced the effectiveness of the current system in reducing poverty.

However, poverty is not dead. For at least 13 million persons, primarily those living in the South Atlantic and West South Central regions of this country, poverty remains a serious problem. For one in five families headed by a black female, poverty remains a daily concern. Similarly, families headed by a female are three times more likely to be in poverty than families headed by a male. While the system has continued to show significant gains in its effectiveness at reducing poverty, large pretransfer inequalities exist and show minor signs of declining.

Table 4.4. Poverty Gap in Fiscal Years 1976 and 1980 under Alternative Income Definitions

	Fiscal Year	Pretax, Pretransfer	Pretax, Post–Social Insurance	Pretax, Post–Money Transfer	Pretax, Post–In-Kind Transfer (no medical)	Posttax, Post–In-Kind Transfer (no medical)
Poverty gap (in billions of dollars)	1976	52.0	25.4	15.5	11.7	12.4
	1980[a]	50.0	21.0	12.4	8.4	8.6
Persons in poverty (in millions)	1976	41.8	25.4	21.2	15.6	17.2
	1980[a]	41.1	22.8	18.8	13.0	13.4
Average poverty gap per person in poverty (in dollars)	1976	1,244	1,000	731	750	720
	1980[a]	1,216	923	658	649	647

[a] Expressed in 1976 constant dollars.

65

Appendix Table 4.A1. Persons in Poverty, Fiscal Year 1976

	All Persons	Pretax, Pretransfer Income	Pretax, Post-Social Insurance Transfer Income	Pretax, Post-Money Transfer Income	Pretax, Post-In-Kind Transfer Income (no medical)	Pretax, Post-In-Kind Transfer Income (with medical)	Posttax, Posttransfer Income (no medical)	Posttax, Posttransfer Income (with medical)
White male								
Greater than 64	15,595,175	7,003,775	1,350,197	874,353	718,457	307,099	746,037	314,824
%	100.00	44.91	8.66	5.61	4.61	1.97	4.78	2.02
Less than 65	142,884,687	12,222,400	7,975,977	7,179,799	6,031,229	5,180,742	6,881,867	5,937,684
%	100.00	8.55	5.58	5.02	4.22	3.63	4.82	4.16
Black male								
Greater than 64	1,515,920	1,036,346	418,611	329,104	261,110	157,966	262,539	170,404
%	100.00	68.36	27.61	21.71	17.22	10.42	17.32	11.24
Less than 65	13,703,684	3,080,668	2,355,565	1,974,556	1,379,652	1,061,277	1,652,209	1,256,290
%	100.00	22.48	17.19	14.41	10.07	7.74	12.06	9.17
Other nonwhite male								
Greater than 64	238,809	132,272	61,771	31,378	22,012	22,012	29,477	29,477
%	100.00	55.39	25.87	13.14	9.22	9.22	12.34	12.34
Less than 65	2,515,953	369,563	319,877	286,674	234,073	200,508	246,858	213,293
%	100.00	14.69	12.71	11.39	9.30	7.97	9.81	8.48

White female								
Greater than 64	7,204,057	4,188,827	1,440,931	1,046,786	799,156	356,237	807,270	357,789
%	100.00	58.15	20.00	14.53	11.09	4.94	11.21	4.97
Less than 65	18,667,138	7,431,173	5,955,338	4,786,841	3,037,892	1,968,010	3,286,195	2,092,816
%	100.00	39.81	31.90	25.64	16.27	10.54	17.60	11.21
Black female								
Greater than 64	1,074,445	890,560	620,434	459,603	351,025	205,199	370,912	205,199
%	100.00	82.89	57.74	42.78	32.67	19.10	34.52	19.10
Less than 65	7,812,731	5,199,432	4,744,369	4,152,719	2,647,807	1,618,456	2,885,814	1,783,061
%	100.00	66.55	60.73	53.15	33.89	20.72	36.94	22.82
Other nonwhite female								
Greater than 64	61,843	46,574	17,697	4,450	4,158	2,909	4,158	2,909
%	100.00	75.31	28.62	7.20	6.72	4.70	6.72	4.70
Less than 65	323,987	153,519	148,041	95,902	65,245	56,619	73,309	56,619
%	100.00	47.38	45.69	29.60	20.14	17.48	22.63	17.48
Total	211,598,429	41,755,109	25,408,808	21,222,165	15,551,816	11,137,034	17,246,645	12,420,365
%	100.00	19.73	12.01	10.03	7.35	5.26	8.15	5.87

Appendix Table 4.A2. Persons in Poverty, Fiscal Year 1980

	Total	Pretax, Pretransfer Income	Pretax, Post-Social Insurance Transfer Income	Pretax, Post-Money Transfer Income	Pretax, Post-In-Kind Transfer Income (no medical)	Pretax, Post-In-Kind Transfer Income (with medical)	Posttax, Posttransfer Income (no medical)	Posttax, Posttransfer Income (with medical)
White male								
Greater than 64	16,954,752	7,855,649	1,011,861	759,234	528,455	90,215	530,513	92,097
%	100.00	46.33	5.97	4.48	3.12	.53	3.13	.54
Less than 65	142,267,263	10,633,062	6,662,021	5,924,940	4,398,105	3,966,670	4,741,090	4,254,106
%	100.00	7.47	4.68	4.16	3.09	2.79	3.33	2.99
Black male								
Greater than 64	1,662,513	979,668	362,392	265,255	185,729	8,669	185,729	8,669
%	100.00	58.93	21.80	15.96	11.17	.52	11.17	.52
Less than 65	13,504,327	1,854,561	1,344,678	1,133,205	794,175	630,759	818,467	674,555
%	100.00	13.73	9.96	8.39	5.88	4.67	6.06	5.00
Other nonwhite male								
Greater than 64	179,438	108,851	44,990	22,938	22,098	4,709	22,098	4,709
%	100.00	60.66	25.07	12.78	12.32	2.62	12.32	2.62
Less than 65	3,037,698	415,036	363,926	342,221	210,484	196,422	226,390	197,654
%	100.00	13.66	11.98	11.27	6.93	6.47	7.45	6.51

White female								
Greater than 64	7,797,343	4,935,022	1,442,646	1,140,339	857,830	85,271	859,416	85,271
%	100.00	63.29	18.50	14.62	11.00	1.09	11.02	1.09
Less than 65	22,535,258	7,972,724	6,286,065	4,994,029	3,517,642	2,227,491	3,610,818	2,334,569
%	100.00	35.38	27.89	22.16	15.61	9.88	16.02	10.36
Black female								
Greater than 64	1,061,057	757,716	478,885	357,761	247,424	28,963	249,155	28,963
%	100.00	71.41	45.13	33.72	23.32	2.73	23.48	2.73
Less than 65	9,038,937	5,291,164	4,583,050	3,678,622	2,076,470	1,192,202	2,087,249	1,206,294
%	100.00	58.54	50.70	40.70	22.97	13.19	23.09	13.35
Other nonwhite female								
Greater than 64	80,474	54,914	28,389	23,768	17,529	2,830	17,529	2,830
%	100.00	68.24	35.28	29.54	21.78	3.52	21.78	3.52
Less than 65	490,151	237,387	202,442	150,884	101,237	61,463	97,101	61,463
%	100.00	48.43	41.30	30.78	20.65	12.54	19.81	12.54
Total	218,609,211	41,095,754	22,811,345	18,793,196	12,957,179	8,495,663	13,445,554	8,951,180
%	100.00	18.80	10.43	8.60	5.93	3.89	6.15	4.09

Appendix Table 4.A3. Persons in Poverty, Fiscal Year 1976, Using New Poverty Cutoffs

	All Persons	Pretax, Pretransfer Income	Pretax, Post-Social Insurance Transfer Income	Pretax, Post-Money Transfer Income	Pretax, Post-In-Kind Transfer Income (no medical)	Pretax, Post-In-Kind Transfer Income (with medical)	Posttax, Posttransfer Income (no medical)	Posttax, Posttransfer Income (with medical)
White male								
Greater than 64	15,595,175	8,115,257	2,397,098	2,053,991	1,958,625	1,094,948	2,010,650	1,116,811
%	100.00	52.04	15.37	13.17	12.56	7.02	12.89	7.16
Less than 65	142,884,687	16,418,545	11,764,171	11,147,614	10,099,767	8,931,219	11,774,071	10,527,152
%	100.00	11.49	8.23	7.80	7.07	6.25	8.24	7.37
Black male								
Greater than 64	1,515,920	1,155,473	638,380	589,401	559,861	338,183	577,589	342,317
%	100.00	76.22	42.11	38.88	36.93	22.31	38.10	22.58
Less than 65	13,703,684	4,009,086	3,353,451	3,167,815	2,836,745	2,393,271	3,318,515	2,802,728
%	100.00	29.26	24.47	23.12	20.70	17.46	24.22	20.45
Other nonwhite male								
Greater than 64	238,809	137,324	111,277	67,430	67,430	39,989	67,430	39,989
%	100.00	57.50	46.60	28.24	28.24	16.75	28.24	16.75
Less than 65	2,515,953	488,841	405,474	367,425	329,107	306,199	360,920	328,079
%	100.00	19.43	16.12	14.60	13.08	12.17	14.35	13.04

White female								
Greater than 64	1,296,077	2,311,855	1,296,077	2,298,374	2,465,088	2,667,464	4,698,206	7,204,057
%	17.99	32.09	17.99	31.90	34.22	37.03	65.22	100.00
Less than 65	4,443,959	6,138,404	4,091,603	5,780,743	6,364,092	7,152,237	8,584,068	18,667,138
%	23.81	32.88	21.92	30.97	34.09	38.31	45.98	100.00
Black female								
Greater than 64	421,057	651,495	413,337	628,760	667,152	754,342	927,108	1,074,445
%	39.19	60.64	38.47	58.52	62.09	70.21	86.29	100.00
Less than 65	3,808,930	4,769,513	3,451,135	4,528,222	5,023,576	5,426,992	5,799,019	7,812,731
%	48.75	61.05	44.17	57.96	64.30	69.46	74.23	100.00
Other nonwhite female								
Greater than 64	8,549	11,469	8,549	11,469	11,469	21,921	46,574	61,843
%	13.82	18.55	13.82	18.55	18.55	35.45	75.31	100.00
Less than 65	104,984	136,281	87,624	126,373	143,938	165,691	170,707	323,987
%	32.40	42.06	27.05	39.01	44.43	51.14	52.69	100.00
Total	25,240,632	32,128,192	22,452,134	29,225,476	32,068,991	34,858,498	50,550,208	211,598,429
%	11.93	15.18	10.61	13.81	15.16	16.47	23.89	100.00

Appendix Table 4.A4. Persons in Poverty, Fiscal Year 1980, Using New Poverty Cutoffs

	Total	Pretax, Pretransfer Income	Pretax, Post–Social Insurance Transfer Income	Pretax, Post–Money Transfer Income	Pretax, Post–In-Kind Transfer Income (no medical)	Pretax, Post–In-Kind Transfer Income (with medical)	Posttax, Posttransfer Income (no medical)	Posttax, Posttransfer Income (with medical)
White male								
Greater than 64	16,954,752	9,211,226	2,236,322	2,074,406	1,918,952	500,244	1,966,833	508,861
%	100.00	54.33	13.19	12.23	11.32	2.95	11.60	3.00
Less than 65	142,267,263	15,029,923	10,536,800	9,863,007	8,517,957	7,731,071	10,392,294	9,489,288
%	100.00	10.56	7.41	6.93	5.99	5.43	7.30	6.67
Black male								
Greater than 64	1,662,513	1,127,743	556,357	504,472	457,543	122,891	481,457	136,260
%	100.00	67.83	33.46	30.34	27.52	7.39	28.96	8.20
Less than 65	13,504,327	2,827,159	2,189,664	2,066,720	1,732,463	1,504,078	2,099,133	1,790,387
%	100.00	20.94	16.21	15.30	12.83	11.14	15.54	13.26
Other nonwhite male								
Greater than 64	179,438	131,769	74,575	62,309	56,044	21,211	56,044	21,211
%	100.00	73.43	41.56	34.72	31.23	11.82	31.23	11.82
Less than 65	3,037,698	595,225	515,241	481,949	387,298	341,008	472,018	421,073
%	100.00	19.59	16.96	15.87	12.75	11.23	15.54	13.86

White female								
Greater than 64	7,797,343	5,529,446	2,932,114	2,842,426	2,464,496	916,986	2,481,591	919,948
%	100.00	70.91	37.60	36.45	31.61	11.76	31.83	11.80
Less than 65	22,535,258	9,503,285	7,848,032	6,797,168	5,995,101	4,463,284	6,234,522	4,698,650
%	100.00	42.17	34.83	30.16	26.60	19.81	27.67	20.85
Black female								
Greater than 64	1,061,057	822,244	655,698	598,170	501,735	223,174	506,533	241,419
%	100.00	77.49	61.80	56.37	47.29	21.03	47.74	22.75
Less than 65	9,038,937	6,133,099	5,507,020	4,855,992	3,898,825	2,809,504	4,029,063	2,915,970
%	100.00	67.85	60.93	53.72	43.13	31.08	44.57	32.26
Other nonwhite female								
Greater than 64	80,474	67,877	41,440	40,960	37,563	22,592	37,563	22,592
%	100.00	84.35	51.50	50.90	46.68	28.07	46.68	28.07
Less than 65	490,151	262,486	233,989	192,021	161,420	113,593	161,420	113,593
%	100.00	53.55	47.74	39.18	32.93	23.18	32.93	23.18
Total	218,609,211	51,241,484	33,327,251	30,379,600	26,129,397	18,769,637	28,918,471	21,279,253
%	100.00	23.44	15.25	13.90	11.95	8.59	13.23	9.73

NOTES

1. Social welfare expenditures are defined to include all federal, state, and local social insurance expenditures; public assistance; health and medical program expenditures; veterans' programs; and education, housing, and social services programs.

2. A "decency standard" at 50% of the median family income — to replace the official poverty index figure — has been suggested by Kenneth Keniston and the Carnegie Council on Children (1978); see also Center for Community Change (1979).

3. Other recent studies that have examined the effectiveness of the current transfer system on reducing the incidence of poverty include Plotnick and Skidmore (1976); Haveman (1977); Paglin (1980); Browning (1975); Smeeding (1975); and Congressional Budget Office (1977).

4. Fendler and Orshansky (1979) have presented updated income poverty cutoff levels, taking into account data from the *U.S. Household Food Consumption Survey, 1965–1966.* These new poverty thresholds are approximately 20% higher than the previous threshold levels, based on the *U.S. Household Food Consumption Survey, 1955–1956.* A comparison of the different poverty counts from these higher poverty threshold levels is given in Appendix Tables 4.A3 and 4.A4.

5. Data presented later for fiscal year 1976 were developed using similar procedures. The fiscal year 1976 data base was produced in 1977 using the March 1975 Current Population Survey.

6. The basic model used to adjust the 1978 CPS for demographic changes, adjust reported incomes, and simulate tax and transfer program data was the Micro Analysis of Transfers to Households (MATH) model, a comparative static microsimulation process.

7. Individual program projections were produced by the CBO to be consistent with the underlying economic assumptions discussed in the text. These program projections were adjusted to the comparable CPS population base. (A complete listing of the individual projection models can be found in Congressional Budget Office 1979.)

8. These estimates do not include the value of low-income energy assistance payments provided during 1980. A total of $1.6 billion has been provided low-income families in 1980 to offset the impact of rising fuel costs.

REFERENCES

Budd, Edward C., and Radner, Daniel B. 1975. "The Bureau of Economic Analysis and Current Population Survey Size Distributions: Some Comparisons for 1964." In *The Personal Distribution of Income and Wealth,* edited by James D. Smith. Washington, D.C.: National Bureau of Economic Research.

Browning, Edgar K. 1975. *Redistribution and the Welfare System.* Washington, D.C.: American Enterprise Institute.

Center for Community Change. 1979. "Beyond the Numbers: The Failure of the Official Measure of Poverty" (December).

Congressional Budget Office, U.S. Congress. 1977. *Poverty Status of Families under Alternative Definitions of Poverty.* Background Paper no. 17, rev. (June). Washington, D.C.: U.S. Government Printing Office.

————. 1979. *Five-Year Budget Projections and Alternative Budgetary Strategies for Fiscal Years 1980–1984* (April). Washington, D.C.: U.S. Government Printing Office.

Doyle, Pat; Edson, David; Pappas, Norma; and Boulding, William. 1980. *Creation of 1980 and 1984 Data Bases from the March 1978 Current Population Survey,* vol. 1. Princeton, N.J.: Mathematica Policy Research.

Fendler, Carol, and Orshansky, Mollie. 1979. "Improving the Poverty Definition." In *Statistical Uses of Administrative Records with Emphasis on Mortality and Disability Research,* U.S. Department of Health, Education, and Welfare, Social Security Administration, Office of Research and Statistics (August). Washington, D.C.: U.S. Government Printing Office.

Haveman, Robert H., ed. 1977. *A Decade of Antipoverty Programs.* New York: Academic Press.

Keniston, Kenneth, and the Carnegie Council on Children. 1978. *All Our Children: The American Family under Pressure.* New York: Harcourt Brace Jovanovich.

Mathematica Policy Research. 1977. *Analysis of Current Income Maintenance Programs and Budget Alternatives, Fiscal Years 1976, 1978, and 1982: Technical Documentation and Basic Output.* Princeton, N.J.: Mathematica Policy Research.

Paglin, Morton. 1980. *Poverty and Transfers In-Kind.* Stanford, Calif.: Hoover Institution Press.

Plotnick, Robert D., and Skidmore, Felicity. 1976. *Progress against Poverty: A Review of the 1964–1974 Decade.* New York: Academic Press.

Smeeding, Timothy H. 1975. "Measuring the Economic Welfare of Low Income Households and the Anti-Poverty Effectiveness of Cash and Non-Cash Transfer Programs." Ph.D. dissertation, University of Wisconsin (Madison).

U.S. Bureau of the Census. 1977. *Projections of the Population of the United States: 1977 to 2050.* Ser. P-25, no. 704 (July). Washington, D.C.: U.S. Government Printing Office.

————. 1979. *Projections of the Number of Households and Families: 1979 to 1995.* Ser. P-25, no. 805 (May). Washington, D.C.: U.S. Government Printing Office.

U.S. Department of Health, Education, and Welfare, Social Security Administration, Office of Research and Statistics. 1980. *Social Welfare Expenditures, Fiscal Year 1978* (14 February). Washington, D.C.: U.S. Government Printing Office.

5 HOW EFFECTIVE IS OUR MULTIPLE-BENEFIT ANTIPOVERTY PROGRAM?

Morton Paglin

A major difficulty in evaluating the effectiveness of our antipoverty program stems from the inadequacy of the poverty statistics used in making program evaluations. It is now recognized that the official poverty series published in the Bureau of the Census *Current Population Reports* significantly overstates the number of persons who are poor because it records only the money income of households. By ignoring the value of in-kind transfers, the census poverty figures fail to register the antipoverty effect of more than 60% of the income-tested transfer budget. Hence our multibillion dollar in-kind programs such as Food Stamps, Medicaid, public housing, rent supplements, and many other noncash welfare programs are assumed to have no value for low-income families.

In the first part of this paper, I report on my revision of the official poverty series. These new figures are compared with the other recent estimates of poverty, focusing on the major conceptual and empirical differences. This is followed by a digression on poverty standards and their welfare implications, and a critical review of such concepts as the *pretransfer poor*. The poverty estimates are also shown to contain a sizable statistical residual of phantom poor — for example, families with substantial property who show negative incomes or accounting losses for some years. The latter part of the paper deals with the target efficiency of our antipoverty programs and the trade-off between target efficiency and other social goals. Finally, the accomplishments and advantages of the in-kind programs in meeting our antipoverty goals are briefly reviewed.

Table 5.1 and Figure 5.1 show the official U.S. poverty estimates along with several revisions that correct the census figures for taxes, underreporting of income, household income basis, and most important of all, for the omission of in-kind transfers. In addition to the two continuous series, each based on a consistent methodological approach, there are some single-year estimates of adjusted census poverty figures. The basis for the variation in the estimates will now be briefly reviewed.

The Census Bureau poverty statistics are derived from an annual sample of more than 50,000 households, which are questioned (mainly through telephone interviews) in March about their money incomes in the previous calendar year; this is referred to as the Current Population Survey (CPS). Families and single individuals whose incomes fall below the Social Security Administration poverty thresholds (changed each year to adjust for inflation) are classified as poor.

A brief inspection of this series reveals that the significant decline in the poverty population occurred in the decade 1959 to 1968; from 1968 to 1979, when there was a major expansion of the welfare transfer budget, the number of persons classified as poor simply moved up and down along a horizontal line. Is it possible that the multibillion dollar antipoverty programs initiated in the late sixties were so target inefficient that they had no impact? The answer is that they had a very great antipoverty effect, but the official statistics failed to measure the improvement in real incomes of the low-income households. A glance at the adjusted series confirms this: from 1959 to 1975 post in-kind transfer poverty fell continuously, declining 75%.

The adjusted census figures reflect a two-stage revision process: first, the revision of CPS money incomes; and second, the cashing out and distribution of household benefits from in-kind programs such as Food Stamps, Medicaid, and so forth.

THE MONEY INCOME REVISIONS

The money income revisions can be summarized under the following headings: (1) conversion of low-income thresholds from a family and

Table 5.1. Official and Final Revised Poverty Estimates: Persons in Poverty

	In Millions			As Percentage of Population		
Year	Census[a]	Paglin Final Revised[b]	Other Revised[c]	Census[a]	Paglin Final Revised[b]	Other Revised[c]
1959	39.5	31.1		22.4	17.6	
1960	39.9	30.7		22.2	17.1	
1961	39.6	30.4		21.9	16.6	
1962	38.6	29.9		21.0	16.1	
1963	36.4	29.0		19.5	15.4	
1964	36.1	27.8		19.0	14.5	
1965	33.2	25.7		17.3	13.3	
1966	30.4	22.3		14.7	11.4	
1967	27.8	18.4		14.2	9.3	
1968	25.4	14.5	19.8	12.8	7.3	10.1
1969	24.1	13.1		12.1	6.5	
1970	25.4	13.1		12.6	6.4	
1971	25.6	11.5		12.5	5.6	
1972	24.5	9.7	12.9	11.9	4.7	6.2
1973	23.0	8.3		11.1	4.0	
1974	23.4	8.0		11.2	3.8	
1975	25.9	7.8	{ 12.4	12.3	3.6	{ 5.8
1976	25.0		{ 10.8	11.8		{ 5.1
1977	24.7			11.6		
1978	24.5			11.4		
1979	26.1			11.7		
1980			8.9			4.1

[a] U.S. Bureau of the Census 1978, p. 15, and advance reports.

[b] Paglin 1980, p. 61.

[c] 1968 and 1972 estimates are from Plotnick and Smeeding 1979, p. 259, Table 1B. The two adjusted CBO estimates for FY 1976 are: (1) persons poor in U.S. posttax, post–all transfers, but without Puerto Rico and the institutional population; and (2) the lower estimate is based on (1) above, but reduces total to adjust for household income basis (see Table 5.2). The 1980 estimate of 8.95 million poor (4.1%) is from Hoagland's Table 4.2 (present volume, ch. 4). Hoagland uses the original CBO approach, corrected as I have done above, to eliminate Puerto Rico and the institutional population. However, he has not adjusted for a household income basis as described in the text for my revision of poverty statistics, 1959 through 1975. When this is done, Hoagland's projected 1980 poverty rate is about the same as my 1975 rate of 3.6%.

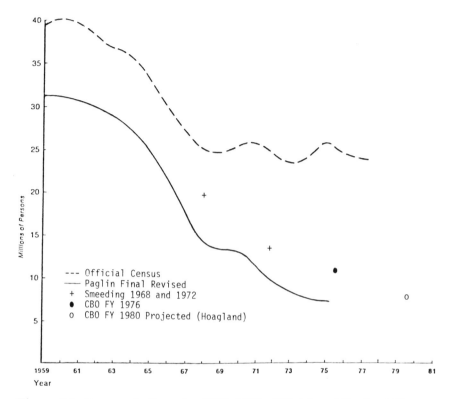

Figure 5.1. Persons in Poverty, 1959–1980, Official and Revised Figures for In-Kind Transfers (Source: Table 5.1)

individual basis to a household basis, (2) adjustment of income for underreporting, and (3) deduction of taxes to arrive at an after-tax income suitable for use with the poverty thresholds.

The CPS uses families and single individuals as consumer units in determining incomes and poverty counts. Unrelated individuals age 14 or older, living in groups or with families, are classified as poor if their incomes are insufficient to meet the minimum income requirements of a single person living alone. Given the fact that there are significant economies of scale in larger living units, and assuming some sharing of facilities and income, the poverty count is too high if it is not based on the income and costs of the functional living unit, namely, the household. (The currently used approach assumes unrealistically that there are no economies of scale and no income sharing unless the persons making up the unit are all related by blood or marriage.) By using the CPS *household* income series that started in 1967, I have recalculated the poverty counts for each household size. For the period 1967–1975, the household concept yields poverty estimates between 93% and 96% of the official figures. For the years 1959–1966, the 1967 percentage revision was used.

The second adjustment of the CPS money income series deals with the problem of underreporting of income. By comparing the CPS income estimates (by type of income) with independently computed totals from the National Income Accounts and administrative budget totals for transfer payments, it is apparent that CPS in recent years reports about 88–90% of total income. Underreporting varies by type of income: wages and salaries approach 98% of the benchmark total; public assistance, 75%; and Social Security payments, 90%. Although underreporting at the low (and high) end of the income scale is usually assumed to be greater than in the middle range, the low incomes were conservatively adjusted upward only by the overall average percentage underreported.

Finally, the CPS cash income concept is based on income before income taxes and Social Security taxes, while the poverty thresholds are based on net spendable income. Since estimates of the number of households not paying federal income taxes match closely with the number of low-income households below the poverty thresholds, particularly in the last twelve years, no revision for income tax was made. Social Security taxes, however, do reduce the net incomes of poor households, close to half of whose total income is derived from earnings. Hence, these earnings have been reduced by the appropriate Social Security tax rate for the period 1959 to 1975. The combined effect of the three cash income adjustments on persons in poverty results in revised estimates that range from 79% to 85% of the official number counted as poor.

ADDING THE IN-KIND TRANSFERS

Two general criteria have been used in selecting the in-kind programs for inclusion in the poverty income estimates:

1. A main purpose of the program should be the provision of services specifically to the low-income population through the use of eligibility tests based on income; or if categorical, as in the case of Medicaid, the eligible categories should reflect previous screening for poverty characteristics.
2. The goods or services transferred should be private, not public

goods, and should be items typically included in the budgets of low-income households. Hence, OEO and HUD Model Cities programs for neighborhood improvement in poor areas are not included because of their public-good characteristics; similarly excluded are legal services for the poor, social work services, subsidized day care, and various educational and training programs, since these are not common elements of the low-income household budget.

3. Only the major federally initiated programs have been included, and all exclusively state and local in-kind services, as well as private charity services, have been excluded because of the paucity of data. Thus, the cashing out of in-kind transfers was limited to the housing, food, and medical programs mentioned below.

For the seventeen years covered in this study, there were four housing programs cashed out and the benefits distributed by income class (low-rent public housing, Section 236 interest subsidies for rental units, Section 235 subsidies for low-income home ownership, and rent supplements for use in both 236 and other rental units). The benefits from six food and nutrition programs were also cashed out and distributed. These were the food distribution or commodity program (now phased out); the Food Stamp Program; the free school lunch, breakfast, and supplementary milk programs; and the recent WIC program (supplementary foods for women, infants, and children). Finally, there were the need-based medical programs: Medicaid and its predecessors (MA and MAA), Medicare, and the maternal and child health care clinics. Not included were OEO neighborhood health clinics and the Veterans Administration health and hospital system, which provides some free general medical services to low-income veterans. The combined effect of all the in-kind benefits added to the revised cash income distribution has a very significant effect on the number of persons below the official poverty thresholds; this is shown in Table 5.1 and Figure 5.1. In the revised series, poverty rates dropped over 75%. In the period 1968–1975, when the official series showed little change, the revised figures continued to drop by 46%.

The alternative single year estimates by Smeeding and the Congressional Budget Office (CBO), also shown in Table 5.1, generally utilize the same data sources as my estimates. Not surprisingly, they are closer to my revised series than to the official figures. But why are there still differences? A brief review of the reasons for the disparities will be useful in highlighting some of the empirical and conceptual differences between the studies.

The CBO Study.   The 5.1% poverty rate shown above is not in the
CBO *published* study, nor is the figure of 10.8 million poor persons. The
CBO published figures indicate post–in-kind transfer poverty in terms of
"family units" and "single-person families," which, when added together, give equal weight to families of different sizes. John Korbel of
CBO kindly provided the computer printouts that reduced all figures to
the more sensible "persons" basis. In addition, the more detailed un-
published data made it possible to adjust the CBO published figures for
conceptual differences with my own study. These mainly were as follows:
The original census (CPS) figures refer to the U.S. noninstitutional population; my revised figures (and Smeeding's) also refer to this population.
CBO, however, *added* the population of Puerto Rico and the long-term
institutional population to the census cash income population distribution
before distributing the in-kind transfers. (Presumably, the reason for
doing this is that some of the in-kind budgets cover Puerto Rico.) This
step alone added a few million poor to their final poverty count. However,
when revising the census estimates of poverty, it would seem better to
retain the census population base and simply cut out from the in-kind
budgets the allocation of funds made to these added population groups.
This procedure was followed in my series. When the CBO figures are
made conceptually comparable to the census population base, and the
number of poor expressed in terms of persons living in poor *households,*
then the 8.3% poverty rate shown in their publication drops to the 5.1%
listed in Table 5.1. (For a detailed comparison of CBO figures and my
own, see Paglin 1980, app. 4, pp. 87ff.) These conceptual differences are
shown in Table 5.2.

Smeeding's 1972 Estimate.   Smeeding's adjustments of the 1972 census
poverty estimate, compared with my 1972 figures, are shown in Table
5.3. His cash income adjustments reduce census poverty counts by more
than mine for reasons (mainly adjustment for underreporting) that I have
discussed elsewhere. However, this larger cash income adjustment is
more than offset by a smaller reduction in poverty attributable to the in-
kind transfers. This difference is explained mainly by two factors.

The first is Smeeding's more limited coverage of the in-kind programs:
Smeeding cashes out only Food Stamps, whereas I cash out five food
and nutrition programs (see above); in housing the coverage is the same;
under medical care Smeeding includes Medicaid and Medicare, but I add
to this the Maternal and Child Health Care Program. In 1972 the programs
omitted by Smeeding amount to over a billion dollars of in-kind benefits
to the poor; I see no justification for such coverage gaps.

Table 5.2. Poverty Estimates after All Transfers and Taxes, Fiscal Year 1976

Population Group	Families (includes single-person units)		Persons	
	Numbers (thousands)	Percentage	Numbers (thousands)	Percentage
1. CBO total poor (U.S., institutional, and Puerto Rico)	6,597	8.3	15,153	7.0
2. Puerto Rican poor	427	53.4	1,744	54.8
3. U.S. institutional poor	806		1,062	45.2
4. CBO total, less Puerto Rico and institutional	5,364	7.0	12,347	
5. Adjustment for household basis			1,560	
6. CBO after all adjustments (line 4 minus line 5)			10,787	5.1
7. Present study (comparable to line 6)			7,762	3.6

SOURCES: Congressional Budget Office 1977, Table 3, p. 8, is the source for family units and percent poor on line 1. All other CBO estimates are from computer printouts provided by John Korbel of CBO. For adjustment on line 5, see text. Line 7 is from my Table 5.1. The Puerto Rican poor on line 2 include Puerto Rican institutional poor.

NOTE: Percent poor always refers to the appropriate population group listed in the left-hand column, expressed in either family units or persons.

Second, and more important than the differences in the scope of programs covered, is the method used in cashing out the transfers. I use a market value approach, while Smeeding deflates the market values to cash-equivalent value and thereby reduces the value of food, housing, and medical care transfers to 88%, 56%, and 68% of their respective market values (Smeeding 1977, pp. 365–66). Hence, in the aggregate, Smeeding allocates (for 1972) $5.772 billion of cash-equivalent transfers to the poor, compared with my allocation of $8.168 billion. It is clear that the method used in valuing in-kind transfers will have a significant impact on the final number of poor, although compared with the zero

Table 5.3. Poverty Estimates for 1972 (number of persons in millions)

	Smeeding[a]	Paglin[b]
Census (1972), persons in poverty	24.555	24.460
Census after adjustments for underreporting, taxes, and household income basis	18.805	20.256
Final revision after all adjustments and cash and in-kind transfers	12.854	9.693

[a] Smeeding 1977, Table 1; Table 5, col. 3.
[b] Paglin 1980, Table 1, cols. 2 and 4; Table 7, col. 3.

value given to in-kind benefits in the official statistics, the difference between the two approaches seems fairly small.

THE PROBLEM OF IN-KIND TRANSFERS

Let us consider the issue of market value versus cash equivalence in greater detail. At first view, the decision to deflate market values seems reasonable. If an in-kind transfer imposes some choice constraint on a consumer (as compared to a cash transfer of like value), why shouldn't the utility loss be translated into lower transfer benefits for the recipient? Smeeding and others have done this, but I believe that their approach is defective both in theoretical conception and in statistical implementation. In our present state of knowledge, the market value approach to in-kind transfers seems the better one.

Households receiving significant components of their income stream in the form of in-kind transfers do have less commodity choice than cash income households, but in a broadly specified model the utility gains may be greater than the losses. In the Becker-Lancaster model of the household, there are two budget constraints: money and time. Consumers purchase commodities and combine them with time in order to produce utility. In this context, we can see that the in-kind transfers have attributes that may make them superior to an earned cash income, which can absorb 35% of the weekly time budget. Although cash transfers are superior to in-kind transfers, the latter may easily be preferred to an *earned* cash income of the same dollar value. Since earnings are the main source of household income, a comparison with earned money income is appropriate. Traditional economic analysis has focused almost exclusively on the *in-kind* attribute, neglecting the transfer and risk-insurance attributes of the noncash government transfer programs.

Although there is some choice constraint, the households receiving a large part of their incomes from transfers-in-kind are free of the work-connected expenses in generating earned income; they have more leisure and are spared the monotony of dead-end jobs. Their in-kind incomes are free of inflation risk: food stamp allotments are revised every six months to keep up with food price changes; public housing tenants do not have to worry about the increasing property taxes, escalating fuel and maintenance costs, and higher interest rates that usually are reflected in higher rents. Since the Sparkman and Brooke amendments to the 1969 Housing and Urban Development Act, local public housing authorities get federal subsidies to meet increased operating costs, and tenants are charged no more than 20–25% of their cash incomes, thus making their rents a declining percentage of real income as in-kind transfers have increased. Despite rapidly rising medical, hospital, and nursing home costs, Medicaid recipients receive a comprehensive package of medical services without concern for meeting the costs through higher charges or increasing medical insurance premiums. Finally, we may note that in-kind and other such need-based transfers are free of the risks of irregularity of earned income and are automatically indexed to the growth in the size of the family, thus eliminating the economic pressures associated with high fertility. Yet, economists in this area have selectively focused on just one dimension of the in-kind transfer: choice on the expenditure side.

The mistake lies in comparing in-kind transfers with a similarly indexed, risk-free, effortless cash transfer. Since most households live on earned income, the proper survey question to ask recipients who could work is this: Would you give up your risk-free, inflation-proof package of food stamps, rent subsidy, and Medicaid coverage (say, market value of $300 per month) for a job at the minimum wage, which after taxes, but before transportation costs, would pay you the same $300? I wonder how many would choose to work an additional 100 hours a month for the benefit of exchanging the in-kind transfers for the cash earnings? I believe most would reject the work as having zero marginal gain, and for some the gain would be negative; if so, then it makes no sense to deflate the market value of the in-kind transfers, since they are preferred to an equal cash–earned income. And for those traditionally outside the labor force, the in-kind transfers still have an added insurance premium of some value, which covers the risks of inflation in food, medical care, and housing, as well as the other risks mentioned.

Finally, the derivation of the cash-equivalent values from old BLS budget data used in combination with the reported monthly incomes of households receiving food stamps and other program benefits raises many questions. Low temporary incomes are poor proxies for permanent incomes or consumption levels. For example, many food stamp households are certified for three months because of lapses of income because of unemployment. Many such families use savings, credit, and food stamps to maintain their normal consumption levels. Yet, Smeeding would deflate the market value of food stamps on the assumption that this family has a permanent income and consumption pattern of the very poor.

DEFINITIONS OF POVERTY

The answer to the question of how effective is our multibenefit antipoverty program depends in part on how we define poverty. We have seen by our review of the alternate poverty estimates that poverty counts based on the more realistic definitions of income show that a large part of the war on poverty has been won, if the official poverty thresholds are used. There is also much evidence (discussed below) that the residual poverty includes a large percentage of persons who are statistical phantoms, who are not in any real sense poor. But aside from data problems, the official poverty standard itself has been questioned. It is worth reviewing some of the alternative definitions of poverty since they illustrate the range of issues raised by a discussion of the war on poverty.

The Pretransfer Poor. Obviously, we need a definition of what transfers are removed from the income distribution before we make the poverty count. In a recent article by Plotnick and Smeeding (1979), the authors arrive at the pretransfer poor by deducting not only the usual income-tested or welfare transfers, but also Social Security, Railroad Retirement, all federal, state, and local government employee pensions, unemployment insurance, and so forth. They discuss groups who "suffer from levels of pretransfer poverty that are well above average" (p. 261), among whom, naturally enough, one finds the retired households. (I wonder if the retired federal government workers with their excellent pensions, some drawing Social Security as well, are aware that they "suffer" from pretransfer poverty?) The authors report that in 1976 there were over 44 million pretransfer poor, and in terms of the poverty deficit, the period from 1965 to 1976 witnessed an "increasing poverty problem that the transfer system has faced" (p. 262).

I suggest that as a social problem geared to elicit our concern, this is a bogus concept of poverty. Furthermore, as an indicator of the dimensions of the poverty problem that must be met by transfers and the growth of the welfare state, the 44 million pretransfer poor are also purely a mythical number. Undoubtedly, government transfers have had a significant impact on poverty. But until we have some firm grasp of the effects of government programs on private pension arrangements, on real savings and economic growth, on early retirement, on labor force withdrawal and unemployment figures, and on family breakups and dependency, it seems to me unwarranted to present such estimates of pretransfer poverty on the assumption of zero income offsets. These hypothetical poverty figures obfuscate the real and declining extent of the poverty problem. A discussion by the authors of possible offsetting factors, which might make their estimates of pretransfer poverty too high, does not suffice to justify using the inflated numbers as if they measured an important dimension of the poverty problem. I suppose that the final step in the escalation of the poverty population will be the concept of the *pre-earnings poor*!

It is interesting to note (Table 5.1, either series) that poverty declined more in the period 1959–1967, *before* the major growth in government transfers, than in the period 1967–1976. But, of course, there is always the possibility that without the growth in transfers the decline might have slowed down; the remaining poverty *may* have been more difficult to eliminate through economic growth.

The Pre-Welfare-Transfer Poor. Some economists attempt to define the numbers who would be poor if the income-tested welfare type transfers were removed. As a poverty concept, this makes better sense than the above approach, since it focuses more exclusively on a group that has a higher probability of being poor in the absence of transfers and that, with them, remains marginally poor. It more reasonably excludes those whose claim to transfers represents in large part an earned right. But even here we must be aware of the significant degree to which the growth in female–headed families and the decline in the responsibility of the male head to share his income with his dependents have been a function of the improved benefits available through welfare transfers. (For a perceptive treatment of AFDC and the male beneficiaries of the system, see Gilder 1980.) New York City, in the decade of the sixties, experienced a 300% increase in its welfare caseload during a period when the unemployment rate was dropping. The tight labor market forced hospitals, which could not recruit laundry workers, to use more disposable sheets and towels. This was also a time when social workers would advise their clients to decline jobs that might result in too large a loss in welfare benefits. (Free choice creates high implicit tax rates on earnings.) So here again, it is questionable to assume that the number of pre-welfare-transfer poor is an independent measure of the problem faced by the welfare system. Rather, the larger and more generous the transfers, the higher the implicit tax on earned income, the easier the conditions of entry into the welfare system, then the larger will be the number of pre-welfare-transfer poor.

Absolute versus Relative Poverty.   The question of how the poverty thresholds should be set (which influences the size of the poverty population) has been actively debated, but is still unsettled. The census poverty figures and the adjusted poverty series shown in Table 5.1 both use the poverty standard developed by the Social Security Administration. This is based on the cost of a nutritionally adequate diet (meeting all the recommended dietary allowances), multiplied by three to provide an income level minimally adequate for other necessities as well. (For a more detailed discussion of the SSA matrix of poverty thresholds and how they were constructed, see Paglin 1980, ch. 1.) The poverty level income is adjusted each year to allow for changes in the price level by applying the BLS consumer price index (CPI).

Advocates of a purely relative poverty standard believe that the thresholds should be raised further in response to gains in real income. (With declines in real after-tax incomes they should be reduced, or not increased as fast as the CPI.) Poverty, in this view, is unaffected by sustained economic growth, and is meaningful only in relative income terms. Hence it is argued that the poverty thresholds should be set at a specified fraction of the median income (typically, one-half the median). Preferably, an equivalence scale should be used to define a set of thresholds, one for each household size.

The real and the relative measure of poverty can be compared by examining the welfare function implicit in each measure. The real income standard implies that a person's welfare (W_i) is a function of his real income (Y_i); hence, $W_i = f(Y_i)$. The poverty income threshold (Y_p), which indicates a minimally acceptable level of welfare, is determined by expert assessment of needs as in the official standard. Although Y_p is usually fixed for a period of time, expert judgment of minimum requirements is determined not only by technical studies of nutritional and other needs, but has a cultural component related to the median level of income (Y_m). Thus, in roughly each generation the poverty threshold has been adjusted upward, although only since 1964 has the threshold received government sanction. This periodic reevaluation of minimum standards implies a belief that an individual's perception of his welfare or poverty status is conditioned both by the absolute level of his income and by the ratio of his income to society's median income, Y_m. Hence, the welfare equation must be expanded to $W_i = f(Y_i, Y_i/Y_m)$; or assuming an additive function, $W_i = aY_i + b(Y_i/Y_m)$. (Note: Y_i/Y_m should first be converted to an index of income rank.) The real issue centers on the weights that should be assigned to a and b.

Those who believe in a real income standard, though also recognizing its relative component, emphasize that the long-run growth in real income has improved economic welfare far more than it has raised our conception of a minimum standard. Therefore, the change in Y_i is given most of the weight in the historical evaluation of poverty. The relativists argue that our conception of the poverty level rises as fast as real income, and hence the low-income individual feels no better off by an increase in Y_i if others in the community also experience the same increase, that is, if his Y_i/Y_m ratio remains the same. For the relativists, poverty is an issue exclusively related to the distribution of income, but for others the goal of raising all households above a specified minimum level of real income is a legitimate and worthwhile social objective. Robert Lampman (1971) has expressed this view:

> I do not think we should engage in frequent changes in the poverty lines, other than to adjust for price change. As I see it, the elimination of income poverty is usefully thought of as a one-time operation in pursuit of a goal unique to this generation. . . . The next generation will have set new economic and social goals, perhaps including a new distributional goal for themselves. (P. 53)

The relativist position has been articulated by Victor Fuchs (1967), who argues that the perception of poverty is purely a matter of "economic distance," which can be measured by the ratio each individual's income bears to the median. Hence the implicit welfare function is $W_i = f(Y_i/Y_m)$. Through a political decision process, the poverty threshold would be set at a fixed proportion of the median income (Fuchs suggests .50), and all households with Y_i/Y_m ratios less than .50 would be classified as poor, no matter what the growth in real income.

There are serious deficiencies in the Fuchs definition of poverty, which make it as unacceptable as an absolute poverty standard that is never revised upward. First, people derive satisfaction from the consumption of goods without *exclusive* reference to the ratio that their consumption bears to the median income. It is difficult to accept the proposition that poverty would be no more extensive or acute in India than in the United States if only the relative dispersions of the income distributions were alike. *There are real income dimensions of poverty (chronic hunger, disease, etc.) that are ameliorated simply by the growth in real income.*

Second, even on a relative basis, the Fuchs measure omits some important comparisons. People frequently compare their present incomes with their earlier incomes; general economic growth therefore makes people feel better off (perceiving improvement over time), even if others are also better off, that is, even if Y_i/Y_m remains stable.

Third, as the general level of income rises, the incremental gains are used to satisfy less important wants, and the welfare or utility differences between persons in the income distribution may become smaller as the whole income distribution shifts to the right. (This applies, for example, if $U = \log Y$.) In welfare terms, the main beneficiaries of economic growth have been the masses, not the elites, even though the elites have also increased their incomes. Our postindustrial society has produced and diffused consumer goods that at one time were available only to the wealthy, thereby reducing the qualitative differences between points on the income scale.

Fourth, the proper implementation of a purely relative standard faces subtle and difficult measurement problems. If we lived in a society where all age-income profiles were horizontal lines, then the age distribution of the population would not matter when estimating the percent poor by applying the .50 median income threshold. Incomes of 20-year-olds could reasonably be compared with 45-year-olds, and the latter with the retired cohort. But as I have pointed out elsewhere (Paglin 1975), our society's average age-income profile is highly arched, the result of heavy invest-ment in education and training. Under these circumstances, one should not ignore stage-of-life-cycle differences when making relative income comparisons. Graduate and professional students generally do not con-sider themselves part of the poverty population, although many fall below half the median income. However, a 40-year-old high school dropout with the same income (but quite different prospects) would justifiably be classified as poor. Relative poverty depends not only on one's present position in the income hierarchy but where one expects to be. Hence stage-of-life cycle and the expected shape of the future income profile are important in assessing relative poverty status; there is a large set of Y_m levels, not a single median income, which is appropriate for such comparisons. As Bradley Schiller (1976) has aptly shown, the income chairs in our distribution are relatively fixed, but the people who occupy these chairs are highly mobile over their life cycle, both within and between age cohorts. This has profound implications for the measurement of long-run inequality and of *relative* poverty when they are calculated from annual income data; both measurements are significantly overstated because they fail to consider a longer time horizon (Paglin 1979).

In the face of such complexities, the real income poverty standard, periodically revised upward by use of survey data on self-assessment of poverty status, seems preferable. The reader should note that both measures discussed are *objective* in the sense that the opinions of the persons being evaluated are not considered. An alternative subjective measure of poverty, which can help resolve the issue of real versus relative elements in the perception of poverty, is discussed elsewhere (see Paglin 1980, pp. 16–20).

The empirical estimates of the change in relative poverty are inadequate, even apart from their failure to recognize such factors as the variety of life-cycle curves, age differences, and number of workers in the household. The recent figures presented by Plotnick and Smeeding (1979, Table 1, sect. C) are deficient in a simple empirical dimension as well — they omit the in-kind transfers that make up over 60% of the income-tested transfer budget and had the highest rates of growth, 1965–1976. (Only the careful reader will catch this because in section B of the same table there is a set of "adjusted" absolute poverty estimates in which posttransfer poverty is defined to include in-kind transfers.) Not surprisingly, the relative poverty rates for 1965–1976 fluctuate around 15.2% and show the same flat trend as the unadjusted official poverty figures. Although we lack specific estimates of relative poverty (defined by Plotnick and Smeeding as .44 of the median income) based on an adequate definition of income (that is, after in-kind transfers), it is easy to show that relative poverty has also declined.

The official poverty rate (without in-kind transfers) went from 17.3% in 1965 to 11.8% in 1976, a drop of 32%. The final revised post–in-kind poverty rates in the same period went from 13.3% to 3.6%, a drop of 73%, much more than the drop in the official figures. This additional reduction in poverty rates is mainly due to the inclusion of the fast-growing in-kind transfers in the definition of household income. As Plotnick and Smeeding indicate, the relative poverty rates without adding in-kind transfers remained flat during the period. If in-kind transfers were 100% target efficient, then they would have no effect on the incomes of the near-poor, or those in the narrow income intervals between the absolute thresholds and the relative thresholds, namely, .44 of the median income for each household size. But, in fact, a large and increasing percentage of the in-kind transfers either went to (1) those whose money incomes were above the absolute poverty thresholds, or (2) those households below the poverty thresholds in money income terms, but pushed above the poverty lines by multiple in-kind transfers. These so-called *spillover effects* have increased as the number and the size of the in-kind programs have grown, thus reducing overall target efficiency. In 1965 the in-kind programs were collectively 56% target efficient; in 1975 this figure dropped to 45%. By examining the program eligibility and benefit schedules, we find that 55% of the transfers (in 1975) went mostly to near-poor households, pushing up their incomes above the relative poverty thresholds in substantial numbers. (Estimates of target efficiency and the distribution of in-kind benefits by income class are given in Paglin 1980, p. 43, Table 7A, and app. 1.) Thus, not only is the level of relative poverty reduced, but also the trend slopes downward. While the specific numbers are not yet available, the proposition that relative poverty has declined is almost indisputable. This conclusion follows logically from the growing magnitude of in-kind transfers going to those just above the absolute thresholds, and the stable percentage of those with money incomes below the relative poverty thresholds. This stable percentage of persons with money incomes below the (relative) poverty thresholds must show a decline when a growing volume and percent of in-kind transfers is added to this segment of the income distribution.

TARGET EFFICIENCY OF IN-KIND TRANSFERS

There is no disputing the fact that the overall target efficiency of in-kind transfers has been declining and seems disappointingly low — about 45% even when the age-based Medicare program is excluded from the income-tested transfer total. (Smeeding, including Medicare as part of the anti-poverty budget even though it is age-based rather than income-tested, found that in 1972 only 31% of the in-kind transfers reduced the poverty gap.) However, these low target-efficiency figures are largely a function of somewhat arbitrary decisions on the test of efficiency. If we raise the threshold a bit in deference to a relative component, as noted in the preceding section, the target efficiency of the transfer programs would go up quite remarkably, since a large part of the benefit spillovers and the initial distribution of benefits go to the near-poor. But this approach is not considered target efficient.

A large part of the spillovers in the programs mentioned earlier is the result of a legislative requirement to meet needs not fully compatible with target efficiency. Note that the poverty thresholds are defined in terms of annual incomes. The Food Stamp and child nutrition programs are geared to respond to short-term as well as long-term nutritional needs. Hence the low-income qualifying period is made very short — one month. Since incomes during a year may fluctuate considerably, especially for low-income households and the unemployed, short-period income poverty may be more than offset on an annual basis; the goal of alleviating short-term poverty conflicts with the goal of high target efficiency.

If we calculated poverty incidence on a short-term basis, the number of poor would rise, but the efficiency of the transfer programs would show significant improvement. Alternatively, we could improve target efficiency by requiring a longer period of low income as a condition of eligibility, or by requiring repayment if income picked up later in the year. Both of these revisions, however, would be impractical. Food, medical care, and other such needs cannot be postponed for a one-year waiting period; other short-term relief centers would have to be organized to fill the gap. Requiring repayment of food stamps or rent supplements if income rose above the poverty line later in the calendar year is equally impractical. It would impose high marginal tax rates and added work disincentives on the very group whose entrance into the labor force we wish to encourage. The desire to improve work incentives is part of the reason why some in-kind transfer programs do not abruptly terminate benefits as households reach the poverty threshold; to do so would impose a 100% tax rate on households who could earn part of their income. Thus, target efficiency and work-incentive objectives are in conflict whether transfers are cash or in-kind. However, the multiple in-kind programs, with eligibility and benefits from each program dependent on household money income, have made the problem of disincentives far worse. In particular, Medicaid, with its categorical coverage for families on public assistance, imposes high marginal tax rates on family heads who leave dependent status to enter the work force. Perhaps a low sliding scale premium for continued Medicaid coverage, paid by each family head who switched from welfare to work, could eliminate the Medicaid all-or-nothing benefit notch.

There is another kind of target inefficiency: the failure of a transfer program to reach all who are poor. Typically, this is measured by comparing the number of poor persons who are enrolled in the program (e.g., Food Stamps) and the official CPS poverty count. Since even the open-ended programs never enroll 100% of the poor, this gap is cited as a need for more "project-outreach" activity. However, such target failure calculations are based on a statistical illusion — that the official number of poor are in fact really poor and are eligible for participation in the program. The following brief rundown indicates some of the groups included in the official census poverty population who are not likely to be eligible for or be in need of transfers.

The Phantom Poor, or Pseudopoor. The phantom poor include those in the under $1,000 income class who had zero census income or loss. Losses are mainly attributable to family farm operations, other types of small businesses, and persons with negative net rental incomes because of accelerated depreciation on real estate, and so on. The Congressional Budget Office provided me with a computer printout of persons in poverty (FY 1976) that excluded the business-loss group from the poverty count; the poverty estimate was thereby reduced by 1,038,000 persons. This group with substantial assets and highly variable incomes is in no way poor and should be removed from the official poverty counts.

A second and related type of overstatement of poverty involves receipts not counted as income and includes all intrafamily transfers, such as payments made to support young adults or elderly parents living on their own. Also included in poverty counts are income-poor who receive lump-sum inheritances or insurance settlements. More recently, the earned income credit, which is paid to large numbers of low-income families, would raise many above the poverty threshold if such payments were counted as income by the Census Bureau.

Finally, there are the newly formed households who in the previous (reference) year were living with their families and may have had little or no earnings; these also are recorded as poor. (For a brief discussion of income definition problems that give rise to phantom poor, see U.S. Bureau of the Census 1976, p. 159.)

The Subterranean Economy. In addition to the nonreporting and underreporting of income mentioned at the beginning of this paper (which was adjusted for in terms of the national income benchmarks), there has been an extensive growth of the subterranean economy. This includes cash income generated by legal activities ("off the books" employment, etc.), but not reported to the IRS, and the whole range of illegal income-generating activities. Peter M. Gutmann of Columbia University estimates that in 1976 there was $176 billion of GNP not recorded. Such income is not likely to be reported to a census telephone interviewer who collects the CPS income data. (See Gutmann 1977.)

The Asset Rich. Most in-kind programs have both income and asset tests for eligibility. This is a fair measure of financial capability. The asset test used in the Food Stamp Program allows the recipient to own a house, a car, and some business property; liquid assets may go up to $1,750, and $3,000 for an aged couple. It should be noted that poverty is measured by income only; hence a certain number of those classified as poor will be ineligible for most transfer programs. In the case of Supplementary Security Income (SSI), an income-tested transfer program for the elderly, it was estimated that 12–15% of those eligible by an income test were ineligible because of the asset test (Federal Council on the Aging 1977).

CONCLUSION

It is evident from the above discussion that there may be a substantial statistical residual in the census poverty population who will be outside the reach of need-based transfer programs. Since none of the adjusted or revised census estimates of poverty (including my own) make a downward adjustment for the phantom poor, actual poverty may well be a few million persons less than the final revised figures.

In the past fifteen years we have witnessed an unprecedented growth of government transfer programs for the needy. Not surprisingly, when the official statistics are corrected for their obvious deficiencies, we see that poverty has declined to a very low level. But even the corrected figures may contain a substantial residual of statistical anomalies — persons with substantial assets, as well as other groups who are not really poor. It is fair to say that despite some substitution of transfers for earned income and private savings, the antipoverty effort has succeeded in accomplishing its primary goal — raising the low-income population above a minimum income floor. The multiple-benefit welfare system has not been conspicuously target efficient or always equitable, but it has accomplished some things that a pure cash transfer system might not have done as well. Dr. Jean Mayer (formerly professor of nutrition at Harvard) has pointed out that "when you look at the problem of hunger in America, it really is not the same country it was ten years ago" (Mayer 1979). He goes on to point out that 19 million persons receive food stamps, 11 million children get free school lunches, and 2–3 million participate in summer food programs. There is the WIC program providing supplementary high protein foods for pregnant women, infants, and young children. Federal and state subsidies go for Meals on Wheels and other food programs for the elderly and the shut-ins.

In the area of medical services, we have largely closed the gap between income classes in terms of doctor visits per year; infant mortality in low-income households has shown a striking decline. Certainly Medicaid/Medicare, Maternal and Child Health Care, and OEO Neighborhood Health Clinics account for a large part of this improvement. Would the antipoverty professionals (or the community generally) have been satisfied if cash incomes were raised, but children missed lunches at school or received inadequate medical care? Or if the needy elderly lacked medical treatment? Perhaps as economists we are too ready to assume that the head of every household allocates income in a way that maximizes the welfare of all persons in the household. The in-kind transfer programs may be a bit more realistic in recognizing human weaknesses and failures.

Through a combination of cash and in-kind programs the war on poverty has succeeded in raising the real incomes and welfare of the poor, though its direct costs and indirect social effects have made it an expensive victory. The fact that it has not reduced "pretransfer poverty" or "pretransfer inequality" should hardly be a matter of surprise to economists. We have relieved poverty through an enormous expansion of income transfers and provided easier access to more generous benefits. Now we express concern that low-income households have raised their incomes by picking up the transfer option rather than by working and earning more. Why be surprised that people make rational choices? Was it unexpected that people would retire earlier to take advantage of improved, tax-free Social Security benefits, that some would substitute Social Security for private savings; that some unemployed workers (especially second earners) would defer returning to work when tax-free unemployment insurance benefits almost equal net earnings? Is it surprising that many women in low-income households find the stability and security of the cash and in-kind welfare package preferable to the less steady income of an erstwhile (or potential) legal spouse? Or that the male hangers-on prefer to keep all their earnings rather than assume a supportive family role? Poverty professionals, who have so tirelessly advocated more generous transfers for the low-income population, now seem appalled by the unreformed extent of pretransfer poverty and are little satisfied by the remarkable reduction in posttransfer poverty.

We have reaped both the benefits and the adverse effects of the growth in the welfare state. Doesn't the present impasse in reforming our complex multiple-benefit welfare system indicate that we may be approaching the limits of effective social policy?

REFERENCES

Congressional Budget Office, U.S. Congress. 1977. *Poverty Status of Families under Alternative Definitions of Income,* rev. ed. Washington, D.C.: U.S. Government Printing Office.

Federal Council on the Aging. 1977. *The Treatment of Assets . . . in Income-Conditioned Government Benefit Programs.* Madison: Institute for Poverty Research, University of Wisconsin.

Fuchs, Victor. 1967. "Redefining Poverty." *Public Interest,* no. 8 (Summer):88–95.

Gilder, George. 1980. "The Coming Welfare Crisis." *Policy Review* (Winter):25–36.

Gutmann, Peter M. 1977. "The Subterranean Economy." *Financial Analysts Journal* 6 (November-December):26–27, 34.

Lampman, Robert. 1971. *Ends and Means of Reducing Income Poverty.* Chicago: Markham.

Mayer, Jean. 1979. Quoted in "Current Reading: Food in America." *Public Interest,* no. 54 (Winter):124.

Paglin, Morton. 1975. "Measurement and Trend of Inequality: A Basic Revision." *American Economic Review* 65 (September):598–609.

———. 1979. "Reply." *American Economic Review* 69 (September):673–77.

———. 1980. *Poverty and Transfers in Kind.* Stanford, Calif.: Hoover Institution Press.

Plotnick, Robert, and Smeeding, Timothy M. 1979. "Poverty and Income Transfers: Past Trends and Future Prospects." *Public Policy* 27 (Summer):255–72.

Schiller, Bradley. 1976. "Equality, Opportunity and 'The Good Job.'" *Public Interest,* no. 43 (Spring):111–20.

Smeeding, Timothy M. 1977. "The Anti-Poverty Effectiveness of In-Kind Transfers." *Journal of Human Resources* 12 (Summer):360–78.

U.S. Bureau of the Census. 1976. *Current Population Reports.* Ser. P-60, no. 101 (January). Washington, D.C.: U.S. Government Printing Office.

———. 1978. *Current Population Reports.* Ser. P-60, no. 115 (July). Washington, D.C.: U.S. Government Printing Office.

III IMPLICATIONS OF CURRENT PROGRAMS FOR REFORM PROPOSALS

In part III we examine three programs — Food Stamps, unemployment insurance, and Aid to Families with Dependent Children — that have in the past occupied and continue to occupy center stage in the political debate on welfare reform.

In the last twenty years or so, Food Stamps — a program allowing one to purchase food with coupons rather than money — has assumed a significant share of the federal welfare burden. J. Fred Giertz and Dennis H. Sullivan review the economic effects of the Food Stamp Program and its relationship to the two major welfare reform efforts in the last two decades, the Nixon Family Assistance Plan and the Carter Program for Better Jobs and Income. The failure of these reform efforts has placed on the Food Stamp Program a burden it was never intended to support: it has become the federal government's guaranteed income. The authors assess the impact of recent reforms and the possibilities for further evolution — or extinction — of the Food Stamp Program.

Has too much attention been paid to labor supply responses at the expense of equally critical areas? Daniel S. Hamermesh believes that economists should turn their attention to evaluating how well social insurance, welfare, and other income maintenance programs meet the goal of preventing hardship. The major focus of antipoverty efforts should be consumption, not income. The author examines how unemployment insurance benefits, in particular, affect consumption of the poor. The results suggest that more efficient targeting is needed. There is an opportunity here either to slice more people from the public dole or to redistribute payments among unemployment insurance recipients so that the goal of alleviating hardship can be met more closely at no additional cost.

James R. Hosek's paper investigates the determinants of family participation in the Aid to Families with Dependent Children–Unemployed Fathers program, and projects the changes in caseload and cost that would arise under selected program modifications. The modifications include extending the program to all states, setting a nationwide benefit floor, and relaxing certain eligibility requirements. An implication of the finding that expanding the Unemployed Fathers program would not raise welfare caseloads dramatically is that our current system is fairly good at aiding nearly all working poor households.

6 THE ROLE OF FOOD STAMPS IN WELFARE REFORMS

J. Fred Giertz and Dennis H. Sullivan

Welfare reform has been a major issue in American political economy for the last twenty years. Over this same period, the Food Stamp Program, which first surfaced as a significant political issue during John Kennedy's West Virginia primary campaign, has developed into a major component of the American transfer apparatus. The growth of in-kind transfers and the counterpoint of reformers' attempts to cash them out are indeed characteristic of the whole period, and the Food Stamp Program is a major example. If we are to think clearly about the future, we must have an appreciation of this significant history.

Our paper analyzes this history in several stages. First, we provide a review of the general public choice approach to the positive analysis of in-kind transfers, then apply this approach to the policy shift from surplus commodity distribution to a national Food Stamp Program. After reviewing the major goals of welfare reform, we review the relationship of food stamps to the two major welfare reform efforts in the last decade, the Nixon Family Assistance Plan and the Carter Program for Better Jobs and Income. The failure of these reform efforts had two effects: Food Stamps began to bear a significant share of the federal welfare reform burden, and the reformers sought to alter Food Stamps so as to carry that burden more fully. We examine these two effects in turn, then provide in the last section an assessment of the possibilities for further evolution — or extinction — of the Food Stamp Program.

REVIEW OF THE PUBLIC CHOICE APPROACH TO IN-KIND TRANSFERS

Until a decade or so ago, economists had very little to contribute to the positive analysis of the reasons for the existence of various governmental transfer programs. Redistribution was usually discussed in a normative framework in which transfers were viewed as a means of achieving improved equity or higher social welfare, as measured by an externally determined social welfare function. Very little was said about the reasons why transfer programs come into existence through the political process. In addition, the form in which transfers are made had received only a cursory treatment.

At that time, the prevailing opinion among economists was that cash or general purchasing power transfers clearly dominated restrictive or in-kind redistribution on the grounds that a recipient, for a given dollar value of redistribution, could achieve at least as much (and very likely more) utility with cash (as opposed to goods-specific) transfers. In-kind transfer programs were labeled as inefficient, and the existence of programs involving such things as food or housing assistance was viewed as an aberration of public policy.

More recently, however, considerable attention has been given to explaining the existence of various transfer programs. One obvious factor contributing to redistribution is the motivation of potential recipients to use the political system to extract resources from unwilling "donors." This motive and the conflicts resulting from it are self-evident and need little explanation. Viewed strictly from this standpoint, redistribution is a zero or, with transactions costs, a negative sum game, with potential recipients attempting to organize coalitions to approve transfer schemes against the defensive efforts of prospective donors.

All redistribution need not fit into this mold characterized solely by conflict. Utility interdependencies among individuals may exist, so that the well-being or possibly the consumption pattern of one person may provide increased (or decreased) utility to others as well. (For a review of the literature in this area, see Collard 1978.) If these sorts of externalities exist in sufficient strength, both the donor and recipient may benefit from transfers. This type of redistribution, sometimes labeled

Pareto-optimal redistribution, can exploit potential "gains from trade." In this situation, redistribution can be explained on the grounds of efficiency rather than equity. The explanation for the collectivization of transfer programs resulting from such motives is based on the free-rider problem. If large numbers of individuals experience utility interdependencies with potential recipients, the disincentives to the private provision of transfers common to most public goods situations may lead to governmentally provided programs where "donations" become tax payments. While this reduces the possibility of individuals (free-riders) receiving the indirect, external benefits of transfer programs without contributing, it means that individuals with no interdependence with the recipients are also taxed. In this context, it is difficult to completely separate Pareto-optimal redistribution from the type based strictly upon conflict that was discussed previously.[1]

Not only does the existence of utility interdependencies help explain the existence of transfer programs; it also is invaluable in clarifying the reasons for the form of such programs. In particular, it can help to explain the existence of in-kind transfer programs such as Food Stamps (Daly and Giertz 1972). Potential donors may receive external benefits from the general level of satisfaction a recipient achieves. This type of interdependency, labeled a *utility externality,* would presumably lead to transfers in cash, since both the donor and the recipient would prefer this form; only the size of the transfer would be in question. On the other hand, donors may derive utility from the various goods and services consumed by the recipient, not just from the level of utility achieved. This type of externality is designated a *goods-specific externality.* This may result from paternalistic feelings on the part of donors who believe recipients are not competent to allocate general purchasing power transfers to serve their own best interests. For example, transfers used for milk might be overwhelmingly supported, while those used for liquor would meet with strong disapproval; likewise, transfers used to provide housing would likely be favored over those that would go for automobiles. In addition, donors may favor in-kind transfers as a technique for achieving other goals that they favor. For example, youth recreation programs may reduce crime, or medical assistance may stop the spread of communicable disease. *Merit goods* is another, older term applied to consumption activities that exert positive external effects.

Both introspection and the casual observation of donors suggest the pervasiveness of goods-specific externalities. A wide variety of both private and public transfer programs have goods-specific characteristics. Polls consistently indicate the willingness on the part of the public to transfer resources for shelter, medical care, education, and especially food, as compared to cash. In particular, food-specific externalities seem to be especially strong with the public, as witnessed by the concern both domestically and internationally, for the problem of hunger. Many people seem to feel that regardless of the deprivation experienced in other areas, no one should be forced, or even allowed, to fail to have access to adequate food.

The existence of goods-specific externalities directly affects the conclusions about the efficacy of cash transfers. In such a case, cash transfers are generally not an efficient technique for achieving Pareto-optimality (Daly and Giertz 1972). When the preferences of both donors and recipients are considered, some type of redistributive program that forces the recipient to depart from the normal maximization conditions, where the marginal rate of substitution is equated to the price ratio, is necessary to achieve Pareto-optimality. Even recipients may favor goods-specific programs if donors have an important role in determining the size of the program. If donors are constrained to make transfers only in the form of cash, this may result in few if any transfers being made. Such programs are by no means easy to devise, however, especially when considered in terms of the cost-effectiveness for the donors. The fact that recipients have additional, unrestricted income over and above their transfer receipts makes it difficult to achieve many of the objectives of donors who are motivated by goods-specific externalities. This problem, which will be explored more fully below, is of crucial importance for the Food Stamp Program (Giertz and Sullivan, 1977; 1978). In addition, the transactions costs associated with in-kind transfers also have to be considered when comparing these programs with cash transfer plans.

FROM SURPLUS COMMODITY DISTRIBUTION TO FOOD STAMPS

Food-specific transfer programs in the United States have been in the form of either commodity distribution plans or food stamp programs. Commodity distribution programs have generally served the dual purpose of making use of surplus agricultural products resulting from government price-support programs while improving the nutritional level of poor people. The first major program came into existence in 1935 and continued until 1939, when it was replaced by an early food stamp program. Another commodity distribution program, adopted after World War II (1949), was also eventually replaced by the current Food Stamp Program in the early 1970s (MacDonald 1977; Clarkson 1975).

The rise and fall of the two commodity distribution programs have, in general, paralleled the availability of surplus farm commodities. Such programs were primarily thought of as a humane way of disposing of virtually worthless commodities, rather than as a direct attempt to deal with the problem of hunger. The quantity of food distributed depended on the level of surplus commodities available, rather than on the level of recipient need. Such programs, however, were successful in providing those that did participate with an assured minimum level of food consumption. Still, the recipients were often less than delighted with the quality and variety of the commodities, while food wholesalers and retailers looked with disfavor on the programs, since the distributions were made at no cost and outside the usual marketing channels (with the final distribution point often at a location inconvenient for many recipients).

Aside from agricultural interests, the commodity distribution plan had few supporters, especially among individuals and groups with a special interest in the problem of hunger. One major criticism was that this federal program, administered by the Department of Agriculture, did not reach many of the most impoverished areas of the country, since state and county governments had to approve and help administer the program to make it operative. In addition, eligibility rules were established locally rather than at the national level. In this situation, there was no assurance to citizens with an interest in the problem of hunger (i.e., those with food-specific externalities) that adequate amounts of food were available to those in need in all parts of the country.

The commodity distribution plan also had more subtle deficiencies. In many cases (especially among the higher income participants), the free distribution did little to increase food consumption, since it merely replaced food that had been previously purchased, making it a very costly way to increase food consumption. The commodity distribution system also had a serious "notch" problem, in that eligibility depended either upon eligibility for public assistance or low income (as determined by the individual states). Since there was no phase-out of benefits near the cutoff point, the all-or-nothing nature of the program created serious disincentives for recipients near the income eligibility level. On the other hand, the commodity distribution scheme had few disincentives for those far below the cutoff levels, since greater earnings in this range had no effect on benefits.

The combination of the opposition of recipients and their proponents and the receding of the agricultural surplus problem during the 1960s led to a gradual replacement of the commodity distribution program with Food Stamps. Congress authorized a pilot Food Stamp Program in 1958, which was eventually utilized by President Kennedy to establish such a program in eight areas around the country in 1961. In 1964, the Food Stamp Program was expanded into a national program (still subject to local government approval) that gradually began to replace commodity distributions. In 1970, benefit levels were greatly increased, giving rise to increased participation in the program, while uniform income and eligibility standards were mandated in a 1971 amendment to the Food Stamp Act of 1964. The program became truly national in scope in 1974, when all counties in the United States were required to have a program in operation.

The Food Stamp Program, as compared with the commodity distribution program, used normal distribution channels (with final distribution in grocery stores) to bring food to the recipient. It kept the food-specific nature of the older program, while giving recipients access to a wide variety of products, as opposed to the limited fare available previously with surplus commodities.[2] The Food Stamp Program employed a gradual benefit-reduction arrangement, which eliminated the notch problem, although this meant that program benefits had to be extended to some recipients who might not be classified as truly poor. The income concept used to determine eligibility was a net concept that included deductions for such items as Social Security and income taxes, 10% of wages and salaries (but not to exceed $30 per month after 1971), medical costs exceeding $10 per month, and shelter expenses that exceed 30% of income after all other deductions. There was also a means test involving household wealth, including a limit of $1,500 on liquid assets.

The design of the program also attempted to stimulate additional food consumption, while at the same time inducing the recipient to bear a share of the cost. Details of the Food Stamp plan (circa 1969–1970) as they affect the recipient can be explained with the use of a diagram illustrating the way in which the program modified the recipient's budget constraint. The program established a minimum purchase requirement (F^*), which every recipient who chose to participate was required to receive. The minimum purchase requirement, which depended strictly upon family size (not the level of the recipient's income), was designed to provide the family with a low-cost, nutritionally adequate diet. This can be seen in Figure 6.1, where a consumer's choice between food (available for purchase with food stamps) and a composite of all other commodities measured in dollars is displayed on the axes. The budget line AB represents a very low income household's pre–food stamp budget line with the monthly food allotment (F^*) set beyond the level of food consumption that families of this income level would (or could) voluntarily choose, thus achieving one goal of individuals with food-specific externalities.

Composite
of Other
Goods
Measured
in $

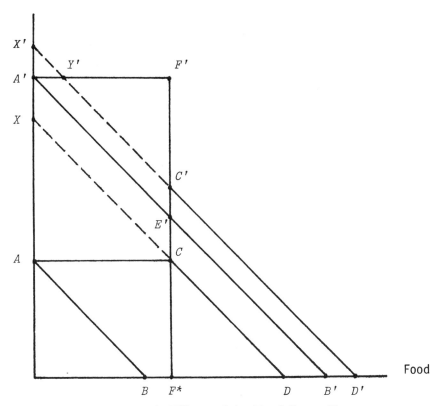

Figure 6.1. The Economic Effects of the Food Stamp Program

The monthly food allotment was not, in general, given to the recipients, but sold at a fraction of the actual cost. The amount paid by the recipient varied according to household income levels from zero (after 1970) to over 85% of the market value of the coupons for those in the highest eligible income categories. In Figure 6.1, free food stamps for extremely poor households would move the effective budget line from *AB* to *ACD* (as compared to *DX* for a cash transfer of the same total cost), where, presumably, every household would participate, aside from lack of information or the stigma attached to the program. The budget line $A'B'$ represents a less poor recipient, of the same family size, and thus the same F^*. In this case, the recipient would have to pay $F'C'$ for the F^* food stamps (whose value is $F'E'$), thus receiving a bonus value of $C'E'$. The relevant budget line would become $A'E'C'D'$ (as compared to $D'X'$ for a cash transfer of the same total cost). It is clear that for many recipients in this category, nonparticipation might be preferable to receiving food stamps. That is, a higher level of utility could be reached along $A'E'$ than along $C'D'$.

From this analysis, it would be expected that participation rates would vary inversely with the level of income. There are also several trade-offs that are faced by donors who experience food-specific externalities, assuming they can affect the design of the program (see Giertz and Sullivan 1977). For example, increasing the minimum amount of food stamps with the same bonus value would increase the nutritional level of participants while reducing the number of those participating. Increasing participation rates could only be achieved by increasing the bonus value or by reducing F^*, neither of which would likely be viewed with favor by many donors. With all the problems, however, food stamps seemed to be a clear improvement over commodity distributions for almost everyone, save those interested solely in the programs as an agricultural subsidy.

The growth of the Food Stamp Program raised many other questions concerning its relationship with other existing transfer programs and particularly with plans for some type of negative income tax emphasizing cash rather than in-kind transfers. These issues are discussed below.

THE GOALS OF WELFARE REFORM

To understand the way in which food stamps and welfare reform interact, one must have some idea of what welfare *reform* tries to reform. From reading the academic discussions in the late 1960s — for example, Green (1967) and the history of the Nixon welfare reform (Bawden, Cain, and Hausman 1971; Moynihan 1973) — the following list emerges:

poverty reduction (either as poverty incidence or poverty gap),
reduction of work disincentives,
equity for the working poor,
reduction of incentives for family dissolution,
reduction of interstate differentials,
fiscal relief for states and localities,

reduction of discretionary power of social workers,
reduction of welfare stigma.

About each a little more needs to be said.

The goal of poverty reduction raises problems of measurement. Much of the Great Society legislation emphasized the incidence of poverty (i.e., the percentage of a population with cash income below the officially established poverty line). This conceptualization predisposes policy discussion toward emphasis on an "adequate" (nonpoverty) income guarantee and against considerations of incentive or of vertical equity. It also fails to distinguish degrees of poverty and fails to take account of in-kind transfers.[3]

Reduction of work disincentives is a widely publicized welfare reform goal. President Nixon called his proposal *workfare*. The usual means are either reduction of the income guarantee for those able, but unwilling to work, or reduction of the benefit reduction rate (often enhanced by an earnings disregard). The former means was a part of both the Nixon and Carter approaches to reform at one point or another, but it is hard to defend politically unless linked (as in the Carter proposal) to a large and expensive public employment program providing the jobs to be offered. The latter means is at the heart of most welfare reform proposals, but it proves difficult to employ in a consistent way. In the first place, lower benefit reduction rates rapidly push the break-even level into heavily populated areas of the earnings distribution, reducing target efficiency. Moreover, the continued existence of some other transfer programs creates severe integration problems, generating high combined benefit-reduction rates and welfare notches caused by income eligibility limits for certain food, housing, and medical benefits. These issues are carefully discussed by Allen (1972), and in less detail by Moynihan (1973). The moral of their story seems to be that lowering benefit-reduction rates is a goal that, while apparently complementary with other welfare reform goals, is expensive to achieve, and thus competitive with other goals for limited funds.

The goal of equitable treatment of the working poor is generally accomplished by combining two reform elements: replacement of categorical eligibility tests with a means test, and employment of a nonconfiscatory benefit-reduction rate. It is important to note that the categorical patchwork that has evolved over the years is often so patently inequitable to the working poor that even very high benefit-reduction rates can constitute a considerable improvement. A rate that appears deficient on work incentive grounds may, therefore, remain defensible as relatively equitable. A more severe problem encountered by the Nixon welfare proposals was the charge that granting equity to the working poor would "expand the welfare rolls" (Moynihan 1973, p. 502). To the extent that the charge was not motivated by political cynicism, it seems to indicate that *any* transfer benefits available on a means-tested basis are going to carry some degree of stigma (a point more recently reiterated in Garfinkel 1979).

Decategorization, necessary for equity to the working poor, is also often a goal of family policy, such as reducing incentives for family dissolution. Early welfare reform debates greatly clarified the practical purposes of the general goal of decategorization.

Reduction of interstate differentials has long been a welfare goal on grounds of equity. The problem of poverty is a national one, as the geographical range of utility interdependence is widespread. There is, moreover, some evidence of migration to attain higher benefit levels. In general, proposals focus on some sort of national minimum benefit, either explicit or in the form of the implicit guarantee in a negative tax.

The national minimum, however, is often seen as differentially beneficial to the least generous states. This has generally led to proposals for fiscal relief to more generous states via higher federal matching rates and for "hold harmless" provisions that prevent state costs from rising. Though generally ignored by academicians, fiscal relief considerations can be of great practical significance because of their budgetary impact.

Issues of stigma and of welfare worker discretion have never played a big role in economists' discussions of welfare reform, but both crop up at important points in welfare reform debates. We have already seen the stigma issue arise in the context of adding the working poor to the welfare rolls, and Moynihan (1973, pp. 302–27) details the vigorous opposition of leaders of the social welfare profession to the Nixon proposals.

WELFARE REFORM AND THE FOOD STAMP PROGRAM

Two major welfare reforms have been proposed in the last decade: the Nixon Family Assistance Plan (FAP) and the Carter Program for Better Jobs and Income (PBJI). Both explicitly addressed the integration of Food Stamps into the comprehensive apparatus. The role of Food Stamps in the debate on the proposals was instructive and often very important.

According to Moynihan (1973):

In the minds of most of the advocates of an income guarantee, food stamps were an anachronism that ought to, as soon as possible, be "cashed out" and incorporated into the primary income-maintenance system. However, within the [Nixon] Administration a major food stamp proposal [viz., complete replacement of surplus commodities by food stamps] had already been presented to the President, who had indicated his general approval. Outside the Administration there was an intense, if limited, political demand for more food stamps, and no discernible demand whatever for a guaranteed income. (P. 137)

More eloquent support for the public choice approach one could not wish. Moynihan himself disliked Food Stamps, largely, it seems, because of the low participation rate, but he certainly recognized the basic point of the public choice analysis: in his words, "food stamps; no beer stamps." He did not, it seems, recognize the corollary point that once food stamps became universally available, the only financial reason for not participating would be a strong desire not to be stuck with all those stamps good only for food — a conscious decision to forego food rather than nonfood.

In any event, FAP emerged as a combined cash/food stamp proposal. The basic combination for a four-person family can be described in a set of three equations (see Bawden, Cain, and Hausman 1971, pp. 331–37):

$$Y = E + 1,600, \text{ if } E < 720. \tag{6.1a}$$

$$Y = E + 1,600 - .5(E - 720), \text{ if } E \geq 720. \tag{6.1b}$$

This equation gives gross income for a negative tax with a \$1,600 guarantee, a .50 benefit-reduction rate, and a \$720 disregard — the original FAP.

$$I = Y - .318(Y - .1E), \text{ if } E < \$3,600. \tag{6.2a}$$

$$I = Y - .318(Y - 360), \text{ if } E \geq \$3,600. \tag{6.2b}$$

These equations show the cash income after meeting the purchase requirement for food stamps, employing the 10% earnings deduction then permitted.

$$B = \$1,272 - .318(Y - .1E), \text{ if } E < \$3,600. \tag{6.3a}$$

$$B = \$1,272 - .318(Y - 360), \text{ if } E \geq \$3,600. \tag{6.3b}$$

The third equation gives the food stamp *bonus value,* the face value of the scrip less the purchase requirement. Most of the contemporary discussions employ either Y or $Y + B$ as their measures of household income. From the public choice perspective, however, the key numbers are the face value of the scrip ($1,272), which is the same for all recipient households of family size 4, and *I*, the household's cash disposable income (ignoring any effects of positive taxes; see Bawden, Cain, and Hausman 1971).

The interaction is outlined in Table 6.1. The benefit-reduction rate rises up to the FAP disregard, though kept down initially by the food stamp earnings deduction. After that the rate takes on its characteristic value of .63, until the food stamp earnings deduction is maximized at $E = \$3,600$. Since in this case the FAP break-even point is below the point at which the food stamp bonus value is zero, the rate drops at $E = \$3,920$ to the food stamp rate. (In fact, however, most such households are not willing to suffer the bother and stigma of food stamps for such small bonus values.)

In terms of our welfare reform criteria, the integration of food stamps and FAP has a couple of real problems. First, the purchase requirement reduces the net cash value of the guarantee. And second, the combined benefit-reduction rate is high across the bulk of the relevant earnings range and changes suddenly at either end (a matter that Anderson [1978], for example, finds most distressing).

The Nixon Administration found it difficult to cope with these problems. The guarantee *was* "inadequate" in some sense. The cash/scrip

Table 6.1.   Interaction of Nixon FAP and Food Stamp Program for Family of Four

Earnings (E)	Cash Transfer	Gross Cash Income (Y)	Net Cash Income (I)	Benefit-Reduction Rate $(1 - [\Delta I/\Delta E])$
0	1,600	1,600	1,091	.29
500	1,600	2,100	1,448	.29
720[a]	1,600	2,320	1,605	.63
1,000	1,460	2,460	1,710	.63
2,000	960	2,960	2,082	.63
3,000	460	3,460	2,455	.63
3,600[b]	160	3,760	2,679	.63
3,920[c]	0	3,920	2,788	.66
4,360[d]	0	4,360	3,088	.32

[a] FAP disregard.
[b] Food Stamp earnings deduction maximum.
[c] FAP break-even point.
[d] Food Stamp break-even point.

combination ($I + \$1,272 = Y + B$) at zero earnings came to $2,363, less than two-thirds of the 1970 poverty line of $3,720. More telling, perhaps, the combination of the low guarantee and the high benefit-reduction rate meant that $3,000 earnings would be required to get the family to a cash/scrip value equal to the poverty line. Consequently, at one point (during the battle in the House of Representatives), the Nixon Administration tried the tack of abolishing food stamps and employing a $2,400 cash guarantee. As Allen (1972) shows, however, this proposal was futile. The likely participation in the cash program would be much higher than with the cash/scrip combination, especially if the .50 benefit reduction were maintained, driving the break-even level to $4,800 (without disregard) or $5,520 (with disregard). Consequently, cost considerations drove the Administration toward a .66 benefit-reduction rate and no disregard. It is hard to see that as much of an improvement on Table 6.1 unless one is very serious indeed about cashing out in-kind programs on principle.

Later, the Nixon Administration tried the opposite tack of liberalizing food stamps to try to lower the combined benefit-reduction rate. Certainly, proposals to liberalize rather than abolish worked better for food stamps than for some of the other in-kind transfers. Their basically negative tax character and the fact that their low guarantee allows a relatively low benefit-reduction rate makes them easier than most to integrate with a cash-negative tax. The stamps, moreover, are generally recognized as a right-in-being, and the liberality of a cash program sufficient to protect this right would certainly increase net program costs. Such an argument seems weak to Friedman "clean sweep" disciples, but retention of some in-kind transfers is a virtual necessity if those with goods-specific concerns are to be kept in the donor coalition.

With the PBJI, the Carter Administration did not share the Nixon scruples about proposing abolition of a program it had just finished reforming. As we shall see two sections hence, the 1977 Food Stamp Amendments actually moved the program away from its food-specific focus and made it correspondingly riper for abolition. The Carter Administration had additional reasons for proposing abolition, however. In part, these involved old arguments about granting recipients freedom in expenditures and about the failure to count in-kind transfers in conventional poverty line analyses.

But there were new arguments, too. First, there was a strong suspicion that most poor people bought almost as much food without the stamps as with them, and those unwilling to do so seemed increasingly able to sell their excess stamps in a black market for 75 cents or so per dollar of face value. This cast into question the value of the extra administrative costs of a separate food stamp program. Second, the Carter Administration stressed the continued stigma attached to food stamps. And third, defensively, the Carter Administration pointed out the thoroughgoing decategorization of PBJI as opposed to FAP (which covered only families), thus refuting the argument for food stamps as a safety net for those falling through the categorical cracks.

It is interesting to see which interest groups and legislators rallied to the support of food stamps, and why (here we follow Weil 1978, pp. 79–86). It is notable that neither farm, nor food store lobbies seem to have shown much interest, although the continued importance of farm interests is indicated by the joint role of such odd bedfellows as Senators Dole and McGovern in the 1977 Reform Amendments. On the other hand, many people clearly continue to consider food stamps as antihunger, not antipoverty *per se*. Moreover, as soon as reform efforts become less than fully comprehensive (PBJI was in hot water from the first), an appreciation often develops for the ability of food stamps to reduce categorical and/or interstate differentials. Even the stigma issue is not as clear as it first appears. The AFL–CIO defended food stamps on the ground that food stamps carry *less* stigma for the unemployed than would means-tested cash transfers, which apparently smack even more heavily of welfare. Also, some conservatives seem to regard the residual stigma as a work incentive and therefore a merit rather than a demerit. The stigma seems to operate most strongly, and with the least incentive effect, on the elderly, and that perhaps explains the popularity of some proposals to cash out food stamps for Supplemental Security Income recipients only.

A review of the role of Food Stamp abolition in the PBJI debate reveals that the continued existence of Food Stamps represents a sort of political saddle point. Liberals fear that Food Stamp abolition will not be fully offset by equivalent cash transfers to all categorical subgroups. Conservatives fear that cashing out Food Stamps will lead to agitation for new food-specific initiatives. It does not appear that either group is anxious to offend those with food-specific concerns; consequently, the legislators seem content to retain this program targeted to those concerns, however much they may then complain about the results.

FOOD STAMPS AS WELFARE REFORM

Despite efforts at abolition, Food Stamps came, by the end of the 1970s, to be recognized as one of the most thoroughly "reformed" elements of the whole transfer structure, a possibility that some, like Paul Mc-Cracken, had foreseen early on (see Moynihan 1973, pp. 174–75). It is worth reviewing the argument for this viewpoint.

First, Food Stamps are a substantial antipoverty program. Federal outlays for Food Stamps will approach $10 billion in FY 1981, more than the federal share of AFDC. Almost 90% of this is targeted to those with cash incomes below the poverty line, for what is, after all, an essential set of expenditures. The allotment for zero income (currently $204 per month for a family of four) is, moreover, a *bona fide* income guarantee, however inadequate, and is indexed for inflation.

Second, the current benefit reduction rates (24% on earned income; 30% on transfers) are about as low as cost-effectiveness will permit, and aid considerably in the integration of Food Stamps with other transfer programs with higher rates.

Third, the Food Stamp Program is noncategorical; in particular, it makes little distinction about work status and none about family status. Its relatively equitable treatment of the working poor is, in fact, probably its most singular virtue from a reformer's viewpoint.

Fourth, Food Stamps fit well with the existing federal structure of welfare payments. They considerably reduce interstate differentials. Blechman, Gramlich, and Hartman (1975, p. 179) showed earlier in the decade that AFDC cash payments varied between the 5 most generous states and the 5 least generous by a factor of 3.5, but cash plus food stamp bonus differed by less than a factor of 2. The real after-stamps differential factor remains around 2, and it would surely be much larger without food stamps. Food Stamps, moreover, provide fiscal relief in that they generate no nonfederal expenditures except a share of administrative costs, while many other programs require partial state matching of actual benefits.

Finally, it is unclear whether the food stamp stigma is more or less severe than other means-tested transfers. This seems to be a question primarily of the recipient's subculture.

THE REFORM OF FOOD STAMPS

In the 1970s, the Food Stamp Program moved toward granting to recipients certain options that had the effect of reducing the food-specific character of the program. In 1971, recipients were supposedly allowed to buy fractional amounts (1/4, 1/2, or 3/4) of the total monthly allotment or minimum purchase requirement. This was done primarily in response to criticism that the single cash payment required for a full monthly allotment of Food Stamps prevented many persons from participating. The strategic use of the fractional purchase option (given that food stamps retain their value indefinitely) would seem to have changed the Food Stamp Program into a price subsidy in which the effective price of food (up to the minimum purchase requirement) was reduced to the recipient by the ratio of the bonus value divided by the monthly allotment. Under these conditions (and aside from the stigma problem), almost every eligible recipient would be expected to participate at least occasionally. People who previously chose not to participate because of the consumption altering effect of the minimum purchase requirement should have found the option highly desirable. Surprisingly, less than 10% of the recipients during the mid-1970s chose this option. The reason for this seems to be that welfare workers tended to encourage or even require recipients of cash transfers to elect the full amount of food stamps. Sometimes this was accomplished by automatically reducing cash transfers by an amount that was then used to buy food stamps. In any event, the fractional purchase option did not mark a major change in the program.

A more thoroughgoing change occurred in 1977, when the minimum purchase requirement was eliminated completely, with recipients given free food stamps in an amount roughly equal to the previous bonus value. This change had been considered previously under what was called the Dole-McGovern Amendment (Sullivan 1976). The effect of this change on the recipient can be seen in Figure 6.1. For the low-income recipient who was already receiving food stamps, the budget line would remain unchanged (although it might change in response to the definition of income also included in the law). For the low-income recipient, the food-specific character of the program remains largely intact. As noted above, the low-income recipient's budget line under this plan is ACD. This recipient's range of choice is considerably restricted, as compared to a cash transfer plan of equal cost, which would give options XCD.

For the higher income recipient (or prospective recipient), free food stamps mean a substantially increased range of choice. Under the old plan, with the purchase requirement, this person's budget line was $A'E'C'D'$. When the bonus value (equal to $C'E'$) is given to the recipient with no additional purchase required, the effective budget line becomes $A'Y'C'D'$, which is almost the same as that resulting from a cash transfer $(X'D')$. Under the present program, food stamps retain their food-specific, consumption-altering character for low-income recipients, while they are basically (aside from administrative and stigma effects) equivalent to a cash transfer for higher-income recipients. As might be expected, there was a marked increase (15%) in the number of participants during the first six months this plan was in effect.

The second important change introduced by the 1977 amendments was an increase in the earnings deduction to 20% of earned income, thus making the effective benefit-reduction rate on earned income .24 instead of .30.

The deduction structure was also changed to provide a standard deduction (now $70), effecting administrative simplification at the cost of equity among recipients. Separate deductions are still allowed, however, for dependent care and "excess" shelter costs (over 50% of income after other deductions). The latter provision is doubtless an attempt to avoid evicting temporarily distressed families from their homes as a price of eligibility, but it does have the odd effect of making Food Stamps a shelter subsidy.

Another important change was imposition of an income eligibility limit at the poverty line, causing a "notch" at an earnings level of $9,020, as opposed to a break-even level of $10,281. This is shown in Table 6.2.

The 1977 amendments affected the Food Stamp Program in two other ways of importance to those concerned with welfare reform. First, the amendments mandated national standards for application, administration,

Table 6.2.   Food Stamp Bonus for Family of Four, 1979

Earnings (E)	Deductions $(D = \$65 + .2E)$	Net Income $(I = E - D)$	Stamp Value $(\$2,448 - .3I)$
0	0	0	2,448
2,000	465	1,535	1,988
4,000	865	3,135	1,508
6,000	1,265	4,735	1,028
8,000	1,665	6,335	548
9,020[a]	1,869	7,151	303
10,000[b]	[2,065]	[7,935]	[68]
10,281[c]	[2,121]	[8,160]	[0]

SOURCE: Figures are based on the amendments of the 1977 Food Stamp reform.
NOTE: Bracketed results are for families receiving a net income above the eligibility cutoff.
[a] Earning cutoff implied by eligibility cutoff of $I = \$7,152$.
[b] Ineligible.
[c] Ineligible; Food Stamp break-even level.

and recipient appeal procedures, the explicit goal being reduction of social workers' discretion. Second, the increased participation will presumably cause administrative costs, only partially borne by the federal government, to rise, with a generally negative fiscal-relief impact.

The most important change other than the abolition of the purchase requirement, however, is the employment of an explicit spending cap on Food Stamps. The operational effect is not altogether clear. The allotment level for each family size is administratively determined by the procedures arising from the aftermath of *Rodway* v. *U.S. Department of Agriculture,* and the allotment is explicitly indexed to food prices. The national standards mandated by the amendments themselves forbid discretionary rejection of eligible recipients. If operative, the cap would therefore require the Department of Agriculture to cut benefit levels arbitrarily because of factors over which neither the Department nor the individual recipients have any control at all. Consequently, the cap seems gratuitous, and it has led to a need for supplemental appropriations each fiscal year. In the long run, annual requirements for supplementary funding virtually guarantee that Food Stamps will become hostage to other legislation sooner or later. It is unclear who will gain from this, but the recipients will be the losers. The proposed FY 1981 budget includes a large increase in the maximum funding level, but if unemployment in 1981 should happen to increase significantly, the appropriation will once again prove utterly insufficient.

ONCE AND FUTURE FOOD STAMPS

From the public choice standpoint, the history of the Food Stamp Program is rich in irony. As Moynihan has pointed out, the support for Food Stamps arose from a concern for *hunger* (food-specific interdependency), quite aside from pressures for an income guarantee. The purchase requirement was a clear result of the food-specific focus, being virtually inexplicable on other grounds. Recipients and those with a more general antipoverty focus (income interdependency) recognized that Food Stamps substantially improved the welfare of most recipients and provided political support for Food Stamps as a clear improvement over surplus commodities. Many antipoverty advocates doubtless hoped to retain Food Stamps and reform the cash transfer apparatus as well.

The bruising battle over the Nixon FAP and its ultimate failure, however, placed on the Food Stamp Program a burden it was never intended to support. It became, in effect, the federal government's guaranteed income. It provided benefits at uniform levels across the nation, without categorical restriction, with a low benefit-reduction rate, and at little cost to states and localities. Though too small to execute its tasks satisfactorily, the Food Stamp Program became the key means by which the overall federal structure dealt with at least two welfare reform goals: equity for the working poor and reduction of interstate differentials. It played some positive role in addressing other welfare reform goals, as well.

Under these circumstances, it was only natural that the Food Stamp Program should cease basking in the limelight as the mainstay of hunger policy and be subjected to the harsher glare of welfare reform criteria. The simple fix for recipients, those with income interdependencies, and those with a preference for a clean sweep, is cashing out. In this event, however, neither liberals nor conservatives are convinced of the beneficial overall effects of so alienating the food-specific donors.

The result is the "reformed" Food Stamp Program, a food program substantially altered to meet welfare reform goals. Taxpayers with food-specific concerns could easily regard this as a hoax. Since a household could scarcely live without *some* other source of income (by earnings or transfer), few households receive stamps worth the maximum allotment or even very close to it.[4] Few households outside the Deep South (where commercial food demand is reduced by greater opportunities for home gardens and where the working poor are especially prevalent) can have their consumption pattern greatly altered.

Conservatives must have very ambivalent feelings about the current Food Stamp Program. Its work incentive features — the low benefit-reduction rate, the 20% earnings deduction, the work registration requirement, and the innate stigma of the scrip — are pretty strong. Greater equity for the working poor is bought at the price of an expanding welfare population, however, and the rapid growth of participation caused by abolition of the purchase requirement can hardly be viewed by conservatives with anything short of alarm.

The combination of the elimination of the purchase requirement and the recent recession has led to rapidly increasing participation in the Food Stamp Program, leading to rapidly escalating costs. It is not surprising that the program has come under the Reagan Administration's scrutiny in its effort to reduce the growth of federal spending. The Administration has not, however, proposed a sweeping reform of the program. Instead, it has put forward a series of measures designed to control program cost without a major restructuring.

These proposals include measures to limit participation by reducing gross income limits to 130% of the poverty level for recipients. In addition, deductions (other than the 20% for earned income) would no longer be indexed for price changes. Inflation would thus erode the value of the deductions, which would reduce both the number of participants and the subsidy received by each participant. The Administration has also proposed that food stamp allotments be reduced to reflect the value of free school meals that family members receive. In an attempt to remove participants who suffer only short periods of lowered incomes, eligibility would be based on prior period income rather than expected income. These and other changes are projected to reduce program costs by over 14% in 1982 and eventually by over 19% in 1986 (Office of the President 1981).

The Reagan Administration faces a dilemma in lowering the maximum gross income for participation. The notch created by the abrupt phaseout of benefits creates disincentives that seem to be incompatible with the Administration's "supply-side" emphasis on promoting incentives for work and saving. One suggestion put forward by conservative members of Congress to address this problem is to require able-bodied recipients to work in low-level public service jobs at the minimum wage to pay for the value of the food stamps received. (Such programs are presently under way on an experimental basis in several parts of the country.) This reflects a general conservative attitude that work incentives for welfare recipients are inevitably so weak that the carrot must be replaced with the stick to generate any real incentive effects. The corollary issue of equity for the working poor seems to have been lost in the rhetorical shuffle. Predictably, this whole approach to the incentive problem is criticized as heavy-handed and demeaning by many liberal observers.

The controversy about the character and purpose of the Food Stamp Program as a food or an income transfer program remains unresolved. The Reagan Administration has criticized the present structure of the program for its tendency "to divert the food stamp program away from this original purpose (of ensuring adequate nutrition) toward a generalized income transfer program, regardless of nutritional need" (Office of the President 1981, p. 1–1); but it proposes little change in the very structural characteristics that have led to the diversion. Senator Helms, Chairman of the Senate Agriculture Committee, has suggested reinstating the minimum purchase requirement, but the currently structured Food Stamp Program, with a low benefit-reduction rate and no purchase requirement, has turned into the main vehicle for welfare reformers, who are therefore expected to defend it vigorously. Given the antipathy of neoconservatives to the received welfare reform approach, the reformers will probably realize that a slightly lower cost Food Stamp Program is the nearest thing to general welfare reform they are soon likely to get. What will become of the hunger issue in this sort of political environment is hard to guess, but we somehow suspect that it will not just fade away.

NOTES

1. In addition to these explanations for redistribution, indirect beneficiaries of governmental redistribution schemes may also be strong advocates of such programs. For example, members of the welfare bureaucracy may support programs that require more personnel, agricultural interests may favor food supplement programs, construction firms and unions may support public housing, and so on. "Insurance" motives are also occasionally adduced.

2. The ability of the recipient to exercise a range of choice generated some reservations of a decidedly paternalistic nature. It was argued that recipients would use their newfound choice to buy foods that were more palatable and more easily prepared, but not necessarily as nutritious as the donors desired.

3. The issue is extensively discussed in Plotnick, "The Measurement of Poverty," in Plotnick and Skidmore 1975.

4. The 1977 change substantially strengthens the case of those who wish to count food stamps at face value in computing the effects of in-kind transfers on posttransfer poverty.

REFERENCES

Allen, J. T. 1972. *A Funny Thing Happened on the Way to Welfare Reform*. Washington, D.C.: Urban Institute.

Anderson, M. 1978. "The Roller-Coaster Income Tax." *Public Interest,* no. 50 (Winter):17–28.

Bawden, D. L.; Cain, G. C.; and Hausman, L. J. 1971. "The Family Assistance Plan: An Analysis and Evaluation." *Public Policy* 19 (Spring):323–53.

Blechman, B. M.; Gramlich, E. M.; and Hartman, R. W. 1974. *Setting National Priorities: The 1975 Budget*. Washington, D.C.: Brookings Institution.

Clarkson, K. W. 1975. *Food Stamps and Nutrition*. Washington, D.C.: American Enterprise Institute.

Collard, D. 1978. *Altruism and Economics*. Oxford: Martin Robertson & Co.

Daly, G., and Giertz, J. F. 1972. "Welfare Economics and Welfare Reform." *American Economic Review* 62 (March):131–38.

Garfinkel, I. 1979. "Welfare Reform: A New and Old View." *Journal of the Institute for Socioeconomic Studies* (Winter):58–72.

Giertz, J. F., and Sullivan, D. H. 1977. "Donor Optimization and the Food Stamp Program." *Public Choice* 29 (Spring):19–35.

———. 1978. "On the Political Economy of Food Stamps." *Public Choice* 33 (3):113–17.

Green, C. 1967. *Negative Taxes and the Poverty Problem*. Washington, D.C.: Brookings Institution.

MacDonald, M. 1977. *Food, Stamps, and Income Maintenance*. New York: Academic Press.

Moynihan, D. P. 1973. *The Politics of a Guaranteed Income*. New York: Random House.

Office of the President. 1981. *America's New Beginning: A Program for Economic Recovery*. Washington, D.C.: Office of the President.

Plotnick, R. D., and Skidmore, F. 1975. *Progress against Poverty: A Review of the 1964–1974 Decade*. New York: Academic Press.

Sullivan, D. H. 1976. "A Note on Food Stamp Reform." *American Journal of Agricultural Economics* 58 (August):560–62.

Weil, G. L. 1978. *The Welfare Debate of 1978*. White Plains, N.Y.: Institute for Socioeconomic Studies.

7 WHAT IS AN APPROPRIATE BENEFIT LEVEL FOR THE UNEMPLOYED?

Daniel S. Hamermesh

Throughout the welter of debate over welfare reform and antipoverty measures, there has been substantial discussion about the appropriate amount of income support to be provided.[1] However, almost the entire debate has been couched in terms of the amount necessary to produce some lessening of inequality in the income distribution without exacerbating work disincentives too greatly (Fair 1971 is perhaps the most explicit formal example of this approach). To my knowledge, none have focused on the questions: Even if we do not care about disincentives, and even if we are unconcerned about the distribution of income *per se,* (1) is there still a justification for transfers? and (2) can our current transfer programs be at least partly viewed as resting upon such a justification?

Research support for this project was provided by the National Commission on Unemployment Compensation under Contract No. 99-9-826-29-5, and by the W. E. Upjohn Institute for Employment Research under a grant to the author. Neither of these institutions is in any way responsible for any conclusions, findings, or opinions expressed herein. Helpful comments were provided by participants in the Middlebury Conference, especially Robert Haveman.

123

Clearly, the major goal of certain of the programs in our income maintenance panoply is altering the distribution of income. Others, particularly those social insurance programs instituted in the 1930s, have the prevention of unanticipated (presumably temporary) hardship as their major goal. As such, they provide the appropriate focus for answers to the two questions presented above. Essentially, they allow us to consider the extent to which such programs are justified as a means of reducing hardship by enabling recipients to smooth consumption, and they give us a framework for measuring whether, in fact, such smoothing occurs.

Our discussion and empirical work focus on unemployment insurance, a system of fifty-three state programs for the temporary relief of experienced workers. (See Hamermesh 1977 for a description of the workings of this system.) We first examine the behavior of the consumer to discover what observed spending patterns might be indicative of underlying hardship, and thus might suggest a justification for the payment of unemployment insurance (UI) benefits. An appropriate benefit is defined as one that removes hardship from those who experience it, but does not provide extra income for those who do not. We then model spending out of unemployment benefits and other income in such a way as to infer the fraction of UI benefits that accrue to workers who otherwise would face hardship in the form of sharply reduced consumption. Because we can infer some objective correlates of whether a particular UI recipient experiences hardship, we can in the conclusion provide some guidelines for policy so that the goal of alleviating hardship can be met more closely at no additional cost.

OUTLINE OF A THEORETICAL FRAMEWORK

In this section we present a simple informal model to motivate the empirical work estimating the response of consumption to income received in the form of unemployment benefits. The model rationalizes a differential response to UI by pointing to liquidity constraints induced by imperfect capital markets within a model embodying perfect foresight.[2] The underlying model describes UI recipients whose behavior is affected by the receipt of UI, in the sense that it is spent differently from other income flows. As such, it provides the basis for constructing empirical models that allow the estimation of the fraction of UI benefits accruing to individuals who are constrained.

The permanent income theory of consumption provides the basis for our model. In its simplest form it implies, for example, that if members of the Jones household expect to work 40 years and live 10 years in retirement, and income is $10,000 per year while working, they will consume $8,000 per year. This means that they will save $2,000 per year during their work lives, so that they have enough savings to keep consumption at $8,000 per year during retirement. We ignore in this example any interest that may be earned on savings, or any preference the household may have for consumption today over consumption in the future. These complications do not qualitatively affect the conclusions. (See Hamermesh 1980 for a formal model that accounts for these difficulties.)

Consider what happens if in one year the household's income drops to $5,000, and in the next it rises (for that year only) to $15,000. The household's lifetime income has not changed; if it can borrow or dip into savings in the first year, it will maintain consumption at $8,000. Similarly, in the second of these two years it will save $7,000 or repay loans.

How will this family, whose consumption is not constrained by capital market imperfections, respond to the receipt of $1,000 in UI benefits during the year in which its other income is only $5,000? Its consumption would have been $8,000 that year, even if no UI benefits had been received. The $1,000 raises the household's lifetime income, but because it is able to borrow or dip into past savings, the UI benefits represent a transitory increase in income that, like other such increases, raises consumption slightly each year of the household's remaining life. For such a family the observed marginal propensity to consume out of UI benefits will be quite low, like its consumption out of transitory income.

Now consider the Smiths, a household identical to the Joneses, except that they have no access to borrowed funds and have no savings to draw upon. Even though their lifetime income is the same as the Joneses', their consumption is drastically reduced, from $8,000 to $5,000 during that year. How will they spend the $1,000 of UI benefits? In their case, it would make sense to spend every penny. Even if they do this, their consumption will only be $6,000, far less than the $8,000 of goods consumed in earlier or later years. Spending the entire $1,000 helps to smooth consumption across the household's life. If they saved part of it, they would increase consumption during later periods, when it is already high, at the expense of current consumption, when it is abnormally low. For this family the observed marginal propensity to consume out of UI benefits will be one.

For the Joneses, we may conclude that the UI benefit is higher than appropriate, as judged by the *objective standard* of how it is spent. Because the Joneses can borrow or dip into savings, the UI benefits do not help to maintain consumption during the spell of unemployment. The

Smiths spend all the UI benefits they receive. Furthermore, even if they got $3,000 in benefits, they would spend it all, for they would still then be consuming only $8,000 per year. For the Smiths the $1,000 in UI benefits is below what is appropriate, in the sense that this amount is insufficient to enable them to maintain their standard of living (at $8,000 per year). It is too low, both because it is meager compared to the size of the lost income and because the household, for whatever reasons, does not have access to borrowed funds or past savings.

The discussion also provides some insight into the justification for a system of UI benefits.[3] The lifetime utility of the family whose consumption is not constrained by lack of savings or access to borrowing exceeds the lifetime utility of the constrained family with the same total income. The difference occurs because the constrained family consumes *too little* during the constrained period and *too much* during the rest of its existence, and because the marginal utility of consumption in any period is assumed to be decreasing as consumption rises.

Consider the situation in Figure 7.1, depicting the utility levels attainable by a family surviving over a lifetime of three periods, two at work and one in retirement. Utility is defined as V per period, and we assume as usual that the family is averse to risk, so the curve is concave. An unconstrained family would, ignoring time preference, consume the same amount C^* in all three periods. This would yield it a lifetime utility equal to $3V(C^*)$. A constrained family cannot borrow in period 1; its consumption is thus $\tilde{C}_1$, and it is $\tilde{C}_2 = \tilde{C}_3$ in the later two periods. Its lifetime utility is

$$[V(\tilde{C}_1) + 2V(\tilde{C}_2)] < 3V(C^*).$$

Even though the monetary values of the consumption streams are equal in both cases (by assumption), the constrained family suffers a shortfall in lifetime utility equal to the vertical distance L.

In this view, UI "tides the family over" by enabling it, through a social mechanism, to smooth consumption over its lifetime. Unless one takes this position, one must view social insurance as a redistributive device. Since the popular discussion and congressional debate prior to the enactment of Social Security held consumption-smoothing to be the goal of UI, viewing redistribution as its purpose is inconsistent with the program's foundations and may be inconsistent with the goals implicit in it today.[4]

This approach provides some direct implications for inferring from actual consumption behavior the fraction of households whose consumption is constrained (and thus whose UI benefit is below what is appro-

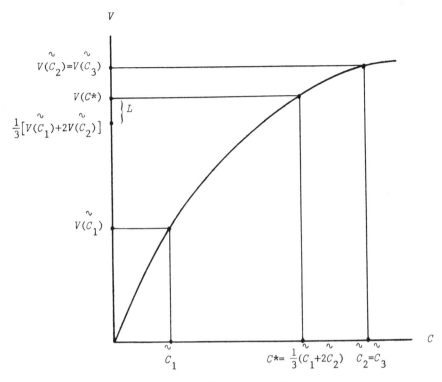

Figure 7.1. Lifetime Utility as a Function of Consumption

priate), and the fraction whose consumption is unconstrained (and thus whose benefits are too high). The greater the aggregate spending propensity out of UI benefits, the larger is the underlying fraction of households whose consumption is constrained. It also provides several testable hypotheses about the kinds of families that will behave as if constrained. First, insofar as access to credit is more difficult for families with low permanent incomes, we should find that low-income families are more likely to consume as if their borrowing is constrained by capital market imperfections, and thus spend each dollar of UI benefits they receive. Second, where and when the earnings loss is proportionately greatest, both because of longer-duration unemployment and lower net replacement of lost earnings, the chance that the family cannot maintain consumption out of prior savings is increased. Given equally limited access to borrowing, such a family is more likely to spend each additional dollar of UI benefits than others. There are other implications of the model that could be tested, but only these two are examined in this study.

ESTIMATES OF THE APPROPRIATENESS OF UI BENEFIT PAYMENTS

In this section, we present two sets of estimates of the fraction of UI benefits that are consumed as if the recipients' consumption is not constrained by lack of access to borrowed funds or lack of sufficient prior savings. The first estimate is based upon aggregate national accounts data for the United States. These data have the advantage that we can measure the impact of all benefit payments upon consumption, and their time-series nature enables us to examine how the fraction of benefits spent as if the recipients were constrained varies with the state of the economy. The data suffer from the obvious drawback that we cannot directly observe the behavior of those persons who are recipients of UI benefit payments.

Many of the drawbacks of the time-series data are missing from the microeconomic data that form the basis for the second set of estimates. These data come from the Longitudinal Retirement History Survey of the Social Security Administration and provide us with observations on individual UI recipients and others. However, they have the drawback that the number of UI recipients in the sample is relatively small, and the data on consumption expenditures are incomplete.

Though each data set is deficient, our estimates should be credible if there is some similarity in the results produced using two such different sources of data. To the extent such similarity exists, we may use the estimated fraction of benefits spent as if consumers were not constrained by capital market imperfections as a guide to inferences about the appropriateness of the average UI benefit. Similarly, any correlation between this fraction and the state of the economy or a family's permanent income can be used to inform policy about benefit levels and potential duration in relation to macroeconomic conditions and personal circumstances.

Time-Series Estimates. The basic model is the standard consumption function, modified to make spending a function of both UI benefits and other disposable income. To embody the permanent income hypothesis, we need to derive measures of permanent UI benefits and permanent other income. (In a pure version of the permanent income hypothesis, only these permanent measures will affect consumption.) The data on income flows are from 1954:I through 1978:II; the series that form the basis for our estimates are government unemployment insurance benefits and disposable personal income less UI benefits, each deflated by the deflator for personal consumption expenditures.[5] To derive the "permanent" component of each of these, equations that efficiently utilize the systematic information contained in the past history of the series were identified and estimated using standard techniques (see Box and Jenkins 1970).[6]

Our time-series model is estimated on the assumption that there is some unobserved fraction α of UI recipients who are not constrained by lack of liquidity. (Implicitly, we assume each recipient has the same UI benefit income.) The estimating equation (see the appendix to this chapter) permits us to infer this fraction, as well as the usual intercept and slope (marginal propensity to consume) from the consumption function. To avoid the need to construct an *ad hoc* measure of the services of durables, we follow Hall (1978) and test the model on spending on non-durables and services only.

The results are presented in Table 7.1. Clearly, the most important finding is that $\bar{\alpha} = .401$. This indicates that a substantial fraction of UI recipients behave as if their borrowing is constrained. Further, the confidence interval around the estimate is fairly narrow. We may conclude that the aggregate evidence is strong that many UI recipients *need* UI

Table 7.1.   Parameter Estimates, Aggregated Data, 1954–1978

	α Fixed	α Depends on UR[a]
Intercept	50.28	49.76
	(6.39)	(6.44)
Marginal propensity to spend on	.712	.714
nondurables and services	(63.47)	(64.63)
Fraction of UI recipients not	.599	
constrained	(9.14)	
α_1		1.265
		(2.80)
α_2 (response to higher UR[a])		.814
		(2.17)

NOTE: t-statistics in parentheses.
[a] Unemployment rate.

benefits, in the sense that their consumption behavior implies they are unable to borrow to maintain their consumption at the levels that would keep them on an optimal consumption path over their lifetimes. However, many other recipients spend in a way that indicates benefits exceed the amount required to remove any liquidity constraint.

We can also examine whether the fraction of UI recipients who are not constrained by liquidity varies cyclically. On the one hand, the fraction may decrease in recessions, as people experience increased hardship when the duration of unemployment spells lengthens. On the other hand, it may increase, as competition from lower-risk borrowers lessens with the decline in capital investment, and as the composition of UI recipients tilts toward the more skilled, more middle-income members of the labor force (see Hamermesh 1977). To examine these possibilities we let

$$\alpha = \frac{1}{1 + \exp(\alpha_1 - \alpha_2 UR)} \, ,$$

where UR is the prime-age male unemployment rate, a fairly good indicator of cyclical changes. This formulation makes the fraction of UI recipients whose consumption is constrained by illiquidity increase (decrease) with rises in the unemployment rate if α_2 is less (greater) than zero.

The estimates of this expanded version of α are presented in the second column of Table 7.1. Both $\hat{\alpha}_1$ and $\hat{\alpha}_2$ are significantly different from zero; $\hat{\alpha}_2 > 0$ implies that the borrowing constraint facing UI recipients becomes less important as the state of the economy worsens. This may be due to the changing composition of the population of potential borrowers that we cited above. It may also reflect the fact that those who are most likely to be constrained have exhausted benefits; their spending patterns are not affected by changes in UI, since they no longer receive benefits. In any event, those estimates imply that increased illiquidity in recessions is not a problem for recipients of regular benefits, and that the appropriate UI benefit amount and potential duration should not, on pure needs grounds, be increased during cyclical downturns for all recipients.

Cross-Section Estimates. Our data come from the Longitudinal Retirement History Survey (LRHS) of the Social Security Administration, a panel study of 11,153 individuals, ages 58–63 in 1969. The surviving individuals were reinterviewed biennially, and we have data from interviews from 1969, 1971, and 1973. However, because measures of past income are required, consumption equations are only estimated for the latter two interview waves. Thus, our tests are conducted on data covering income and consumption for 1970 and 1972. Of the 11,153 people initially in the sample, and the 8,928 left in 1973, the majority had to be eliminated from our estimation because of errors in coding and gross inconsistencies between the various spending flows.[7] We are left with 2,458 observations in 1972 and 3,188 in 1970. Of these older Americans, 113 received UI benefits in 1972, and 175 received benefits in 1970. Eliminating the majority of the original sample does not appear to have greatly changed the demographic characteristics of the sample.[8]

For 1972, the original data allow the construction of observations on the sum of spending on food, transportation and gasoline, vacations and trips, and housing.[9] Together these four consumption categories comprised 49% of average after-tax income in the sample, a figure that suggests there is some underreporting of consumption spending in these categories. Whether there is a systematic relationship with income cannot be determined. For 1970, the consumption data contained so many errors in the food expenditure category that the sum of reported consumption of only three commodity groups could be used — transportation, vacations and trips, and housing expenditures. (With the exception of the deletion of gasoline from the first of these three, the categories are measured exactly as in the 1972 data.)

In addition to the income flows specified in the appendix, we also include a number of demographic and work-status variables that capture individual differences in spending propensities not due to income differences. Dummy variables for race, sex of the household head, the head's marital status, and whether the head is fully retired, partly retired or not retired, are included, as are continuous variables for the head's age and the number of children living in the household. The coefficients of these control variables are shown in the appendix.

The equation specified in the appendix allows us to estimate $(1 - \alpha)$, which can be viewed as the probability that a recipient of UI benefits faces a liquidity constraint and thus exhibits altered consumption behavior. Estimates of this parameter and of the marginal propensities to spend out of permanent and transitory income are presented in Table 7.2 for the two subsamples from the LRHS. For the 1972 subsample, we find that $\hat{\alpha} = .45$. This is quite similar to the estimate in the previous section, and it reinforces the conclusion that a fair part of UI payments, though by no means all, does serve to tide households over periods of hardship that cannot be alleviated because of capital market imperfections. (How-

Table 7.2. Estimates of the Fraction Constrained and of Marginal Spending
Propensities out of Permanent and Transitory Income, All Households, 1970
and 1972

	1970, N = 3188		*1972, N = 2458*	
$1 - \hat{\alpha}$	.05		.55	
	Marginal Propensity to Spend out of			
	Permanent Income	*Transitory Income*	*Permanent Income*	*Transitory Income*
Three consumption categories (four in 1972)	.2784 (51.02)	.0367 (2.03)	.3246 (46.55)	.1874 (8.90)

NOTE: t-statistics in parentheses.

ever, the confidence interval for the cross-section estimate $\hat{\alpha}$ would include most of the range $0 < \alpha < 1$. This probably results from the paucity
of observations for which we observe positive unemployment benefits.)
Also, the relative magnitudes of the propensities to spend out of permanent and transitory income, and the significance of the latter, are
consistent with the expectation that our measure of transitory income
contains some component of permanent income.

The estimates from the 1970 LRHS sample show that $\hat{\alpha} = .95$. Unlike
our other data sets, the 1970 data for older Americans imply that nearly
all UI benefits are spent like other transitory income, and that most UI
recipients do not find their consumption spending constrained by problems of liquidity. There is no good reason why such a large difference
should exist between the $\hat{\alpha}$ for the two years, but it is worth noting that
here, as in the 1972 estimates, the confidence interval around $\hat{\alpha}$ is very
wide. Also, as in the 1972 data, the response of spending to changes in
permanent income exceeds that to changes in "transitory" income.

The probability α is assumed in the estimates in Table 7.2 to be
identical for all sample observations. It is likely, though, that it varies
with each individual's characteristics, particularly with income, as we
discussed above. We thus specify $\alpha = \alpha(YP)$ as

$$\alpha(YP) = \frac{1}{1 + \exp(\beta_1 - \beta_2 YD)} \, ,$$

where β_1 and β_2 are parameters to be estimated, and YD is the deviation (in thousands) of the household's permanent income from the sample mean. This formulation makes the fraction of UI recipients whose consumption is constrained by illiquidity increase (decrease) with permanent income if β_2 is less (greater) than zero.

We find that $\hat{\beta}_1 = 6.5$ and $\hat{\beta}_2 = .45$ for the 1972 sample. The estimate of β_2 implies that α is increasing with YP, and thus that the probability of being constrained decreases as permanent income is higher. (Again, as with the estimates of α, no useful statements of significance can be made about $\hat{\beta}_1$ or $\hat{\beta}_2$.) The extent of variation in α by income is shown in the top row of Table 7.3. The estimates imply that the spending of most of the people in the sample is constrained by illiquidity when we specify α as a function of permanent income. Only for those with incomes well above the mean does the probability of being constrained become small. For the 1970 sample, we estimate that $\hat{\beta}_1 = 3.5$, $\hat{\beta}_2 = .75$. In these data, as for 1972, the probability of being constrained decreases with income, according to our hypothesis. As the second row in Table 7.3 shows, this decrease is quite slow over most of the range of the sample, though the probability is high for people with the lowest incomes in the sample.

Whether our results on older workers can be easily extrapolated to the general population is unclear. On the one hand, the older unemployed worker is more likely to have savings to tide himself over spells of unemployment; this suggests α is lower for the population as a whole than in our samples. Also, the older worker is better known by potential lenders and has established a credit history. On the other hand, the older worker has a shorter remaining worklife over which to repay a loan. So

Table 7.3. Probability That a UI Recipient Is Constrained by Illiquidity, as a Function of Permanent Income

Permanent Income =	0	5,000	Average[a]	One Standard Deviation above Average[b]	Max.[c]
1972 $1 - \hat{\alpha} =$	.99998	.99997	.9985	.9755	.0001
1970 $1 - \hat{\alpha} =$	.889	.160	.023	.001	.0001

[a] $8,756 in 1972; $7,453 in 1970.
[b] $15,011 in 1972; $12,682 in 1970.
[c] $47,395 in 1972; $54,872 in 1970.

too, the younger worker is more likely to have relatives (parents) who can provide credit. These factors imply our estimates of α are too high. Given these offsetting considerations, we must conclude, absent additional information, that our estimates are the best available.

CONCLUSION

We have argued that an appropriate benefit for the unemployed is one that prevents drops in consumption during the spell of unemployment. The most important empirical finding from our two sets of tests is that, according to this notion of appropriateness, around half of all UI benefits go to households that spend them as if they exceeded the appropriate level. If the purpose of UI is to prevent recipients from suffering declines in living standards (in consumption), our evidence suggests that a substantial portion of benefit payments are not target efficient toward this goal. That is, payments could be redistributed among recipients so that more are prevented from suffering sharp declines in living standards while unemployed, yet no more benefits are paid out.

The basic implication for UI policy stems from our finding that the likelihood that a household's consumption is constrained by lack of savings or an inability to borrow during a period of unemployment is negatively correlated with its income. In terms of our concept of an appropriate benefit, households with lower incomes are more likely to have benefits that are too low. It implies that the welfare of the population of UI recipients as a whole can be improved by any policy that targets payments more toward low-income eligible households. (This is independent of any redistributive, or antipoverty, effects.) Thus, for example, legislative changes that increase net replacement rates for low-income families and decrease them for high-income families would accomplish this end. This could be done by simultaneously changing benefit formulas to increase gross replacement still further among beneficiaries whose family incomes are low, while taxing UI benefits, as was legislated for higher-income households in the Revenue Act of 1978.

Our time-series results suggest that there is little case, based on the notion of economic need, for extended programs *that are generally applicable* during periods of high unemployment. (We saw that the probability that the average UI recipient is constrained by illiquidity declines as unemployment rises.) Instead, the changing composition of the population of UI recipients over the cycle argues for extended programs that are more target efficient than the extensions of UI benefits that were legislated during the 1974–1975 recession.

Taken together, our results and discussion imply that UI payments in the United States are not target efficient in terms of aiding eligible households that are most likely to suffer the hardship of reduced consumption during periods of unemployment. This target inefficiency can, of course, be rationalized by the realization that purposes other than that of maintaining consumption have always been suffused through the program. Nonetheless, maintenance of consumption has been viewed as a major consideration, and the accretion of changes that make UI increasingly resemble a welfare program (shortened waiting periods, maximum weekly benefits, extended benefits) strengthens this objective. And so, perhaps the best approach is to attempt to improve the program by better targeting benefits toward households whose consumption is most severely affected by spells of unemployment. This can be accomplished, without increasing disincentives, by raising benefit maximums, improving gross replacement for low-wage workers, and by taxing all benefits. Our basic result suggests it is worth exploring, lest UI benefits continue to be paid at increasing levels to the majority of households that appear to anticipate unemployment and use UI benefits to increase consumption in periods other than that in which the benefits are received.

If it were politically feasible, our results imply that a loan program would be a reasonable substitute for UI benefits. If, as we demonstrate, lack of savings or access to credit markets results in hardship, establishing such a program would target aid to those who most need it, since only they would be willing to participate. While attractive *in vacuo,* such an approach is so revolutionary, and so undercuts one of the most widely accepted transfer programs, as to prevent further consideration. As a compromise, however, state UI programs should begin moving back toward longer waiting periods. (In the late 1930s no state had a waiting period of less than 2 weeks, and many had 4-week periods. Today, one week is the maximum, and 12 states have no wait.) A return to longer waiting periods is consistent with the insurance aspects of UI and with our view of UI as a transfer designed to maintain consumption.

Our findings suggest the fruitfulness of this approach that examines the effects of social insurance, welfare and other income maintenance programs on consumption. While we have constructed the model to apply to UI, the approach should also be applied *mutatis mutandis* to evaluating other programs. Rather than continuing the torrent of work on the labor market effects of these programs, economists should turn their attention to evaluating them on their own terms — how well do they meet the goal of preventing hardship. After all, the major focus of antipoverty efforts must be consumption, not income. It is time to begin to remedy the startling absence of research on consumption among the poor and how it is affected by transfer programs.

APPENDIX

The estimating equation for the time-series data is derived as follows. We assume that the behavior of unconstrained UI recipients is described by

$$C = a_0 + a_1(YP + UP) \qquad (7.A1)$$

and that of nonrecipients by

$$C = a_0 + a_1 YP , \qquad (7.A1')$$

where YP and UP are the predictors of other income (Y) and unemployment benefits (U), and C is personal consumption expenditures other than durables. Remembering that the discussion above (in "Outline of a Theoretical Framework") implied that individuals whose consumption is constrained by liquidity will spend each dollar of UI benefits and transitory income, we can describe their behavior as

$$C = a_1 a^*(Y + U) = a_1 a^*(YP + YT + UP + UT) , \qquad (7.A2)$$

where YT is the deviation of Y from YP, UT is the deviation of U from UP, and a^* is the inverse of the marginal propensity to spend on all items, including durables.[10]

Let I be the ratio of insured unemployment to the civilian labor force. We then can combine (7.A1), (7.A1'), and (7.A2) to derive the estimating equation

$$C_t = a_0(1 - I_t + \alpha I_t) + a_1\{YP_t[1 - I_t + \alpha I_t + (1 - \alpha)a^*I_t] \\ + UP_t[\alpha + (1 - \alpha)a^*] + a^*(1 - \alpha)[YT_t + UT_t]\} , \qquad (7.A3)$$

where a_0, a_1, and α are parameters to be estimated; the subscript t is appended to each time series.

The model is estimated by nonlinear least squares on series that have been transformed using a first-order autoregressive process.[11] We find $\overline{R}^2 = .9767$; for the results in which α is specified as a function of UR, $\overline{R}^2 = .9775$.

The estimating equations for the cross-section model are derived by dividing after-tax income into UI benefits and all other income. For each

UI recipient, let Z be the minimum of UI benefits received in years t and $t - 2$ (a 2-year lag because of the 2-year hiatus between interviews in this panel of data). Then we define transitory UI benefits as $U'_t = U_t - Z$.[12] Permanent income is defined as

$$YP_t = .5(Y_t + Y_{t-2}) + .5(2U_t + 2U_{t-2}) + Z .$$

The first term is an average of income flows other than UI in the 2 years. The second term is designed to reflect the lost income replaced by UI, and it implicitly assumes a constant replacement rate of .50. The third term is just that part of UI benefits that can be viewed as permanent. Transitory income is simply $YT_t = Y_t - YP_t$.

The equations to be estimated are quite similar to (7.A3). We assume each UI recipient who is not constrained by illiquidity consumes according to

$$C = a_0 + a_1 YP + a_2(YT + U') ,   \text{(7.A4)}$$

where U' is that part of UI benefits that represents replacement of lost permanent income. Here and below, the term a_0 represents a linear function of demographic and other variables that control for differences in spending propensities. Because our cross-section data include income observed only biennially, part of any measure of transitory income may contain permanent components.[13] To capture this possibility, we include transitory income even for the unconstrained UI recipient, but we expect $a_1 > a_2$. We assume that an individual who does not receive UI will consume according to (7.A4), except that for him, $U' = 0$.

The constrained UI recipient consumes as

$$C = a_0 + a_1 YP + \gamma(YT + U') ,   \text{(7.A5)}$$

where $\gamma = a^* a_1$, and a^* is the same as in the time-series equations. (We assume that the constant term belongs here because we cannot completely separate permanent from transitory income.) Taking a weighted average of (7.A4) and (7.A5),

$$C = a_0 + a_1[YP + (1 - \alpha)(YT + U')a^*] + a_2\alpha(YT + U') .$$

Since we wish to include observations that have no UI benefits, and because nonrecipients are assumed to be unconstrained, this equation can be respecified as

$$\begin{aligned}C = a_0 &+ a_1[YP + (1 - \alpha)a^*(YT + U')D] \\ &+ a_2[(1 - D) + \alpha D](YT + U') ,\end{aligned}   \text{(7.A6)}$$

where D is an indicator variable equaling one if the individual receives UI benefits.

Table 7.A1. Estimates of Effects of Demographic and Work Status Variables on Spending by Older Workers, 1970 and 1972

	Effects on Spending	
	1970[a]	1972[b]
Married male	33.3	496.0
	(.38)	(3.71)
Female	323.0	−80.3
	(3.52)	(−.57)
Children in	5.51	−181.0
household	(.11)	(−2.82)
Fully retired	19.7	−177.0
	(.39)	(−1.96)
Partly retired	157.0	11.4
	(1.83)	(.10)
White	−34.9	269.0
	(−.42)	(1.90)
Age in years	3.29	32.8
	(.22)	(1.41)

NOTE: t-statistics in parentheses.
[a] Transportation, vacations and trips, housing.
[b] Food, transportation and gasoline, vacations and trips, housing.

Equation (7.A6) is estimated by ordinary least squares for fixed values of α on the grid (0, .05, .1, . . . , 1) to find that value of α that maximizes the likelihood function. The specification of α as a function of YP is estimated by a two-round procedure that first searches a broad lattice of values of (β_1, β_2) and then searches a finer lattice around that pair of values that maximized the likelihood function on the first round. For 1972, we find that $-2 \log \lambda$, distributed as $\chi^2(11)$, when α is assumed invariant to YD, is 2226.7; when α is specified as a function of YD, then $-2 \log \lambda = 2227.8$. Analogous statistics for 1970 are 2317.6 and 2317.8. Table 7.A1 presents the estimates of the coefficients of the demographic and retirement-status variables included in equation (7.A6).

NOTES

1. For example, the McGovern demogrant proposal found its political inspiration — and demise — in considerations of the support level appropriate for maintaining living standards in low-income families.

2. The view of the world implicit in this approach — behavior under constraints induced by market imperfections — is in many ways analogous to the discussion in Abowd and Ashenfelter (1981) of the adjustment of wage differentials to constraints imposed by workers' inability to obtain the optimal number of hours of work.

3. Baily (1977) attempts to justify UI benefits in the context of optimal resource allocation by considering the program as an insurance mechanism that pools the risks of unemployment. Flemming (1978) builds a model in which the optimality of UI depends on how well capital markets function.

4. Feldstein (1974) raised questions about whether UI benefits equalize the distribution of income, but a reanalysis of his results (Hamermesh 1977, ch. 2) suggests his data show they do so. Unfortunately, this evidence deals only with the distributional effects of UI benefits, and it is very difficult, as the work of Ehrenberg, Hutchens, and Smith (1978) indicates, to discover the distributional impact of the partly experience-rated payroll taxes that finance those benefits.

5. Since UI benefits are not taxed, subtracting them from disposable personal income does not induce errors in the data.

6. The estimated filters are

$$\log Y_t = .008096 + 1.11836 \log Y_{t-1} - .11836 \log Y_{t-2}; \quad \chi^2(18) = 14.58,$$
$$(.00137) \phantom{+ 1.11836 \log Y_{t-1} - } (.10125)$$

and

$$\log U_t = 1.5592 \log U_{t-1} - .5592 \log U_{t-2}; \quad \chi^2(19) = 11.60.$$
$$\phantom{\log U_t = 1.5592 \log U_{t-1} - }(.0856)$$

The χ^2 test of the autocorrelation functions for both models indicates that the hypothesis that the residuals generated by the models are "white noise" cannot be rejected at any reasonable significance levels.

7. A large number of the observations had alphabetical characters in fields for which only numerical characters should have been present.

8. Of the original records from the LRHS sample, 27% represent unmarried women, 11% were unmarried men, and 62% were married men. White men comprised 89%, and median household income was $8,555 for married men in the labor force in 1968, $4,610 for married men out of the labor force, and $5,555 and $1,530 for unmarried men in and out of the labor force, respectively (see Irelan et al. 1976). In our 1970 sample, 29% of the people were unmarried women, 9% unmarried men, and 62% married men. Whites accounted for 90%, and the *average* household income was $8,565 in 1968.

9. Expenditures on food and transportation were calculated by multiplying by 52 the respondent's reported usual weekly expenditures. Gasoline expenditures were estimated by multiplying by 12 the reported monthly spending. Housing spending is an amalgam of blown-up monthly rent or mortgage and taxes, plus annual spending on utilities, plus 6% of the net value of owner-occupied housing. Vacation and trip expenditures are the amount the respondent reported as allocating to this category. These categories are not consistent with one another, but they appear to be the most sensible given the way the data are reported in the survey.

10. a^* is estimated as the inverse of .897 from the Cochrane-Orcutt estimate of

$$CTOT = a_0' + \frac{1}{a^*} \cdot YP,$$

where $CTOT$ is total personal consumption expenditures.

11. The autoregressive parameter is estimated from an OLS regression of consumption on permanent and transitory Y, and permanent and transitory U.

12. To make the income data comparable, Y_{t-2} and U_{t-2} were blown up by the change in average income in the sample between years $t-2$ and t. Between 1968 and 1970 this was 6.57%, and between 1970 and 1972 it was 7.39%. The income figures used are an approximation to disposable income that also includes the imputed net value of owner-occupied housing. Disposable income is derived by applying the relevant year's aggregate data on average federal personal income and OASDHI payroll tax rates by income group to all income flows other than UI and retirement income. (See U.S. Department of the Treasury 1968, 1970, 1972.)

13. Holbrook and Stafford (1971) treat transitory income received in nonconsecutive years as uncorrelated, and assume people have a horizon of two years or less. This suggests that the deviation from the average of incomes in two nonconsecutive years may be viewed partly as a component of permanent and partly as a component of transitory income.

REFERENCES

Abowd, John, and Ashenfelter, Orley. 1981. "Anticipated Unemployment, Temporary Layoffs, and Compensating Wage Differentials." In *Studies in Labor Markets,* edited by S. Rosen. Chicago: University of Chicago Press.

Baily, Martin. 1977. "Unemployment Insurance as Insurance for Workers." *Industrial and Labor Relations Review* 30 (July):495–504.

Box, G. E. P., and Jenkins, Gwilym. 1970. *Time Series Analysis: Forecasting and Control.* San Francisco: Holden-Day.

Ehrenberg, Ronald; Hutchens, Robert; and Smith, Robert. 1978. "The Distribution of Unemployment Insurance Benefits and Costs." U.S. Department of Labor Technical Analysis Paper no. 58 (October).

Fair, Ray. 1971. "The Optimal Distribution of Income." *Quarterly Journal of Economics* 85 (November):551–79.

Feldstein, Martin. 1974. "Unemployment Compensation: Adverse Incentives and Distributional Anomalies." *National Tax Journal* 27 (June):231–44.

Flemming, John S. 1978. "Aspects of Optimal Unemployment Insurance." *Journal of Public Economics* 10:403–25.

Hall, Robert. 1978. "Stochastic Implications of the Life-Cycle-Permanent Income Hypothesis." *Journal of Political Economy* 86 (December):971–88.

Hamermesh, Daniel S. 1977. *Jobless Pay and the Economy.* Baltimore: Johns Hopkins University Press.

———. 1980. "Social Insurance and Consumption — An Empirical Inquiry." National Bureau of Economic Research, Working Paper no. 600 (December).

Holbrook, Robert, and Stafford, Frank. 1971. "The Propensity to Consume Separate Types of Income." *Econometrica* 39 (January):1–20.

Irelan, L., et al. 1976. *Almost 65: Baseline Data from the Retirement History Study.* Washington, D.C.: Social Security Administration.

U.S. Department of the Treasury. 1968, 1970, 1972. *Statistics of Income.* Washington, D.C.: U.S. Government Printing Office.

8 THE AFDC–UNEMPLOYED FATHERS PROGRAM:
Determinants of Participation and Implications for Welfare Reform

James R. Hosek

The U.S. income transfer system provides less coverage for married, spouse-present families than for single-parent families. One reason for this is the limited scope of coverage for such families within the Aid to Families with Dependent Children (AFDC) program. The AFDC program has two components, Family Group (FG) and Unemployed Father (UF). The UF component, created in 1961, serves husband-and-wife families in adverse economic circumstances. In contrast, the FG component, dating from the beginning of AFDC in 1936, primarily aids single-parent families. UF tends to furnish less coverage than does FG because UF families must satisfy certain eligibility requirements (discussed below) beyond those of FG. Also, many states do not offer the UF program;

This paper derives from earlier studies (Hosek 1978; 1979a) that were prepared under a grant from the U.S. Department of Health, Education, and Welfare. The 1978 study also appeared in the *Review of Economics and Statistics* (November 1980). The material presented here is published with the permission of the Rand Corporation and North-Holland Publishing Company. The author would especially like to thank John Antel, Philip Armstrong, David Arnaudo, Richard Buddin, David Lyon, and John Maniha for their insight, support, and encouragement.

141

only 26 states and the District of Columbia had a UF program in 1975, and the total has changed little since then.

The UF caseload has grown far less rapidly than the FG caseload (Figure 8.1). In 1979 FG provided aid to over 3.5 million families while UF aided only 120,000 families. UF states, shown in Figure 8.2, are typically populous and are generous in their AFDC benefits. Many non-UF states lie in the Sun Belt and the Rocky Mountains. The average AFDC level of assistance for a family of four in 1975 was over $100 a month more in UF states than in non-UF states: $330 a month versus $227.

To some, the slow growth of UF raises a concern about whether the program has been effective, or could be effective if its coverage were expanded. An implication of my research is that slow UF growth is not a sign of ineffectiveness, but instead reflects the relative attractiveness of market opportunities as a means of shoring up economic well-being among husband-and-wife families.

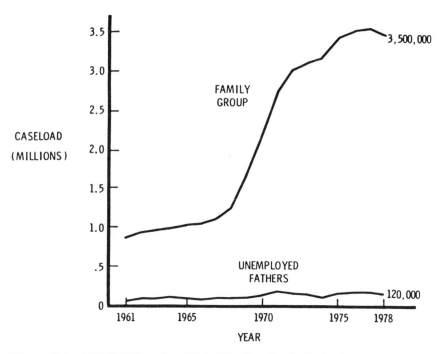

Figure 8.1. AFDC-FG and AFDC-UF Caseload, United States, 1961–1978

Figure 8.2. States with AFDC-UF Programs in 1975

A straightforward way to increase the coverage of married, spouse-present families would be to mandate UF for all states. An important variant of this policy option would be to introduce a nationwide floor on the level of assistance. This paper examines those alternatives. After briefly describing the conditions for participation in UF, I discuss the results and implications of an empirical analysis of the determinants of family participation in UF. The discussion, which focuses on the roles of market earnings opportunities and unemployment insurance (UI) benefits, emphasizes the importance of earnings opportunities as a determinant of family decisions not to participate in UF. Also, with regard to UI benefits as an alternative to UF, data presented below indicate that several hundred thousand low-wage, long-term unemployed fathers apparently draw no UI compensation. The overall number of unemployed fathers (short plus long term) who receive no UI would be still larger. While not all of these families would be eligible for UF, an expanded UF program might be a well-targeted and cost-effective means of improving their income support.

Drawing upon the model of family participation in UF, I then present estimates of the caseload and cost of three policy options: (1) instituting UF in non-UF states subject to existing benefit schedules; (2) establishing a nationwide benefit floor equal to 75% of the poverty line; and (3) establishing a nationwide benefit floor equal to 100% of the poverty line. The analysis shows that such changes in UF policy will not cause large increases in either UF caseload or cost. Moreover, these results are contrasted with previous research on the negative income tax, an alternative and better-known option for increasing the income support system for husband-and-wife families. The paper offers reasons why the prospective size (hence cost) of a nationwide UF program falls roughly an order of magnitude below that of a negative income tax. This finding, in conjunction with the potential for UF to aid low-wage, unemployed fathers, not otherwise helped by UI benefits, suggests that policy interest in UF may actually increase, particularly during the present austere fiscal climate.

DETERMINANTS OF FAMILY PARTICIPATION IN AFDC–UF

Conditions of Participation in AFDC–UF.   Table 8.1 summarizes the eligibility requirements and benefits available under UF. To a degree, UF is very similar to FG: Both programs serve low-income, low-asset families with children; within a state both programs use the same income test, assets test, and AFDC benefit schedules; and both automatically make families eligible for Food Stamps and Medicaid. UF and FG differ crucially, however, in their eligibility requirements pertaining to family heads.

Federal regulations require that a UF family head — a husband — have a work history of steady attachment to the labor force. He must

Table 8.1.   AFDC–UF Program Eligibility Criteria and Benefits, 1975

---

1. *Eligibility Requirements*
    a. Family must be husband-and-wife family with children under 18 years, or under 21 years if attending school.
    b. Husband must
        • Be "unemployed" — work less than 100 hours per month.
        • Have worked at least 6 of 13 calendar quarters prior to welfare application, or have been eligible for or received unemployment insurance benefits during the 13-quarter period.
        • Have worked less than 100 hours during the 30 days prior to application.
        • Register with the state employment office and the Work Incentive Program (WIN).

Table 8.1. *Continued*

- Be able to work and not refuse an offer of employment or training without good cause.
c. Income test
    - Countable income must be less than the standard of need defined by the state.
    - For determining initial eligibility, countable income (monthly basis) equals earned plus unearned income less deductions:

$$Y_c = (Y_e - D_e) + (Y_u - D_u).$$

  - For recertification of eligibility, countable income (monthly basis) equals two-thirds of earned income, less a $30 set-aside, minus allowable deductions for work expenses, plus unearned income less deductions:

$$Y_c = [.67(Y_e - 30) - 30 - D_e] + (Y_u - D_u).$$

  - Income received unexpectedly or irregularly is not counted.
  - Deductions for work expenses include local, state, and federal taxes on earnings, union dues (if mandatory), contributions to pension funds, Social Security, and other mandatory payroll deductions.
d. Assets test
    - Real and personal property must not exceed a federal maximum value of $2,000 per AFDC recipient.
    - Many household furnishings and appliances are typically excluded.
    - Many states exclude the home from countable assets.
    - States establish their own assets tests.
e. Strikers: States may, at their discretion, permit otherwise eligible workers on strike to participate in AFDC–UF.
2. *Benefits*
    a. AFDC benefit schedules vary by state. A family's AFDC benefits depend on the difference between the state's needs standard and the family's countable income; however, the formula for computing AFDC benefits varies by state.
    b. AFDC families are automatically eligible for
        - Medicaid.
        - Training and rehabilitation through WIN (if offered).
        - Other social services (day care; family planning; ways to improve housing and money management; utilization of other community services such as health and legal services).
        - Emergency assistance.
    c. Food Stamps
        - Until 1978 AFDC families were automatically eligible for Food Stamps; they must now apply for them.
        - The purchase requirement was eliminated in 1978.

have worked in 6 of the 13 calendar quarters prior to application for welfare,[1] or have qualified for or received unemployment insurance benefits. "Worked" means that he earned at least $50 during the quarter, a requirement easily met by most. Further, he must have been unemployed for at least 30 days before applying for welfare. (He may apply prior to that time, but may not receive aid until the time limit is met.) The UF program defines unemployment as working no more than 100 hours per month. This differs from the usual Bureau of Labor Statistics definition, which counts a person as unemployed if he is not at work (either jobless or on temporary layoff) and has actively sought a job within the previous month.

After enrolling in UF, the husband still must not work more than 100 hours per month — the so-called *one-hundred-hour rule*. He may exceed 100 hours in some months, but not regularly. The intent of the rule appears to be to target UF on the jobless and underemployed, but it limits the range of jobs that can be held while on welfare.

Empirical Analysis of Participation.   Desiring to maximize its utility, a family decides to participate in UF depending on the utility from being on UF, subject to the eligibility requirements and available benefits, versus the utility of being off UF. On UF the family must satisfy the income test, the assets tests, the one-hundred-hour rule, and other requirements listed in Table 8.1. These constraints are not relevant when the family is off UF, and the family may prefer to work more, earn more, and save more than it could under UF.

An earlier study, Hosek (1978) examines the relationship between the probability of participation[2] and four kinds of variables suggested by the model: UF benefits (including the Food Stamp bonus); variables reflecting the husband's earnings capability; variables reflecting the wife's earnings capability; and UI benefits (including the Food Stamp bonus). The model suggests that the chance of UF participation should rise with UF benefits and decline with family earnings capability. Moreover, the chance of participation should decline as UI benefits increase, if families tend to treat UI as a substitute for UF.

The analysis of family participation in UF was based on family-level data. The data were drawn from a choice-based sample collected at three sites: the Chicago, Detroit, and Los Angeles metropolitan areas. With only three sites, the effects of variables that vary strictly by site (such as unemployment rate and the AFDC assets limit) could not be tested.[3] Neither could the effect of relaxing the one-hundred-hour rule, because the rule is invariant across state UF programs.

UF and UI benefit variables were created for each family. These variables represent *prospective* benefits (including the Food Stamp bonus), should a family decide to participate in UF or UI, respectively.[4] Also, variables for hourly wage and years of school were chosen to reflect the husband's earnings capability. For wives, many of whom do not work and therefore report no hourly wages, age, years of school, and variables indicating the presence of young children (0 to 5 years) and older children (15 to 20 years) were selected. The choice of these variables is common among studies of earnings, labor supply, and human investment (e.g., Mincer and Polachek 1974 and references therein).[5]

The UF participation model was estimated by probit, and Table 8.2 reports the elasticity of the change in the probability of participation evaluated at the means of the explanatory variables, as well as the means themselves. As the table indicates, the hypotheses based on the model were confirmed on the whole, with the size and statistical significance of the effects often being larger for white families than for nonwhite families.

A major finding is the high elasticity of UF participation with respect to UF benefits. As seen in Table 8.2, a 1% increase in UF benefits causes a 3.6% increase in the white participation probability and a 2.4% increase in the nonwhite.[6] Also, the elasticity on UI benefits is consistent with the hypothesis that families treat UI as a substitute for UF.[7]

Table 8.2 further shows that UF families tend to be younger, have less education, and have a lower wage rate for the husband than do non-UF families. That is, the kinds of families who participate in UF are those with low earnings capabilities. This pattern is reflected in the effects of these variables on the probability of UF participation: increases in age, schooling of either spouse, and the husband's wage all reduce the family's likelihood of being on UF. Each effect is significant for whites, but only the age effect is significant for nonwhites.

The weaker showing for nonwhites draws attention back to the means in the table. Between UF and non-UF white families, the differences between mean age, education, and wage are pronounced, but not so for nonwhites. The likeness between UF and non-UF nonwhite families, as well as the weak effects of the earnings capability variables, may be due to the greater variance of earnings among nonwhites, as opposed to whites with the same observed characteristics. One factor to consider is unemployment. The unemployment rate is twice as high for blacks as whites, and studies document a higher incidence and longer duration of unemployment among nonwhites after controlling for age, education, wage rate, and other factors (Hall 1972). Viewed over the span of a year, these differences can generate sizable racial disparities in the chance of

Table 8.2. Model of Family Participation in AFDC–UF: Means and Elasticities of Explanatory Variables, by UF Status and Race

	White			Nonwhite		
	Mean			Mean		
Variable	Off UF	On UF	Elasticity	Off UF	On UF	Elasticity
Benefits (in dollars per month)						
UF	445	502	3.59***	462	502	2.39***
UI	557	524	−2.03*	477	485	−0.84
Husband						
Wage rate (dollars per hour)	8.63	5.35	−0.70*	5.91	4.87	−0.39
Years of school	13.2	10.6	−3.21***	10.8	10.5	−0.09
Wife						
Age	38.5	32.6	−1.60***	34.7	33.4	−1.95*
Years of school	12.6	10.8	−2.38***	10.6	10.7	−0.47
Presence of children						
0–5 years	0.37	0.60	−0.02	0.57	0.55	−0.38***
15–20 years	0.46	0.24	−0.54***	0.36	0.35	−0.18*
Hispanic/other	—	—	—	0.71	0.31	−1.60***

NOTE: Statistical significance of coefficient on which elasticity is computed: * = .10; ** = .05; *** = .01.

ever being unemployed in a given year and, among those unemployed, in the total weeks of unemployment.

Another factor behind the small size and significance of nonwhite earnings variables concerns their earnings behavior. Evidence on this has been assembled by J. P. Smith (1978), who finds a negative correlation between the earnings of white husbands and their wives, but a positive correlation for blacks. Thus, in white families the wife's earnings even out variations in the husband's earnings, so that family income is relatively stable. But in black families the husband and wife are typically both major contributors to family earnings, and the income-stabilizing role of the wife tends to be absent. Given this pattern of behavior, nonwhites may be more likely than whites to seek welfare benefits as a means of maintaining income.

The remaining explanatory variables indicate the presence of younger and older children, and whether a nonwhite family is Hispanic or other than black. The presence of older children who can take care of themselves as well as younger brothers and sisters reduces the family's probability of participating in UF. The home time of the older children may substitute for the wife's, thereby encouraging her participation in the labor force, raising family earnings, and reducing the likelihood of poverty-level family income. The presence of young children has essentially no effect on the UF probability of white families and a strong negative effect for nonwhite families, a finding that requires further research for clarification. The large and significant negative elasticity associated with the Hispanic/other variable reveals that their chance of UF participation is below that of blacks: a 1% increase in the proportion of Hispanic/other reduces the probability of participation among nonwhite families by 1.6%.

SOME IMPLICATIONS OF THE MODEL OF FAMILY PARTICIPATION IN UF

Market Opportunities. Although families are more likely to participate as UF benefits rise, it appears that most of them choose not to participate because the husband and wife have higher earnings opportunities in the job market.

The pull of market opportunities is revealed in the small percentage of husband-and-wife families with children that are predicted to participate in UF in a given month. These predicted percentages, which derive from the model of family participation in UF, are displayed in Table 8.3 by the wage class of the husband. For these families, the husband is

Table 8.3. Predicted UF Participation, Husband's Potential Earnings, and Actual Family Earnings, by Husband's Wage Class, 1975

Husband's Wage Rate (dollars per hour)	Predicted Monthly Percentage of All Husband-and-Wife Families with Children on AFDC–UF[a]	Husband's Potential Annual Earnings[b]	Family's Actual Annual Earnings[c]
<2.00	1.67	3,120[d]	7,516
2.00–2.99	1.00	5,200	9,344
3.00–3.99	0.76	7,280	11,149
4.00–4.99	0.71	9,360	12,849
5.00–5.99	0.55	11,440	15,239
6.00–6.99	0.46	13,520	17,515
7.00–7.99	0.36	15,600	20,243
8.00–8.99	0.28	17,680	22,943
9.00+	0.21	24,960[e]	30,286

[a] Based on model of family participation in AFDC–UF presented in this report.

[b] Midpoint of husband's wage class × 40 hours per week × 52 weeks per year.

[c] Arithmetic average of family earnings, taken over all families in each wage class. Families are husband and wife with children less than age 21; husband less than age 65, not incapacitated, not in armed forces or institution. (Source: Survey of Income and Education).

[d] Wage rate assumed to be $1.50 per hour.

[e] Wage rate assumed to be $12.00 per hour.

typically the primary earner, and his wage rate affords a ready measure of his earnings capacity. As the table shows, the higher the husband's wage rate, the lower is family participation in UF.

Women's earnings further reinforce the point. Over the past decade, the labor force participation rate of women has risen substantially. Much of the increase can be attributed, surprisingly, to married women with children. To understand the effect of this trend on family earnings, and hence on a family's decision not to participate in UF, compare the column of *husband's potential annual earnings* with that of *family's actual annual earnings* in Table 8.3. The former indicates what the annual earnings of the husband would be if he worked full-time (40 hours a week) throughout the year (52 weeks, including paid vacation). The latter column, by contrast, presents the average value of actual family earnings. In every case, actual family earnings exceed the husband's potential earnings by a considerable amount. For example, a husband earning $3.50 an hour could gross $7,280 a year, but average family earnings in that wage class exceeded $11,000 in 1975. Less than 1% of all families in the $3.00 to $3.99 per hour wage class are predicted to participate in UF in any month.

Further support for the importance of family earnings opportunities may be found by comparing average family earnings with the level of benefits a family might expect on UF. Participation in UF in 1975 automatically entitled a family to AFDC, Food Stamp, and Medicaid benefits. AFDC benefit schedules vary from state to state, as does the sum of AFDC benefits and Food Stamp bonus. Assume for illustration that an average family could receive up to $400 a month in AFDC, plus Food Stamp bonus. That would imply an annual benefit income of $4,800, which falls far below average family earnings even in the lowest wage class. However, if the family has an illness that generates high health costs, the availability of Medicaid as an adjunct to UF could be a significant inducement to participate.

Summarizing, the UF participation rate is low partly because many families prefer work over welfare, and as family earnings opportunities increase, the expected percentage of families on UF diminishes. Also, many families have multiple earners, and as a consequence, actual family earnings tend to overwhelm benefits available under UF.

Unemployment Insurance versus Unemployed Fathers. When the husband becomes unemployed, the family often can seek income assistance from unemployment insurance (UI) and, in states offering the program, UF. According to the empirical results in Table 8.2, families appear to treat UF and UI as substitutes: As UI benefits increase, families are less likely to participate in UF. Two factors bolster this finding and suggest why families would tend to choose UI over UF.

First, UI benefit schedules are often more generous than those of UF and tend to grow more so as the husband's wage rate rises and family size declines. Only in the case of low-wage husbands with large families do UF benefit schedules tend to be the more generous. These patterns arise because of the way UI and UF benefit schedules are defined. Roughly speaking, UI benefit schedules rise with wage rate up to a benefit ceiling and do not depend on family size, while UF benefit schedules rise with family size and do not depend on wage rate.

Second, UI benefit schedules are person-specific, but UF benefit schedules are family-specific. The computation of UI benefits for the unemployed husband will ignore any family income deriving from the wife's earnings or from unearned income (interest, dividends, and rent, for example); not so the UF benefit computation. Under UF, unearned income and the earnings of other family members would by and large be deducted from the UF benefit schedule amount in arriving at the family's actual UF benefit payment. Thus a family's actual income could easily be higher with the husband on UI than with the family on UF, particularly if the wife or other family members work or if there is a substantial amount of unearned income. Table 8.3 has shown that many husband-and-wife families with children do have multiple earners who account for a sizable fraction of family earnings. With respect to unearned income, I find that in every wage class the total amount of unearned income exceeded $1,000 a year on average in 1975.[8] Upwards of three-fourths of this income comes from nontransfer sources, implying that many — though surely not all — families have sources of income available to augment UI benefits and help tide them over periods of joblessness. In sum, when choosing between UI and UF, many families have good reason to select UI — a further explanation for the low rate of participation in UF.

Although UI may often be preferable to UF, many unemployed families could be ineligible for UI. Consequently, a special role for UF might be in offering support to those families. In 1975, a year of high unemployment, significant percentages of unemployed, low-wage husbands reported no UI benefits. This was especially true among the long-term unemployed (15 or more weeks), who made up about 40% of all unemployed husbands from husband-and-wife families with children. Among the long-termers, over 40% of husbands in the wage class earning less than $4.00 an hour apparently drew no UI benefits, in contrast to 25% in the $4.00 to $7.00 an hour range and 20% in the over $7.00 an hour range who apparently drew none. The total number of long-term unemployed husbands reporting no UI benefits amounted to over 425,000. I was unable to study how many of the long-term unemployed would qualify for UF.

CASELOAD AND COST PROJECTIONS

The federal government could increase the income support available to married, spouse-present families with children by mandating UF to non-UF states. An important variant of this policy option would be to also introduce a nationwide floor on the level of benefits, which is assumed to be accompanied by an easing of the income test in each state to a level commensurate with the benefit floor. Under the assumption that existing eligibility rules are unchanged, apart from adjustments in states' income tests, I have thus estimated the caseload and cost of three policy options: (1) instituting UF in non-UF states subject to existing benefit levels by state, (2) establishing a nationwide benefit floor equal to 75% of the poverty line, and (3) establishing a nationwide benefit floor equal to 100% of the poverty line.

Throughout these projections, benefit levels are defined as the state's AFDC level of assistance for each family, given its size, plus the net Food Stamp benefits corresponding to the level of assistance. Medicaid, housing, and other benefits are not included, nor are there any adjustments for cost-of-living differences between states. Because of the way the cost estimates have been constructed, the figures should be viewed as upper bounds on the direct program costs.

The estimates are based on the statistical analysis of the determinants of family participation in UF. If future family behavior differs markedly from past behavior, or if legislation changes the basic character of the UF program, the estimates presented here may differ greatly from future reality.

If the UF program, which was offered in 27 states in 1975, had been mandated to all states, the UF caseload would have risen by 34,000 families, from 117,000 to 151,000 (Table 8.4). The small size of the

Table 8.4. Projected Total and Incremental UF Monthly Caseload, by Policy Option

Policy	Non-UF States	UF States	All States
A. Projected Total UF Caseload (1975)			
Base			
Mandating UF to all states	34,100	116,900	150,900
Add-on			
Benefit floor = 75% poverty line	37,600	117,100	154,700
Benefit floor = 100% poverty line	61,100	130,000	191,100
B. Projected Incremental UF Caseload (1975)			
Base			
Mandating UF to all states	34,100	0	34,100
Add-on			
Benefit floor = 75% poverty line	3,500	200	3,700
Benefit floor = 100% poverty line	27,000	13,100	40,200

NOTE: Totals may not add up because of rounding.

increase can be traced to the fact that non-UF states tend to be less populous and to have lower AFDC benefit levels than UF states. If, in addition to mandating UF, a nationwide benefit floor equal to 75% of the poverty line had been established, another 3,500 families would have participated in UF. In this case, the increment in caseload is modest because only about a dozen states fall below the 75% floor. In contrast, a more generous benefit floor of 100% of the poverty line would have affected all but a few states and would have added 40,000 families, bringing the total UF caseload to 191,000.

These projections demonstrate that UF caseload is not overwhelmingly sensitive to even large increases in the benefit level, and that a nationwide UF program, under existing eligibility requirements and plausible benefit levels, would entail only a small caseload. The 151,000 cases represent 0.56% of the 26.5 million working-age, husband-and-wife families with children in the United States in 1975.

Turning to costs, option (1), mandating UF to non-UF states under existing benefit schedules, would have added 70% to federal outlays for AFDC–UF in 1975. The total cost to all governments would have been $13.4 million per month, or $161 million per year (Table 8.5). Of the monthly amount, $9.2 million arises from AFDC benefits and $4.2 million from Food Stamp bonuses. Assuming that existing AFDC cost-sharing arrangements were maintained, the federal government would pay about 60% of the $9.2 million, or $5.5 million. The Food Stamp Program is wholly federal, so the added federal outlay under option (1) amounts to $9.7 million per month ($116 million per year), or just over 70% of the monthly cost of $13.4 million. Option (2) (benefit floor = 75% of poverty line) would have been slightly more expensive, whereas option (3) (benefit floor = 100% of poverty line) would be double the cost of option (1). Most of the extra cost would appear as federal expenses in the form of supplemental payments to reach the benefit floor.

As mentioned above, the policy projections are based on the assumption that UF eligibility rules remain constant. I note here that a recent U.S. Supreme Court ruling, *Califano* v. *Westcott* (June 1979), has the effect of extending the UF program to families with unemployed wives. I expect the increase in cases brought about by the ruling to be severalfold below the 630,000 poor families with working wives in 1975. Some of these families, although below the poverty line, will nevertheless have incomes that exceed the AFDC income limits and hence will be ineligible. In other cases, the unemployed wife may be eligible for and choose to participate in unemployment insurance rather than in the AFDC–Un-

Table 8.5.   Projected Incremental Monthly Cost, by Policy Option (In millions of dollars per month)

Policy	Non–UF States	UF States	All States
A. Projected Incremental Cost (1975)			
Base			
Mandating UF to all states	13.4	0	13.4
Add-on			
Benefit floor = 75% poverty line	1.8	0.1	1.9
Benefit floor = 100% poverty line	16.4	9.3	25.7
B. Sources of Incremental Cost (1975)			
Base			
Mandating UF to all states			
AFDC benefits	9.2	0	9.2
Food Stamp bonus	4.2	0	4.2
Total	13.4	0	13.4
Add-on			
Benefit floor = 75% poverty line			
AFDC benefits	0.6	0.04	0.6
Food Stamp bonus	0.5	0.03	0.6
Federal supplement	0.7	0.04	0.7
Total	1.8	0.11	1.9
Benefit floor = 100% poverty line			
AFDC benefits	5.4	4.5	9.9
Food Stamp bonus	4.0	1.8	5.8
Federal supplement	7.0	3.0	10.0
Total	16.4	9.3	25.7

employed Parent (née Unemployed Father) program. And in still other cases, the family may simply not want to participate in UF.

Moreover, an earlier Supreme Court ruling, *Philbrook* v. *Glodgett* (June 1975), bore on the question of joint participation in UI and UF. The ruling led to new legislation, the so-called Corman Amendment, which took effect after the year to which my estimates pertain, 1975. The Corman Amendment assures jointly eligible families the right to participate in both UI and UF, but in effect stipulates that the family must participate in UI, so that UI income is counted in the computation of UF benefits. Prior to Glodgett, many states prohibited participation in

UF until a family had exhausted its UI benefits. Had the effect of the Glodgett decision and Corman Amendment been embodied in my policy analysis, the projected caseload and cost figures probably would have been slightly higher.

AFDC–UF VERSUS NEGATIVE INCOME TAX PROGRAMS

Negative income tax (NIT) programs have occupied center stage in debates over welfare reform during the three previous administrations. NITs' potential virtues include horizontal equity and administrative efficiency, to mention two. Horizontal equity involves extending income maintenance to married, spouse-present families, as well as to individuals (single family heads), and instituting a nationwide benefit schedule, perhaps adjusted for regional differences in cost of living. States could choose to supplement the level of benefits available under an NIT; specifically, states could retain their AFDC programs, albeit probably without federal cost-sharing, in order to target added benefits on certain groups as defined by state-set eligibility criteria.

The prospects for horizontal equity under an NIT resemble those attainable under the UF policy options considered above. Mandating UF to all states would result in universal income maintenance for married, spouse-present families with children. In addition, setting benefit floors of 75% or 100% of the poverty line would even out some of the interstate disparities in benefits available under AFDC and Food Stamps. Still, the UF options would leave the scope of UF smaller than that of NIT, because UF would continue to exclude individuals or husband-and-wife families without children. Of course, UF could be broadened to include them, and the one-hundred-hour rule could be removed as well.

There is scanty evidence on the relative administrative efficiency of an NIT versus the existing (or incrementally modified) set of welfare programs. Even if an NIT did not require an assets test, the need for frequent and accurate income accounting remains.

Moreover, recent attempts to control fraud and reduce duplication of effort in processing AFDC case records appear promising, as witnessed by the Colorado Monthly Reporting Experiment (Williams 1978). Given these developments, there seems to be no prima facie case that an NIT administration would be more efficient than the decentralized administrations of AFDC, Food Stamps, and possibly other programs (SSI, housing) that an NIT might replace.

Proposed changes in the federal income maintenance package raise numerous behavioral questions, ranging from effects on participation to labor supply, fertility, family stability, nutrition, and education/training decisions. Foremost among these, judging from the quantity of research, are the effects on labor supply. Recent research based on income maintenance experiments (Cogan 1978; Spiegelman, Groeneveld, and Robins 1978) leaves little question that labor supply reductions occur among recipients. In aggregate, these reductions cause substantial increases in NIT program cost in the form of foregone wages (less work effort). Because of similarities in benefit level and marginal tax rate, one would also expect labor supply reductions from UF.[9] But the diminutive size of the predicted UF caseload implies that the absolute cost of the program, including the ''hidden cost'' of foregone earnings, will be an order of magnitude below the cost of an NIT.

Equally important, the comparisons below underscore the importance of the participation decision as a determinant of program cost. It is suggested that past microsimulations of NITs exaggerate the caseload and cost of these programs, as a consequence of the nonempirical methodology used to determine whether a family participates. An empirical approach, such as the one employed in this study, may be a preferable foundation for policy evaluation.

Comparison of AFDC–UF and NIT Participation Estimates. Table 8.6 displays the predicted number of participating families and participation rates under nationwide UF and alternative NITs (Keeley et al. 1977; Greenberg and Hosek 1976). As seen on the right-hand side of the table, UF participation equals less than 1% per month. With an average duration of stay on UF of about 9 months, the number of different families on UF during a year would be about 2.1 times the monthly caseload.[10] As a result, annual participation rates would be less than 2% per year, as shown in panel A of Table 8.6. In contrast, the studies of NIT predict annual participation rates ranging from 5% to 60%, an enormous difference.

The difference is partly due to the inclusion of families without children in the NIT studies. In 1975 there were 41.8 million husband-and-wife families with heads below age 65 (U.S. Bureau of the Census 1977); of these, 26.5 million had children less than age 21. Even if the NIT participation rates were halved as a gross adjustment for the difference in base populations, large differences between UF and NIT participation rates would remain. Such differences cannot be attributed to benefit

Table 8.6. Numbers and Percentages of All Married, Spouse-Present Families with Children, Participating in AFDC–UF and Negative Income Tax Programs

Marginal Tax Rate	Benefits		

A. Hosek Study: AFDC–UF (1976 Data)

	AFDC Benefits, Food Stamp Bonus, Plus		
	No Further Supplement	Benefit Floor = 75% of Poverty Line	Benefit Floor = 100% of Poverty Line
About 0.7			
Number of families per month	151,000	155,000	191,000
% of all families	0.56	0.58	0.72
Number of families per year	317,000	326,000	401,000
% of all families	1.18	1.22	1.51

B. Keeley et al. Study: Negative Income Tax (1975 Data)

	Guarantee for a Family of Four		
	50% of Poverty Line	75% of Poverty Line	100% of Poverty Line
0.5			
Number of families per year	2,400,000	7,600,000	15,700,000
% of all families	9.1	28.7	59.2
0.7			
Number of families per year	1,300,000	2,800,000	5,800,000
% of all families	4.9	10.6	21.9

C. Greenberg-Hosek Study: Negative Income Tax (1973 Data)

	Guarantee for a Family of Four	
	80% of Poverty Line	100% of Poverty Line
0.5		
Number of families per year	4,300,000	7,300,000
% of all families	16.2	27.5
0.7		
Number of families per year	2,300,000	3,700,000
% of all families	8.7	14.0

levels, for the UF programs in conjunction with the benefit floor are at least as generous as the NIT programs. Marginal tax rates, however, are only roughly comparable across programs.

Under UF, the marginal tax rate depends on whether the family also participates in Food Stamps, Medicaid, or housing assistance; the tax rate is endogenous to the family. Much the same is true under an NIT, but simulations of NITs have not taken full cognizance of the point. Instead, Medicaid and housing program participation have been disregarded vis-à-vis their effect on the marginal tax rate, while the Food Stamp Program itself is assumed to be rolled into the NIT benefit schedule. The effects of Medicaid and housing have been omitted, not because authors are ignorant of the interdependence between program participation and tax rates, but because of data deficiencies. Thus in Table 8.6 the marginal tax rates of alternative NITs should be interpreted as program-specific tax rates rather than as the exact tax rate facing each family. Similarly, the UF tax rate of about 0.7 is comparable to the AFDC program tax rate of 0.67 (above the first $30 per month of net earnings and other employment-related deductions) and the Food Stamp Program tax rate (decline in the Food Stamp bonus as income rises). It seems likely that the caseload projections of the present study are more comparable to an NIT having a marginal tax rate of 0.7 rather than 0.5, but either NIT rate could be chosen here for comparison. At the higher tax rate the break-even income of NITs is lower and fewer families are eligible for benefits; consequently predicted NIT participation is smaller, although still far larger than predicted UF participation.

Beyond benefit levels and tax rates, other factors differentiating predicted participation in UF and NIT programs include methodology, eligibility requirements, unemployment insurance, participation costs, and welfare stigma. Both the Keeley et al. and Greenberg-Hosek studies base the participation decision on a comparison of current with predicted income and hours of work. Predicted hours of work, hence predicted income under an NIT, derive from defensible statistical analyses of hours of work behavior (Keeley et al. use experimental data and Greenberg-Hosek use survey data). In contrast, the present study relies on an empirical analysis of the participation decision itself. The full analysis (Hosek 1979b) takes direct account of an assets limit and unemployment insurance and indirect account of other eligibility rules, participation costs (information gathering, time costs of applying for a recertification), and welfare stigma insofar as they are embedded in the constant term of the family participation model. Although the NITs being simulated had no eligibility requirements other than an income test, in practice there

still would be UI, participation costs, and welfare stigma to consider. By
not empirically evaluating the effects of these variables on participation,
the NIT participation rates may be biased upward from true rates.

With respect to the effect of UF eligibility requirements on participation, I would argue that the prior-work rule and WIN registration
requirements of UF are easily satisfied by most husbands. Also, the role
of an assets test in limiting the UF participation rate may be small.[11] The
one-hundred-hour rule confines the program to families experiencing a
transitory reduction in income due to unemployment or underemploy-
ment of the head, as well as to some families in which the head simply
prefers to work part time. The one-hundred-hour rule may be effective
in restraining UF participation, but its effect is mitigated by the presence
of the income test, which would have to be satisfied even if the hours
test were removed. Consequently, if the assets test, hours limit, prior-
work rule, and WIN registration requirements are only weak deterrents
to family participation in UF, then the UF and NIT programs emerge as
fairly close relatives. Moreover, the large discrepancy in participation
reported in Table 8.6 might then serve notice of a potentially gross
overestimation of NIT enrollment and, by the same token, program cost.
Whereas past research has focused on the labor supply effect of NITs,
there is now the suggestion that participation behavior could be the
preeminent factor governing size and cost.

But this is not to deemphasize the potential policy role of UF. As
shown, the extension of UF to non-UF states can initiate the process of
extending income maintenance to married, spouse-present families with
children at relatively low cost. Other modifications in UF — mitigating
the one-hundred-hour rule and the assets test, for instance — could be
done sequentially, while monitoring the cost and effectiveness of the
program over time. Thus the UF program contains the potential for
expansion into a virtual NIT; at the same time, selective modifications
could increase the role of UF as a source of support for low-wage,
unemployed fathers not receiving UI benefits.

NOTES

1. This applied as of 1975, the year to which the data in this study refer. The current
regulation states that the husband must have worked in 6 of the 17 calendar quarters prior
to application, and so is less restrictive.

2. The probability of participation refers to the "unconditional" chance that a husband-
and-wife family with children will participate in UF. That is, in contrast to most existing

analyses of program participation, where the decision to participate is first conditioned on the family's being eligible, my analysis investigates the joint outcome of eligibility and participation. (For further discussion, see Hosek 1978.)

3. Another analysis using UF caseload data across states showed no large or statistically significant effect of unemployment rate or assets limit on caseload (Hosek 1979a).

4. The UF benefits variable equals the maximum AFDC and Food Stamp benefits available to a family, given its size and location, should the family decide to participate in UF. If the family were to work while on UF, its income, including actual benefits paid, would be higher than its potential benefits as measured here. But the level of benefits paid would tend to be less than the maximum. Thus, the benefit variable should be thought of as a measure of benefit opportunity, or maximum potential benefits, while on UF. Note that a UF benefits variable is computed for each family, whether or not it is on UF. The UI benefits variable was developed in an analogous fashion.

5. Were data available, other variables also could have been included — for example, health status, years of work experience, stability of employment, special training, foreign-born origin, difficulty speaking English, and migration experience.

6. These particular effects, although statistically significant, can change when other variables are added to the equation. The addition of a variable for the number of children increases (decreases) the size and significance of the white (nonwhite) elasticity (Hosek 1978). This sensitivity should be borne in mind when interpreting caseload projections. However, the other coefficients (and elasticities) vary little when number of children is added to the specification.

7. The UI benefits variable is not statistically significant for nonwhites because many nonwhite husbands have a wage rate leading to UI benefits below the UI benefit ceiling and approximately equal to a constant fraction (about 50%) of their wage. Even with the Food Stamp bonus added, the UI benefit variable then becomes more colinear with the wage. This problem does not arise for whites, whose higher wage rates place many families at the UI benefit ceiling. When the UI benefits variable is deleted from the equation, the wage-rate effect strengthens to the point of statistical significance for nonwhites as well as whites.

8. See Appendix Table 8.A1. This table also shows, by wage class of the husband, the total number of families, predicted UF caseload, predicted percent of families on UF, total income per average family, nonearned income (transfer vs. nontransfer), and percent of families that participate in the Food Stamp Program.

9. Leonard Hausman (1976) did a small scale study of labor market search effects of UF and Food Stamps.

10. An average duration of stay of 9 months implies that, in equilibrium, 1/9 of the UF caseload is replaced each month. If the number of UF cases in January equals C, then the number of UF cases during the year equals $C(1 + 11/9)$. But some of these cases will consist of the same families reentering UF; so the number of different families on UF will be less, say $C(1 + 10/9)$, roughly. Therefore, multiplying the monthly caseload by $(1 + 10/9) = 2.1$ approximates the number of different families on UF during a year.

11. The assets test can be viewed as a residual screen. Most families passing the income test and the one-hundred-hour rule seem likely to pass the assets test. To the extent the assets test constrains UF participation, it tends to focus the program on *persistently poor* working families. In contrast, families with temporarily low income would have greater assets and are therefore more likely to be screened out by the assets test. (See Hosek 1979b for further discussion.)

Appendix Table 8.A1. UF Participation and Family Income, by Husband's Wage Class, 1975

Husband's Wage Rate (dollars per hour)[a]	Total Number of Families[b]	Predicted Monthly Caseload	Predicted Monthly Percent on UF	Average Income, All Families (dollars per year)				Percent Ever on Food Stamps January–June 1976
				Earned Income	Nonearned Income I[e]	Nonearned Income II[d]	Total Income	
A. All States								
<2.00	563,148	9,396	1.67	7,516	283	955	8,753	16.95
2.00–2.99	1,539,945	15,433	1.00	9,344	211	837	10,392	13.19
3.00–3.99	2,967,796	22,423	0.76	11,149	293	808	12,250	8.99
4.00–4.99	4,300,369	30,674	0.71	12,849	319	922	14,092	5.88
5.00–5.99	4,910,606	26,879	0.55	15,239	286	1,067	16,593	3.65
6.00–6.99	4,200,331	19,339	0.46	17,515	216	1,218	18,950	2.22
7.00–7.99	2,957,484	10,503	0.36	20,243	161	1,207	21,613	1.31
8.00–8.99	1,913,078	5,367	0.28	22,943	117	1,330	24,393	0.78
9.00 +	3,918,838	8,101	0.21	30,286	97	1,815	32,227	0.54
B. UF States								
<2.00	282,019	6,589	2.34	8,045	377	1,053	9,476	15.16
2.00–2.99	708,298	10,722	1.51	9,834	267	906	11,008	11.25
3.00–3.99	1,482,334	15,919	1.07	11,294	364	884	12,542	10.01
4.00–4.99	2,492,568	23,759	0.95	12,706	396	960	14,063	6.87
5.00–5.99	3,090,556	21,205	0.69	15,139	353	1,039	16,532	4.52
6.00–6.99	2,849,686	15,998	0.56	17,395	254	1,192	18,842	2.55
7.00–7.99	2,037,348	8,506	0.42	20,042	191	1,148	21,382	1.36
8.00–8.99	1,357,436	4,548	0.34	22,861	131	1,326	24,320	0.88
	2,735,667	6,790	0.25	30,058	109	1,787	31,971	0.54

C. Non-UF States

<2.00	281,129	2,807	1.00	6,984	188	856	8,028	18.75
2.00–2.99	831,647	4,711	0.57	8,926	164	778	9,867	14.84
3.00–3.99	1,485,462	6,504	0.44	11,005	222	732	11,958	7.98
4.00–4.99	1,807,801	6,915	0.38	13,047	213	870	14,131	4.51
5.00–5.99	1,820,050	5,675	0.31	15,409	174	1,114	16,698	2.16
6.00–6.99	1,350,645	3,340	0.25	17,768	137	1,273	19,179	1.53
7.00–7.99	920,136	1,997	0.22	20,689	93	1,336	22,124	1.21
8.00–8.99	555,642	819	0.15	23,142	81	1,339	24,573	0.54
9.00 +	1,183,171	1,311	0.11	30,812	70	1,878	32,817	0.55

SOURCE: 1976 Survey of Income and Education.

[a] Husband's wage rate = annual earnings ÷ (weeks worked × usual hours per week).

[b] Married, spouse present, with children less than 21 years; husband less than 65 years, able to work, not institutionalized or in armed forces.

[c] Nonearned Income I = AFDC, public welfare, and the sum of employment insurance benefits and veterans' pension if the husband received unemployment insurance benefits. (UI benefits and veterans' pension income are not reported separately on the SIE.)

[d] Nonearned Income II = other nonearned income (interest, dividends, property income, pensions, plus veterans' payments if the husband did not receive UI benefits).

REFERENCES

Cogan, John F. 1978. *Negative Income Taxation and Labor Supply: New Evidence from the New Jersey–Pennsylvania Experiment.* R–2155–HEW. Santa Monica, Calif.: Rand Corporation.

Greenberg, David H., and Hosek, James R. 1976. *Regional Labor Supply Response to Negative Income Tax Programs.* R–1785–EDA. Santa Monica, Calif.: Rand Corporation.

Hall, Robert E. 1972. "Turnover in the Labor Force." *Brookings Papers on Economic Activity,* no. 3:709–56.

Hausman, Leonard J. 1976. "Impact of Work Tests on Employment Behavior of Welfare Recipients." Mimeographed. Brandeis University, Waltham, Mass.

Hosek, James R. 1978. *Family Participation in the AFDC–Unemployed Fathers Program.* R–2316–HEW. Santa Monica, Calif.: Rand Corporation.

———. 1979a. *The AFDC–Unemployed Fathers Program and Welfare Reform.* R–2471–HEW. Santa Monica, Calif.: Rand Corporation.

———. 1979b. *An Introduction to Estimation with Choice-Based Sample Data.* P–6361. Santa Monica, Calif.: Rand Corporation.

Keeley, Michael C., et al. 1977. *The Labor Supply Effects and Cost of Alternative Negative Income Tax Programs: Evidence from the Seattle and Denver Income Maintenance Experiments, Part II.* RM–39. Menlo Park, Calif.: Stanford Research Institute.

Mincer, Jacob, and Polachek, Solomon. 1974. "Family Investments in Human Capital." *Journal of Political Economy* 82, no. 2 (Supplement March/April):S76–S108.

Smith, James P. 1978. *The Distribution of Family Earnings.* P–6249. Santa Monica, Calif.: Rand Corporation.

Spiegelman, Robert G.; Groeneveld, Lyle P.; and Robins, Philip K. 1978. "The Work Effort and Marital Dissolution Effects of the Seattle and Denver Income Maintenance Experiments." In *Materials Related to Welfare Research and Experimentation,* Senate Finance Committee, Subcommittee on Public Assistance. Washington, D.C.: U.S. Government Printing Office.

U.S. Bureau of the Census. 1977. "Characteristics of the Population below the Poverty Level: 1975." In *Current Population Reports.* Ser. P–60, no. 106. Washington, D.C.: U.S. Government Printing Office.

Williams, Robert G. 1978. "Statements." In *Materials Related to Welfare Research and Experimentation,* Senate Finance Committee, Subcommittee on Public Assistance. Washington, D.C.: U.S. Government Printing Office.

IV EVALUATING NEXT STEPS

The emphasis in the last few years of reform effort has been on an integrated approach to cash and jobs assistance. The papers in part IV evaluate the next steps in welfare reform with an eye to the still-unresolved questions and issues that will determine whether the jobs-oriented approach cum "safety net" of cash assistance will succeed or fail.

The integrated approach to jobs and cash assistance finds its clearest expression in the paper by Larry L. Orr and Felicity Skidmore. The authors provide a concise and insightful treatment of the integrated approach as it has evolved over the last forty-five years. Their history of the legislative effort to show where we came from is a useful prologue to the remaining papers.

Measures to directly create jobs targeted on low-wage workers is a relatively recent turn of public policy. The bulk of these measures involve direct public service employment (PSE) programs and employment subsidies. The Robert H. Haveman paper reviews the redirection of labor market policy to demand-side initiatives and speculates on the reasons why they have come to replace education-training and income transfer policies. The federal responsibility for job creation will be diminished if Congress approves the phasing out of CETA-funded public jobs. Yet, direct job-creation measures that remain intact must ultimately confront the issues of displacement and administrative difficulties. These potential problems are the realities of direct job creation as we enter the 1980s.

Economic theory is useful in determining the direction of policy impact, but not always the magnitude. A case in point is the work disincentive effect of a negative income tax (NIT). The implicit tax associated with an NIT decreases the price of leisure and thus discourages employment as a result of a *substitution effect* unfavorable to work effort. So long as leisure is a "normal" good, the receipt of income engenders an *income effect* also unfavorable to work effort. Thus, economic theory predicts that an NIT will result in some loss of work incentive relative to no program at all. Robert Moffitt's review of the experimental results addresses the quantitative question of *how much*. The policy implications of the clear disincentive effects that the author finds are to shift emphasis toward "NIT-sticks," which impose work requirements on the recipients of benefits.

The first three papers in part IV consider either jobs programs or cash transfer programs in isolation. But because future welfare reform is likely to contain elements of both policies, it would be remiss to ignore the possible interactions between them. This remaining gap is filled by David M. Betson and David H. Greenberg, who consider the policy implications that derive from various NIT–PSE schemes.

9 THE EVOLUTION OF THE WORK ISSUE IN WELFARE REFORM

Larry L. Orr and Felicity Skidmore

Concern with the work effort of low-income families — and the effect on that work effort of public cash assistance — has been a dominant force in shaping the existing welfare system and thirty years of efforts to reform and improve that system. In the past ten years, this concern has led to a radical change in the policy approach to welfare reform: from an emphasis on raising and extending cash welfare benefits while attempting to minimize work disincentives, to an emphasis on an integrated approach that would actively facilitate the employment of low-income family heads through job-search assistance and creation (on a very large scale) of public service employment opportunities, while providing a "safety net" of cash assistance for all families. In this paper, we describe the (initially independent) historical streams of policy development in cash assistance and employment and training programs that have now come together to produce this shift in welfare policy; analyze the difficult policy trade-offs that underlie the new approach; and discuss the still-unresolved questions and issues that will determine whether the new approach will succeed or fail.

THE WORK ISSUE IN LEGISLATIVE HISTORY

The Concern. Any receipt of cash or goods that is not a reward for work by definition makes work less necessary, because the recipient can enjoy a given level of consumption while working less than would otherwise be the case. Any program whose benefits fall as other income rises — as indeed they must in any program designed to aid low-income families — intensifies this disincentive by reducing the net reward for work.

That this matters is attested to by the prominence of the work issue and efforts to deal with it throughout the history of federal welfare policy. On the moral level, work is considered to have intrinsic value in our society. Thus, having a job or being supported by someone who is earning can be expected to be important to the self-esteem of society's members. In addition, since work is valued, those who feel that society has a responsibility to ensure certain minimum living standards, and are working and paying taxes to fulfill this responsibility, are likely to feel that those benefiting from society's help also have a responsibility to work. On the economic level, work is important, in that any reduction in earnings means that the cost to the taxpayers of providing a given standard of living is increased. It is also important because any reduction in work reduces the nation's production — reducing the amount of goods and services that society as a whole can consume and, thus, the standard of living of us all. On the political level, work is important because these moral and economic considerations are not lost on the voting public, who are therefore less likely to support generous income support programs that do not take these considerations into account.

The federal government entered the welfare policy arena in 1935 with the passage of the original Social Security Act. In the four and a half decades since, efforts to deal with the work issue in welfare and welfare reform have gone from a relatively straightforward concern to ensure that those expected to work did in fact work by denying them eligibility for cash transfers, to the recent realization that cash transfers, combined with jobs in an integrated income support system, can achieve more effectively than cash alone the "uneasy triangle" of income support policy objectives: (1) adequacy, (2) desired incentives, and (3) economy (Smith and Heffernan 1972).

Transfer Policy. The Social Security Act of 1935 marked the beginning of federal income support policy and its contours can still be seen in the basic structure of our income support system. The act was based on the following perception of the work issue: most individuals are either capable of and thus expected to work, or they belong to families that include such a worker. They can, therefore, be expected to command adequate living standards from private earnings.

Certain groups or categories are not expected to work, however, for various socially acceptable reasons, and these are deserving of help. In 1935, the categories defined as not expected to earn their own way were the aged, mothers of dependent children (i.e., children with no father in the house), and the blind. The Social Security Act thus included three welfare programs: Aid to the Blind (AB), Aid to the Aged (OAA), and Aid to Dependent Children (ADC). It should be noted, however, that these were considered short-term programs for residual groups rather than the mainstay of the act. The central programs were designed on the assumption that even the deserving categories had been workers or dependents of workers. Thus, the elderly were assumed to have had a lifetime of gainful employment, mothers of dependent children were assumed to be the widows of former workers, and the unemployed were assumed to have fallen on hard times that were temporary. These circumstances were provided for by a series of social insurance programs that, when in full operation, were to be self-financing in the form of payroll deductions during the breadwinner's working life: Old Age Insurance, Unemployment Insurance, and (in 1938) Survivor's Insurance.

In 1950, a set of amendments added to the categories of the deserving — by introducing Aid to the Permanently and Totally Disabled (APTD) and including benefits to the caretaker (usually the mother) of dependent children in the ADC (now AFDC) program, as well as to the children themselves — but did not change the basic approach to the work issue. The addition in 1956 of the Disability Insurance program followed the same pattern.

By the 1960s, however, it was clear that dealing with the work issue simply by separating the workers from the nonworkers and only providing income support for the latter was causing distortions that were in fact defeating the objectives of encouraging work. The AFDC program was the focus of the criticism. In spite of the establishment of Survivor's Insurance, the AFDC caseload had grown steadily. It was increasingly recognized, in consequence, that women on AFDC were not predominantly widows, but women who had been left by the fathers of their children. The suspicion was also growing that the categorical division that led to only single parents with children being eligible for support was causing men to leave their wives and children simply in order to qualify them for public support. In addition, views had changed somewhat since

1935 with respect to whether women should stay home with their children at public expense or whether they should, rather, work to contribute to their own support.

All this led in the 1960s to a new scrutiny of AFDC and the work issue, and three major new initiatives to deal with it. The first came in 1961, when the AFDC program was expanded, at state option, to cover two-parent families when the breadwinner was unemployed. The explicit objective of such a step was, in the words of the Secretary of Health, Education, and Welfare, to "keep families together." However, concern lest this money would allow fathers to be idle who would otherwise be gainfully employed led to such restrictions on eligibility with respect to prior attachment to the labor force that few families at any one time were able to qualify.[1]

The second major change came in 1962, with the recognition that regulations governing the benefits could themselves be a factor in inhibiting work. Up to this point, recipients could in fact become worse off by working if expenses were incurred in connection with that work, because the grant was reduced by the total amount of the recipient's earnings. The 1962 amendments allowed the deduction of work-related expenses from the income offset against the welfare benefit. There was, in addition, some seed money for day care and some provision (not much used) for federal matching funds for employment and training programs.

The year 1967 saw the third change — basically a substantial extension of the 1962 beginnings with respect both to deductibility from earnings as an incentive to work, and training and services to increase the employability of AFDC mothers. The work incentive (WIN) program was passed as part of the 1967 amendments, to provide training, work experience, and jobs. And the *30 and ⅓ rule* was introduced, whereby the first $30 of earnings (in addition to the work expenses) and one-third of each additional dollar earned was to be disregarded in computing the benefit. The belief that recipients differed in their suitability for work, and that this difference should be recognized, was still evident in the 1967 legislation in the provision requiring only AFDC recipients judged appropriate to be referred to WIN. By 1972, views about the responsibility of AFDC recipients to work had hardened, and the so-called Talmadge Amendment was passed, requiring all AFDC recipients to register for work or training.

As these Social Security Amendments were changing the legislative approach to the work issue, in the late 1960s the war on poverty was leading to a parallel development that was very important in its influence on the treatment of the work issue in the 1970s. Policy planners in the

Office of Economic Opportunity began to favor a concept espoused by a variety of academic economists throughout the 1960s: a universal, noncategorical negative income tax.[2] The universal negative income tax proposal was a direct response to the recognition that a categorical system that treated different groups differently created incentives to change categories, that a substantial group of families was poor even though they contained an able-bodied breadwinner working full-time and not covered by any significant transfer option, and that any feasible transfer option for that group had to pay careful attention to work incentives.

The OEO group was concerned, however, that public fear of the work-disincentive consequences of providing a negative income tax for the working poor would defeat any such proposal. A series of income maintenance experiments was therefore funded, in the expectation that the work disincentive resulting from an experimental negative income tax would turn out to be small and that this evidence would further the cause of reform.

As it turned out, just two years after the first experiment was initiated, a negative income tax proposal was introduced in Congress — the Family Assistance Plan (FAP), designed to replace AFDC and extend benefits to all poor families with children. It had no jobs component, but it did have a work requirement specifying that employable family members who refused to accept training or employment would forfeit their share of the benefit; and some additional funding for training under WIN was provided. FAP failed to pass for many reasons, but probably crucial to its defeat was the unrelenting concern with work incentives displayed by the Senate Finance Committee and the damage done to the FAP cause by the demonstration that, when combined with existing programs, FAP recipients could make themselves actually worse off by working. Concern was also expressed by the committee about the absence of a jobs component. A revised version of FAP (H.R. 1) was introduced in 1971, transferring the administration of payments to employable families from HEW to the Department of Labor and including some better integration of its tax rate provisions with those of existing programs. Criticism of its incentive features, again, was a prominent factor in its defeat.

That the crux of the problem was cash assistance for the working poor is supported by examination of the successful legislation that did flow from the FAP–H.R. 1 effort. The Supplemental Security Income Program — originally proposed in the FAP legislation — was passed in 1972, to replace the categorical programs for the aged, blind, and disabled with a uniform federal negative income tax. The Food Stamp Program was reformed by executive action in 1970 and legislative amendments in 1971 and 1973 into a national, universal negative income tax program, with a work test, but no categorical exclusions from eligibility. It was thus the first guaranteed income program to include all families headed by able-bodied working age males — but the currency was earmarked vouchers rather than cash. And in 1974, the Earned Income Tax Credit (EITC) was passed, the effect of which was to raise the incomes of the poor families who worked by supplementing *earnings* up to $8,000 a year.

Whatever its legislative success, the introduction of FAP was a landmark event in welfare policy with respect to the work issue, signaling a shift from the exclusionary, categorical policies that had been followed since the 1930s to a principle of universal coverage with reliance on work requirements and incentives (primarily, "low" tax rates) to mitigate reductions in work effort. As we have seen, the policy shift did not go so far as to attempt to actually *increase* work effort or employability in any major way. But during the same period, seemingly unrelated policy developments were under way in the areas of employment and training, which in the 1970s would come together with the movement for a universal negative income tax and culminate in a second major shift in welfare policy.

Employment and Training Policy.   Unlike the Social Security Act, which formed the basis of transfer policy, the major employment and training programs of the 1930s — the Works Progress Administration (WPA), Public Works Administration (PWA), Civilian Conservation Corps (CCC), National Youth Administration (NYA), and Civil Works Administration (CWA), among others — did not outlive the immediate urgent needs of the Depression. Except for some relatively modest public works programs intended to combat the recessions of the late 1940s and 1950s, the use of direct provision of employment and training to alleviate economic hardship was largely nonexistent until the early 1960s. The return to these policies took form largely in response to the steady decline of the dominant industries in certain areas. The key pieces of legislation that made up this initiative were the Area Redevelopment Act and the Public Works Acceleration Act. These were both designed to address structural unemployment on a regional basis, rather than defining and focusing on the employment problems of particular types of individuals. The passage in 1962 of the Manpower Development and Training Act (MDTA) — although its focus was still on structural unemployment and the consequences of technological change — marked the beginning of efforts to enhance the employment opportunities of individuals.

In the mid-1960s, the nation's training and employment policy again shifted, this time from workers unemployed (or in danger of losing their jobs) because of technological change to individuals who had few skills and in many cases little education or training of any kind. The Equal Opportunity Act of 1964 and the establishment of the Office of Economic Opportunity led to a series of job assistance and training programs for the disadvantaged. In keeping with the times, the emphasis of MDTA was also shifted in 1967 from retraining to initial skill development and remedial education for people with few labor market skills.

In 1973, the various employment and training programs stemming from MDTA and the antipoverty initiatives of the mid and late sixties became, under the Comprehensive Employment and Training Act (CETA), a single decentralized, decategorized program. National guidelines contained in federal program regulations, however, as well as strong local program support, helped to maintain the emphasis on services to disadvantaged populations in spite of the change in the service delivery system.[3]

Concomitant with the increased targeting of employment and training programs on the poor with few labor market skills as an antipoverty strategy was the macroeconomic concern with the difficulty of keeping unemployment low without running into unacceptably high rates of inflation. This search for ways to "cheat on the Phillips curve" provided an additional reason for interest in public service employment (PSE) as a cure for structural unemployment — the hope that the hard-to-employ who are not reached by macroeconomic stimuli can be placed into jobs that do not compete with the private sector and therefore do not drive up wages and prices.

Acting on these concerns, in 1978 Congress moved to substantially tighten eligibility provisions in the CETA Reauthorization Act. The act defined separate titles (and appropriations) for the structurally and cyclically unemployed, made more stringent the income and unemployment requirements for eligibility, and placed stricter restrictions on CETA PSE wage rates. The effects on eligibility were dramatic: in 1978, almost 19 million persons met the CETA PSE eligibility requirements; in 1979, only about 4 million persons qualified for CETA PSE jobs under Title II (the title covering the structurally unemployed).

There was still, however, no direct link between CETA and the income transfer programs. The increasing targeting of employment and training programs on hard-to-employ, disadvantaged workers meant that these two sets of programs were increasingly serving the same clientele. Because of the categorical nature of cash assistance and the continued

exclusion of most of the working poor, even with the 1978 CETA amendments only about 15% of CETA enrollees actually received cash assistance. But in 1979, over 90% of new CETA PSE enrollees were
economically disadvantaged (Committee on Evaluation 1979).[4] Extension
of cash assistance to all low-income families would therefore result in a
near-identity between the two target populations.

Recognition of the convergence of objectives and clientele in these
two policy areas, together with the inherent difficulties of designing cash
transfer programs that would enhance — or even preserve — work
incentives, led in the late 1970s to the second major shift in welfare policy
since the 1930s: innovative attempts to design an integrated income sup-
port/employment system that would combine CETA-type employment
and training opportunities with universal cash assistance. The first was
the unsuccessful Program for Better Jobs and Income (PBJI), introduced
in Congress in 1978. The second, a scaled-down version of PBJI, was
introduced in 1979 as two separate bills, the Social Welfare Reform
Amendments of 1979 and the Work and Training Opportunities Act.

The basic approach of the two now-defunct proposals was the same.
They again preserved the distinction between those expected and not
expected to work, but were designed to provide income support to both
groups. The latter were eligible for a cash transfer program with no work
component. For the former, the work concern was addressed by providing a combined cash and jobs program for the principal earners in *welfare
eligible* families, and welfare eligibility was significantly expanded by
mandating AFDC–UP in all states.[5]

ADEQUACY VERSUS INCENTIVES IN A CASH PROGRAM

This new approach to welfare reform promises a way out of the vexing
dilemmas that arose in previous attempts to provide adequate income
support to low-income families through cash assistance alone. It is well
known that the more generous a cash transfer program, as measured by
the guarantee level, and the more target efficient, as measured by the
break-even level, the higher must be the marginal tax rate — and therefore the greater the disincentive. This problem became glaringly clear
during the FAP debate. Although FAP nominally had only a 50% marginal tax rate, when it was considered in combination with the other tax
rates facing many would-be recipients (Food Stamps, 30%; public housing, 25%; the positive income tax, 14%; Social Security tax, 6%; etc.),
the combined marginal tax rate could actually exceed 100%, as was
pointed out in the Senate Finance Committee hearings on FAP.

Of course, one way to lower tax rates is to allow the break-even level to rise. Why can't we give adequate benefits *and* have low tax rates? The first reason is that Congress and the public don't want income support benefits to go to people much above the poverty line, as can be seen from the current break-even levels of the major income-tested programs. (The Food Stamps eligibility ceiling is $9,840 in annual earned income for a family of four, the Earned Income Tax Credit phases out at $10,000, and federal SSI benefits stop at $8,515 of earnings for a couple.) The second reason has to do with cost and caseload size. As the break-even level rises, it reaches into the dense part of the income distribution, which means that very large numbers of people become eligible for benefits. This, of course, increases the cost. But the overall cost is not the only consideration. Congress is also acutely sensitive to the *numbers* of people on welfare; this sensitivity was one of the major reasons for opposition to both FAP and PBJI.

So, lowering the tax rate does not appear to be feasible, at least politically. But perhaps the emphasis in the last ten years of reform effort on the importance of lowering the tax rate has been misplaced, even from the point of view of incentives. Recent evidence casts increasing doubt on the presumed advantages of lowering the marginal tax rate. Evidence from the most recent and largest of the income maintenance experiments (the Seattle-Denver experiment) suggests that, at least for male heads, the substitution effect (the ''pure'' effect of tax rates on net wage rates) is almost zero. For this politically important group, it turns out to be primarily the income effect of higher transfers that leads to decreases in work effort. And lowering the marginal tax rate has the effect of *increasing* benefits, and therefore the income effect, for all recipients except those with no income. In addition, lowering the tax rate raises the break-even point and, for a given budget, reduces the poverty-efficiency of the transfers. Finally, raising the break-even point has the paradoxical effect of *increasing* the number of people subject to the ''high'' tax rates of welfare; thus, while lowering the tax rate may reduce the work disincentive for a given recipient, it may well increase work reductions in the aggregate.

According to simulations based on the Seattle-Denver results applied to the national population, an income support program with the parameters of the cash component of PBJI would lead to average reductions in hours worked for husbands in two-parent families of 3%, for wives in two-parent families of 9%, and for single parents of 2%. Much of this reduction, according to the Seattle-Denver evidence, would come in the form of more time unemployed or out of the labor force. These reductions may seem modest, but it should be emphasized that even a small percentage decline in hours worked by family members can lead to large increases in budget cost, but only small gains in disposable income for the families. Consider the example of a family with $8,000 in earnings before the implementation of a transfer program with a 50% rate. If the program were to induce a 5% ($400) decline in earnings, the cash payment the family would receive would increase from $200 (when earnings were $8,000) to $400 — a 100% increase. The family's net income, however, would remain the *same* as in the absence of the program, with a net cost to the federal treasury of $400.

This *leverage effect* of work-effort reductions on benefit costs means that even modest percentage decreases in earnings can substantially increase aggregate program costs for those recipient groups whose earnings are large relative to their benefits. Simulations of a negative income tax with a guarantee equal to 75% of the poverty line and a 70% tax rate indicate that a 20% reduction in hours of work among husband-wife families would translate into a 32% increase in net transfer costs. Viewed in these terms, the "modest" labor supply reductions anticipated (and found) by the designers of the income maintenance experiments turn out to be a major disadvantage of the universal negative income tax approach.

Attempts to mitigate these costs by lowering the tax rate, while maintaining the same income guarantee, are doomed to failure for the reasons described above.[6] Simulations of alternative programs with income guarantees fixed at 75% of the poverty line and tax rates of 50% and 70% show that, while the percentage earnings reduction falls from 20% to 13%, as the tax rate is reduced, the aggregate transfer costs attributable to labor supply response rise from $.95 billion to $1.10 billion, and total net program costs increase from $3.9 billion to $6.4 billion — with much of the increase going to the least needy families, made eligible because of the rise in the break-even level. (All costs are in 1974 dollars; for a detailed discussion of those results, see *Summary Report: Seattle-Denver 1978*.)

These results played a major role in the policy decision by the Carter Administration to shift from a cash-only welfare reform strategy to a combination of jobs and cash. Adding public job creation to the available options changes the picture substantially.

ADEQUACY VERSUS INCENTIVES IN AN INTEGRATED CASH-PLUS-JOBS PROGRAM

It is important to bear in mind that the guarantee is not the only measure of adequacy and, indeed, may not in all cases be the best. Take the case

of a family with positive earnings. The relevant measure for them is the
income they actually receive at their current earnings level. Figure 9.1
shows two cash transfer schedules: ACD (with guarantee OA) and BCD
(with guarantee OB).[7] While ACD has a much lower guarantee, it is just
as generous as BCD for families with earnings above Y_0; in that range,
the two schedules coincide. The problem is, of course, that not all
families have earnings of Y_0 or greater, and those who do always face
the risk of earnings losses through unemployment. If, however, earnings
of at least Y_0 could be assured, then ACD would be just as generous as
BCD — when generosity is measured by the income that the family could
reasonably be expected to earn plus the cash supplement at that level.

This concept of adequacy underlies the distinction between *expected-
to-work* and *not-expected-to-work* families embodied in most recent welfare reform proposals. For those families who are not expected to work,
the guarantee is the appropriate measure of adequacy because, by definition, they are expected to live on it. For those families who are expected to work, the guarantee can be much lower, *provided that*
employment opportunities are guaranteed and the cash assistance tax

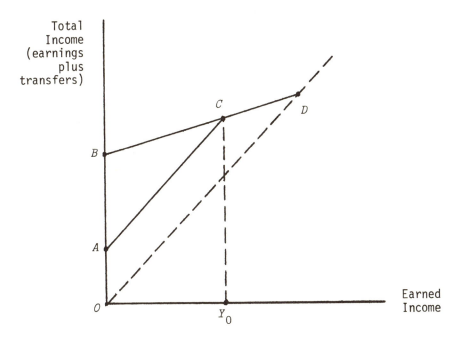

Figure 9.1. Hypothetical Cash Transfer Plans

rate is sufficiently low that the combination of minimum guaranteed earnings and cash assistance provide an adequate income level.

Transfer schedules like ACD for the expected-to-work population are attractive on several grounds. First, as compared to BCD, they substantially reduce the income effect of transfers on work effort, especially with respect to decisions to work or not to work in a particular month. And as we have seen, much of the work-effort reduction observed in the income maintenance experiments took the form of lengthened spells of unemployment or time out of the labor force. Second, they are much more acceptable on political grounds. Congress and the public have consistently shown a marked resistance to allowing able-bodied recipients of cash assistance to stop working entirely and live on a generous guarantee. Indeed, discussions of welfare reform in the popular press sometimes treat the guarantee — which is far and away the most widely discussed parameter of any plan — as if it were the actual transfer to every family. The combination of a schedule like ACD with guaranteed employment opportunities would virtually eliminate the fear of large numbers of families living on the dole, without unduly penalizing the families of workers who become involuntarily unemployed.

The original PBJI proposal embodied a cash transfer schedule for expected-to-work families of this form, along with sufficient PSE job slots to provide employment for all cash assistance recipients who could not find jobs in the regular labor market. The argument does not depend crucially on the nonlinear form of the transfer schedule, however. Much the same considerations would apply to a low-guarantee, low-tax-rate schedule, which would cross the high-guarantee, high-tax-rate schedule BCD at some earnings level.

For example, if the cash guarantee is set at 75% of the poverty line for a family of four ($5,560), with a 50% tax rate, and a guaranteed job paying $3.65 an hour is provided, total family income will be $9,356, or about 126% of the poverty line — and this income level *is guaranteed* as long as one family member is willing to work full-time. The cost of guaranteeing that level of income through cash alone — that is, of setting the cash guarantee at 126% of the poverty line — is well beyond the range of political feasibility.

Moreover, the cash-plus-jobs approach virtually reverses the work disincentives present in a cash-only program. Because the income guarantee now takes the form of guaranteed earnings, rather than transfers, the income effect of a high cash guarantee is largely eliminated, and the family's incentive to work — as well as its employment opportunities — is greatly enhanced. The tax rate can also be lower than in an equivalent cash-only program (although, as noted earlier, the work-incentive effects of lowering the tax rate are probably small, at least for the male heads who have the bulk of earnings in low-income families). Simulations of the PBJI proposal indicated that the jobs component of that program would have increased the work effort of covered families by about 5% as compared to the cash component of PBJI alone.[8] Finally, the provision of guaranteed employment allowed adoption of a work requirement that is neither punitive nor unenforceable, further enhancing the political acceptability of the cash-plus-jobs strategy.

The promise of enhanced work incentives along with improved income security led to the incorporation of substantial jobs components in virtually all of the welfare reform proposals — both by the Carter Administration and in Congress — over the past several years. The common element of those plans has been a *two-tier cash component,* with lower guarantees for families with members expected to work (that is, all families with children with 2 able-bodied adults and single-parent families with no children under 6), along with a substantial number of subsidized jobs for those families who are unable to find employment in the regular labor market.

Under the Carter Administration's proposals, for example, assistance in finding a job in the regular labor market would have been provided for an 8-week period. Those who were unsuccessful in finding unsubsidized jobs after 8 weeks in the job-search stream would have received necessary training or a public service job with wages set at about 110% of the minimum wage. Along with this would have gone the provision of any supportive services, such as child care or transportation, necessary to enable the work or training requirements to be met. Principal earners in all welfare eligible families would have been eligible (and companion legislation proposed mandating AFDC–UP in all states). It was estimated that under these provisions, 95% of all welfare recipients in families with a member working in a PSE job would have been above the poverty income level, and 65% would have been above 125% of the poverty level.

A particularly noteworthy feature of this reform initiative was the development of the 8-week job-search provision. The job-search period was originally viewed as just a waiting period, to screen applicants so that the jobs program could be focused on the neediest and the least employable. As the proposal evolved, however, that thinking changed. There was a serious commitment at both the federal and the program-operator level to provide real job-search assistance (JSA) during this period.

The idea of JSA was not in itself new. The Employment Service and

WIN have provided such assistance for many years. But the commitment to assist *all* welfare eligibles in this way, and to tailor new JSA techniques specifically to the disadvantaged population was indeed new. Since JSA costs only $250–$500 per participant for an 8-week period (compared with about $10,000 per public service employment slot), it is still potentially a very cost-effective way of reducing dependency, unemployment, and federal costs.

The integrated cash-plus-jobs approach is, thus, exciting as a new welfare reform idea. As with all new approaches, however, since no *guaranteed* public employment program has been tried before in this country, there are many issues on which much more needs to be known. To these we now turn.

UNRESOLVED ISSUES IN GUARANTEEING JOBS TO LOW-INCOME FAMILIES

The cost, political and administrative feasibility, and desirability of a guaranteed-jobs program, as well as its optimal design, all turn on a number of issues about which little is currently known. A major pretest of the Carter Administration welfare reform proposal — the Employment Opportunities Pilot Project (EOPP) now underway in fifteen sites across the country — should help to resolve many of these outstanding questions. This section enumerates the major issues to be addressed by further research.

Feasibility. It is not entirely certain that the government *can* create sufficient jobs to guarantee employment to all eligible workers who cannot find unsubsidized jobs. The estimated number of job slots required under PBJI was about 1.4 million.[9] Direct job creation on this scale has never before been attempted in this country. We do have some experience with moderately large jobs programs, however.

CETA, which would have been the administrative mechanism for the Carter Administration welfare reform proposal, until recently provided about 550,000 PSE jobs for long-term unemployed workers, a high fraction of whom were from low-income families. The Work Opportunities and Training Act would have added about 400,000 slots to this total. A build-up of this magnitude seemed quite feasible, based on recent CETA experience: over a one-year period in 1977–78, under the Emergency Employment Act, CETA provided 346,000 additional PSE jobs. Nevertheless, it remains to be seen whether jobs can be created to fully satisfy demand, especially given the fiscal budget cuts envisioned under the Reagan Administration.

Participation Rates. A crucial factor influencing total job-slot requirements, and thus the feasibility of the program, is the participation rate among eligibles. The unknowns here include not just the fraction of eligibles who enroll in the program, but also the portion of enrollees who can be placed in unsubsidized employment during the job-search period, and the length of time those who ultimately are placed in subsidized jobs stay in those jobs. The latter is particularly important; if turnover in the jobs is low, it may be necessary to create an ever-increasing number of jobs to employ all who need them.[10]

An important influence on both the initial participation rate and turnover in the subsidized jobs is the attractiveness of the jobs relative to jobs in the regular labor market. Some workers may find it advantageous to leave low-paying, unsubsidized jobs to enter the jobs program. The degree to which this occurs will be heavily influenced by the wages, working conditions, and security of the subsidized jobs, and the length of the job-search period. At present, however, very little is known about the number of employed who would "come out of the woodwork" to take the jobs.[11]

Finally, participation in the job component will be directly affected by the success of job-search assistance during the initial eight weeks. This is a major unknown, since highly structured, concentrated job-search assistance for low-wage workers is a relatively new undertaking. Recent EOPP demonstrations tested a variety of job-search approaches, some of them in a controlled experimental setting. The initial experience in the EOPP sites yielded a wide range of outcomes, with anywhere from 20% to 60% of those entering job search being placed in unsubsidized jobs. A good deal of analysis will be required to sort out the effects of alternative JSA approaches and local labor market conditions, and to net out the proportion who would have found jobs without assistance, in order to determine the added contribution of JSA.

Net Job Creation. In addition to providing income support for low-income families, welfare-reform jobs are intended to increase total employment opportunities (in a noninflationary manner) and total social product. To achieve these goals, the subsidized jobs must be designed so that they do not compete with existing economic activities — that is, they must produce goods and services that would not be produced in their absence. Otherwise, it is likely that subsidized workers will displace other workers indirectly through the workings of the market, or be substituted for them directly, particularly in the public sector. Estimates of *net job creation* (the proportion of subsidized jobs not offset by displacement and substitution) in previous PSE programs vary widely — a variety of studies has placed the rate of substitution and displacement after one year anywhere from 9% to 120%. This range reflects both the analytical difficulty of the problem and the methodological weaknesses of the studies. Clearly, more and better research (and/or data) is needed on this issue.

It should be borne in mind, however, that even substantial displacement and substitution would not necessarily vitiate the *income redistribution* objectives of a jobs program. To the extent that unemployment is simply redistributed in favor of primary earners in low-income families, the effect on the income distribution would still be equalizing. Nevertheless, it is important to know the level of net job creation that can be attained, and to find ways to minimize displacement and substitution.

Labor Market Effects.   As we noted earlier, it is hoped that by targeting PSE jobs on low-skilled, unemployed workers, additional employment can be created without generating upward pressure on wages in the regular labor market and, consequently, on prices. However, to the extent that workers are drawn out of private (or regular public) sector employment, shortages of low-skilled labor may be created and wages bid up, at least at the lower end of the wage distribution. The level of the PSE wage is critical in this regard, since it in effect creates a floor below which workers (at least principal earners) need not accept alternative employment. Even if the PSE wage is set at the legal minimum, it is not clear that there would not be substantial shifts of workers from existing jobs into the program. Not only is it well known that large numbers of workers are now employed at less than the minimum wage (or — what may be more relevant — below the weekly wage implied by the minimum hourly wage), but even for workers in existing minimum wage jobs, the security and working conditions of a PSE job might prove attractive.

At present, very little is known about the relative attractiveness of PSE jobs at alternative wage rates and existing employment opportunities in the regular labor market. A major effort will be made in the EOPP demonstrations to measure these effects, both through analysis of labor market dynamics in the pilot sites and their matched comparison sites, and through an experiment in which randomly selected subsamples of the low-income population are made eligible for PSE jobs at alternative wage rates.

Optimal Mix of Jobs and Training. Direct provision of jobs targeted on low-wage workers is, as we have noted, a relatively recent turn of public policy. The more traditional approach, followed throughout the 1960s and early 1970s, was to attempt to remedy through training programs the lack of skills that presumably prevented these workers from finding jobs in the regular labor market. Clearly, there are some workers whose skills and education are so limited that they would not be productive even in subsidized jobs tailored to their abilities; for them, some training is necessary and appropriate. Equally clearly, there are many workers who can be productive without further training, but either lack employment opportunities in the regular labor market or are unable to find or take advantage of the opportunities that exist. The relative proportions of these groups among unemployed low-income workers is a major unknown in designing a large-scale employment and training program targeted on this population. Moreover, it is not clear that we know how to discriminate between these two groups, in order to select those workers who would benefit from training.

Long-Run Effects on Participants. While recent policy deliberations have viewed job creation as primarily a short-run income maintenance strategy, it is clearly important to know as well whether it can be expected to further the traditional goals of employment and training programs: enhancement of the labor force participation, wage rates, hours, earnings, and employment stability of participants once they return to the regular labor market. While little is now known about these long-run effects on participants, there is some rather tentative preliminary evidence that is encouraging. Recent analyses of the Continuous Longitudinal Manpower Survey data show fairly impressive gains in earnings and (to a lesser extent) wage rates of CETA participants (*Impact of CETA* 1980, pp. 3.27–64). While there are, as usual, some methodological weaknesses in these studies, these results are fairly robust with respect to alternative specifications of the comparison group, and are therefore encouraging. In any case, much more analysis of these issues, using better and longer-term data, is clearly in order.

Value of Output. From a social point of view, there is little distinction between jobs and cash transfers unless the jobs produce output of some value. Of course, the lower the *net* cost of job creation the greater the value of output, and the attractiveness of job creation (as opposed to cash transfers as an income security approach) is enhanced accordingly. Empirical valuation of the output of subsidized jobs is exceedingly difficult; it's simply a special case of the well-known problem of valuing government services. Only limited attempts have been made to date to place a value on the output of CETA PSE jobs, but these attempts have been encouraging. For example, a study by the National Academy of Sciences reported that over 70% of local CETA administrators felt that the job performance of CETA workers was "about the same" as the other workers performing similar tasks (Committee on Evaluation 1979). There is, of course, obvious potential for bias in querying administrators about the performance in their own programs, but these responses are at least suggestive — and there are very few other data to rely on at this point.

Administrative Procedures.   Coordinating and integrating the administrative structures that dispense cash, on the one hand, and provide job-search assistance, training, and employment, on the other, is not a trivial undertaking. At present, there are two entirely separate programmatic structures — the public assistance agencies (including their employment and training component, WIN) and the CETA prime sponsor network — each with its own personnel, procedures, eligibility criteria, and clientele. In many cases, the geographic boundaries of the local agencies of the two systems do not ever coincide. Yet, in an integrated system, the interaction between the two must be smooth and swift. A host of questions arise in designing an integrated administrative structure: What agency will have the final responsibility for eligibility determination? For determination of employability? For certification that essential services, such as child care and transportation, are available? For determining that the work requirement has not been met? Should the job-search, employment, and training components be merged into WIN, or should CETA replace WIN, or should the two work in parallel? Should CETA provide job-search assistance to welfare applicants, or wait until they have been certified eligible for cash assistance — a process that can take weeks or even months? What record system and data processing capabilities are necessary for tracking participants in the two systems?

Beyond the interaction of the cash-plus-jobs programs themselves, there are a number of other linkages that must be worked out with other public and private sector agencies and organizations. Among the more important of these are the state employment services, public and private social service agencies, and public and private employers.

While some of these questions can be addressed in the abstract, the only sure test of solutions is through learning by doing in the field. Right now, we are confronting, and attempting to resolve, these issues in the EOPP demonstrations.

CONCLUSION

The work issue has been a dominant factor in shaping the evolution of both cash assistance and employment and training policy over the past forty-five years. In both spheres, policy has come to focus much more strongly on enhancing the employability and employment opportunities of disadvantaged and low-income families with members who, by popular consensus, are expected to provide a substantial proportion of family income through earnings. In the last few years, this confluence of policy emphasis has produced a new breed of welfare reform proposal, which holds forth the promise of reconciling the goals of income adequacy, target efficiency, and enhanced work effort and employment opportunities. These new approaches present complex and unresolved issues of feasibility, impact, and program design, which will define the agenda for welfare research and policy analysis for the coming decade.

NOTES

1. This concern also prevented 23 states from adopting the program at all and led some that established it initially to drop it. In 1978, when 2.5 million two-parent families had incomes below the poverty line, only about 120,000 families were receiving AFDC–UP in any given month.

2. A negative income tax, of course, is a transfer system under which a certain level of support is guaranteed to recipients with no other income; this guarantee is then reduced by a (usually) proportional tax rate on earnings until, at a certain earnings level, known as the *break-even level,* the guarantee has been completely eliminated and benefits cease. AFDC is a categorical negative income tax with guarantees that vary from state to state and with a tax rate and break-even level determined by the "30 and ⅓ rule" and the treatment of work-related expenses.

3. Only in a few specific cases — such as the countercyclical public service employment initiatives in Title IV — has this legislative and policy emphasis been relaxed.

4. As used here, the term *economically disadvantaged* includes persons with family incomes below the poverty level (in 1979 about $7,400) or 70% of the BLS lower living standard (in 1979 about $8,100 for a family of four), the handicapped, and the institutionalized.

5. The cash assistance bill also set national minimum benefit levels and tied AFDC–UP eligibility to income rather than prior labor-force attachment.

6. It should be noted that similar considerations apply to earlier attempts at welfare reform. For example, the 1967 AFDC amendments, which lowered the tax rate from 100%

to 67% and were hailed as a major work incentive, may have actually reduced work effort in the aggregate by raising the break-even level and increasing the number of families facing the welfare tax rate, and by increasing benefits, and therefore the income effect, for recipients who were working prior to the amendment. Similarly, the Earned Income Tax Credit, passed in 1974 as an inducement to increased earnings, is probably a net disincentive, because there are far fewer earners in the *phase-up range,* where benefits rise with earnings, than in the *phase-out range,* where benefits are taxed away as earnings rise, and because it, too, has an income effect on work effort at all earnings levels.

7. For the uninitiated, transfer diagrams like Figure 9.1 are interpreted as follows: at any given level of earnings along the horizontal axis, the family's total income is the sum of earnings, measured by the vertical distance between the horizontal axis and the (dotted) 45° line, plus transfers, measured by the vertical distance between the 45° line and the transfer schedule. As can be seen in Figure 9.1, transfers decline as earnings rise until, at point D (the break-even level), transfers are zero; above that level, total income equals earnings. The marginal tax rate at any earnings level is given by 1 minus the slope of the transfer schedule at that level.

8. The increase in work effort compared to a cash-only plan providing an equivalent income guarantee would, of course, have been much greater.

9. The demand for subsidized jobs is, of course, quite sensitive to the wage rate. Increasing the PBJI wage rate from $3.00 per hour (1975 dollars) to $4.00 per hour, for example, would have increased job-slot requirements from 1.5 to 2.5 million. This demand sensitivity, as well as the desire to target the jobs on workers with the poorest alternative job prospects, argues strongly for keeping the wage rate close to the minimum wage, at least initially. (See Smolensky and Haveman 1978.)

10. To avoid this "stockpiling" effect, the Carter Administration proposal provided for ongoing job-search assistance while the worker was in a subsidized job, and required another 8-week job-search period after 52 weeks in the subsidized job.

11. Concern about this phenomenon was a principal motivation for the Carter Administration's decisions to limit eligibility to principal earners — who are less likely than secondary workers to find the jobs attractive — and to keep the wage rate relatively low.

REFERENCES

Committee on Evaluation of Employment and Training Programs, National Academy of Sciences. 1979. *The New CETA: Effect on Public Service Employment Programs.* Washington, D.C.: National Academy of Sciences.

The Impact of CETA on Participant Earnings. 1980. Working Paper no. 1. Rockville, Md.: Westat Corporation.

Smith, Robert F., and Heffernan, W. Joseph. 1972. *Work Incentives and Welfare Reform.* Reprint Series, no. 78. Madison: Institute for Research on Poverty, University of Wisconsin.

Smolensky, Eugene, and Haveman, Robert. 1978. "The Program for Better Jobs and Income: An Analysis of Costs and Distributional Effects." Reprint Series, no. 275. Madison: Institute for Research on Poverty, University of Wisconsin.

Summary Report: Seattle-Denver Income Maintenance Experiment. 1978. Washington, D.C.: U.S. Department of Health, Education, and Welfare.

10 DIRECT JOB CREATION:
Potentials and Realities
Robert H. Haveman

In the area of labor market policy, the 1970s have seen a major redirection of policy away from programs designed to change the productivity of individual workers and toward direct job-creation policies. For fiscal year 1980, nearly $4 billion was obligated for direct job-creation efforts, three-fourths of it for public sector job creation. This outlay reflects a major change of emphasis from the earlier training-education-placement efforts in the manpower field, and an expansion of income support policy in the transfer program area. The effort to provide jobs directly to the unemployed would appear to reflect dissatisfaction — perhaps, frustration — with policies to increase income and employment via increasing earnings capacity, and to maintain the income of those for whom work is unavailable. This increase in the direct provision of jobs can be viewed as a

Research reported here was supported in part by the Institute for Research on Poverty at the University of Wisconsin (Madison) by funds provided by the U.S. Department of Health, Education, and Welfare. John Bishop, Robert Lampman, and especially Sheldon Danziger provided useful comments on an earlier draft.

This is a revised version of a paper that appeared in *Employing the Unemployed,* edited by Eli Ginzberg, pp. 142–59. © 1980 by Basic Books, Inc., Publishers, New York. Reprinted by permission.

major commitment to the Full Employment Act of 1946. It reflects the same commitment as that which resulted in passage of the Full Employment and Balanced Growth Act of 1978 — more commonly known as the Humphrey-Hawkins Bill.

Direct public provision of jobs is a relatively unorthodox venture for the market-oriented U.S. economy. It represents an admission that the current structure of the market economy, despite aggregate monetary and fiscal measures, is unable to secure adequate economic performance. Support for direct public job provision comes in part from a belief that this instrument can reduce some of the current constraints on labor market performance. It is by improving this performance that direct job creation holds promise as an effective instrument for reducing income poverty, and for solving what has come to be known as the structural unemployment problem.[1]

In this paper, the concept of direct job creation is first defined and the primary job creation activities of the federal government during the 1970s are identified. Then I discuss the rationale for direct job-creation measures; a rationale that has both a political and economic dimension. This rationale suggests substantial potential for direct job-creation measures — a potential involving increased employment, a lower inflation rate, and a more equitable income distribution. This potential, however, may be deceiving, because major policy interventions often carry with them unintended and unforeseen side effects. After discussing these side effects and marshalling existing evidence on the effectiveness of direct job-creation measures, I suggest a few speculative alternative approaches for direct job-creation efforts in the United States.

WHAT IS DIRECT JOB CREATION?

It is perhaps easier to indicate what direct job-creation policy *is not,* than what it is. First, it does not refer to normal public employment — that employment which provides direct public sector services — even though standard public employment can include a direct job-creation aspect. Here, *direct job creation* is defined by measures that are undertaken to accomplish two major objectives. They are, first, an increase in labor demand for specific groups in the economy, such as youths, minorities, the handicapped, or those with little education or skills. Because normal labor demand for these groups is often inadequate when other groups are fully employed, they are referred to as the structurally unemployed. Second, the reduction of income poverty is an objective of direct job-creation efforts, because these groups tend to be found at the bottom of the earnings distribution. In short, then, any policy measure designed to increase the demand for the labor of specific groups experiencing high unemployment (or nonemployment) or income poverty will be considered direct job creation.[2] This includes direct public service employment programs and employment subsidy programs designed to create jobs in the private sector.

Most prominent among the recent policies fitting this definition is the Comprehensive Employment and Training Act — CETA. As originally developed in 1973, CETA was designed to enable local officials to coordinate manpower programs so as to meet their particular concerns and to provide jobs for unemployed and disadvantaged workers. Although the original act included a provision for public service employment for those with low skills, the major thrust of CETA came with a 1974 revision that established an untargeted, countercyclical public employment program. With federal support provided to areas experiencing high and sustained unemployment, transitional employment opportunities were provided by state and local government agencies at close to prevailing wage rates. Of the nearly 300,000 slots created in the first year of the program, less than one-half were filled by persons from low-income families, and nearly three-fourths were filled by high school graduates.

After 1976, the emphasis in CETA shifted toward disadvantaged and hard-to-employ workers. The 1976 amendments reserved 250,000 job slots for disadvantaged workers, and with Carter Administration sponsorship a target of 750,000 public service jobs was established with eligibility criteria targeted toward disadvantaged workers, welfare recipients, and the long-term unemployed. By 1979, 43% of the nearly 700,000 CETA jobs were being performed by the structurally unemployed, and by 1980 this stood at about 60%.

Although CETA is the most prominent direct job-creation program, it is not the first. One predecessor was Operation Mainstream, which by the mid-1970s was directly employing about 40,000 older, disadvantaged, and chronically unemployed workers in community service activities at wage rates slightly above the minimum wage. As in CETA, little training was provided. Moreover, relatively few workers were placed in regular public or private jobs.

An even larger predecessor was the Neighborhood Youth Corps (NYC), which was perhaps more a work experience than a public employment program. As part of the war on poverty in the 1960s, NYC provided short-term summer and during-school employment at low wage rates to over 6 million poor youths during a ten-year period. Another predecessor (which has received publicity out of all proportion to its magnitude) was the Work Incentive (WIN) program. This publicity came from the 1971 legislative requirement that welfare recipients register for work. While over 2 million recipients were so registered by the mid-1970s, only a few thousand were given public jobs, and most of those were in work experience or on-the-job training programs rather than regular public employment. Another direct job-creation program, but with a countercyclical emphasis, was the Public Employment Program (PEP) of the early 1970s. During its two-year life, PEP employed 340,000 workers in transitional public jobs and an additional 300,000 workers were hired in summer jobs. Targeting to specific groups in PEP was not extensive, and while nearly one-half of the workers had been unemployed for a long time, over three-fourths were high school graduates, and relatively few were from low-income families.

All of these direct job-creation programs involved the special provision of work by the public sector. Technically, workers in these programs were public employees. In the 1970s, however, direct job-creation efforts were also aimed toward the provision of jobs in the private sector — in part, because the magnitude of the problem exceeded the potential of the public sector to provide jobs. The major private sector program designed to increase the demand for labor, particularly for low-wage labor, was the New Jobs Tax Credit (NJTC) enacted in 1977. The NJTC provided a tax credit equal to 50% of the first $6,000 of wages paid to the 50 workers hired in a firm above 102% of the firm's previous year employment level. While this two-year program (1977–1978) did not distinguish among workers by their unemployment or poverty status, the subsidy — and hence the incentive to hire low-wage workers — was a higher percentage of their wages than it was for more skilled workers.

In 1979, the NJTC was replaced by a directly targeted employment subsidy program, the Targeted Jobs Tax Credit (TJTC). For the first year of employment, this tax credit equals 50% of the first $6,000 of wage cost for any newly hired person from a designated set of categories — youths from low-income families, disabled workers, Vietnam era veterans, and SSI and general relief recipients. The subsidy falls to 25% for the second year of employment. By eliminating the 102% employment threshold and explicitly designating target groups, the substitution of TJTC for NJTC represents a shift in emphasis from cyclical unemployment toward structural, low-wage unemployment.

One final direct job-creation measure — proposed, but not enacted — should be mentioned. In 1977, President Carter proposed direct job creation as an integral part of his welfare reform plan — the Program for

Better Jobs and Income (PBJI). Work, he stated, would be substituted for welfare as a primary source of income for many current welfare recipients. In his plan, 1.4 million new minimum-wage jobs would have been created by the government and would have been filled by able-bodied welfare recipients not encumbered with substantial child care responsibilities. To continue receiving income support payments, these recipients would have been required to find employment in regular public or private sector jobs or to participate in the PBJI jobs program. Among other reasons, congressional concern with the budgetary cost of PBJI led to its demise.

In both labor market and income support policy, then, the direct creation of jobs through public employment and employment subsidy programs has played a pivotal role during the 1970s. While training remained a component of some of these programs, work *qua work* was seen as their primary purpose. For recipients, the work provided was viewed as having value in itself as an alternative to unemployment, as human capital in providing experience in the world of work and some on-the-job training, and as earned income rather than income support from transfer programs. For taxpayers, direct job creation was viewed as more desirable than cash grants with no quid pro quo in providing income support to the disadvantaged, and in producing outputs meeting some private or social need.

These recipient and taxpayer gains were judged to be at least equal to the costs of creating work where no real — or at least well-articulated — demand for output exists. The costs of creating jobs are not trivial, and estimates range from an annual budget cost of about $3,500 per job in the NYC program to over $10,000 per job in the WIN and CETA programs. These per job costs, however, are substantially below the government outlays required to create employment by means of tax cuts or general spending increases.

WHY DIRECT JOB CREATION?

High unemployment rates among certain groups, large and growing welfare rolls, and substantial and concentrated income poverty are not new phenomena. Why, then, did the government wait until the 1970s to turn to direct job creation to combat these problems? The answer, it seems, is not one that fosters confidence in either policymakers or economists.

Though rarely admitted, the political rationale for direct job creation rests on a pair of less than inspiring propositions. The first is frustration over the apparent failures of early labor market programs. The decisions made in the 1960s to provide education, training, and skills to poor and unskilled workers were optimistic ones, based on the human-resource-investment notions of economists and other social scientists. The poor, it was believed, could earn their way out of poverty if given additional education and skills. The problem was thought to arise on the supply side of the labor market — and tens of billions of dollars were spent during the decade after the war on poverty was announced to correct supply-side deficiencies. To supplement this strategy, income transfers were expanded through increased coverage, additional programs, reduced eligibility requirements, and more generous benefits. From 1965 to 1981, income transfers targeted on poor and disadvantaged workers grew from about $30 billion to about $300 billion (Danziger, Haveman, and Plotnick 1981).

This period also saw the rising importance of evaluation research. Hundreds of evaluation studies were made of the numerous education, training, and income support programs — and the results were not positive. Participants in the training programs generally recorded earnings increases, but they were often not large enough to cover the costs of providing training. Gains in educational attainments were also recorded, but these were largely short-lived and insubstantial (Levin 1977). Welfare and transfer benefits expanded and incomes were supported, but serious work disincentives were created, horizontal inequities remained severe, and administrative complexities and claims of fraud supported the belief that there was a "welfare mess." Perhaps most serious, the national poverty count did not fall markedly, especially after 1969, and the unemployment rates for minorities, youths, women, and other groups remained several times larger than the average rate. After all of these efforts, the supply-side training, education, and income support strategy apparently had not really worked. The failure of the supply-side approach increased the relative attraction of a demand-side strategy — hence, direct job creation, in part by default.

The other political rationale for direct job creation arises from dissatisfaction with the growth in the income support system. The substantial increase in education, training, and other social welfare expenditures brought with it the strong opposition of those nonpoor who were paying the bill. Failures were emphasized, work disincentives cited, and the absence noted of tangible reductions in poverty and unemployment. Income transfer and social policy came to be viewed as encumbering the economy, restraining initiative, investment, and growth (Feldstein 1974a; 1974b). This opposition also argued against what it saw as the senseless strategy of "give-aways." Little could be expected from a system of money or food or housing or medical care gifts in which no quid pro quo in the form of effort was required or expected, and in which the gift was withdrawn as effort increased. The remedy was clear — provision of income support should be granted only in payment for work provided. Again, direct job creation — the new "putting out" system — met this concern. Unfortunately, what was required to satisfy the political need for a quid pro quo was the presence of an individual in a job slot, an input, and not the value of the output that his/her services yielded.

This characterization of the political rationale for direct job creation may be too cynical, but perhaps not by a great deal. Arguments concerning the self-esteem associated with work as opposed to welfare were raised, as was the value of work experience and the outputs produced. Moreover, the provision of jobs would reduce a primary constraint on the success of training programs — the lack of jobs — and offset the work disincentives of standard transfer programs. It is difficult, however, not to believe that these arguments were little more than dressing for the real need for a policy alternative to the discredited supply-side strategy — an alternative that entailed some quid pro quo for income support. Direct job creation was such an alternative.

While the political rationale for direct job creation is a questionable one, the economic rationale failed to be clearly articulated in time to have substantial impact on legislation. With but few exceptions, economists had neither fully thought through, nor convincingly argued this rationale until well after major public service employment and wage subsidy programs were in place. And as we will see, that rationale is not an unimpressive one. Henry Aaron's (1978) characterization of policy-making guiding social science — rather than the reverse — is nowhere better illustrated.

What, then, is the economic rationale for direct job creation? This rationale starts from a perception of the adverse economic effects of existing legal and institutional constraints on the operation of the labor market. Because of these constraints — minimum wage laws, employer discriminatory behavior, union power and influence, supply disincentives caused by income transfer and by income and payroll tax programs, and the demand disincentives caused by unemployment insurance and payroll taxes — labor markets do not respond quickly to changes in labor supply or demand, and a wedge is created between the gross wage paid by employers and the net wage received by workers. Employer-borne gross-wage costs are increased relative to the perceived marginal product of low-skill workers, and the net wage received by workers is reduced relative to the supply price of labor for these workers; the market clearing effect of flexible wages is not permitted to operate. In this context, high unemployment among groups of low-skill workers — youths, minorities, women — is inevitable, as is the persistence of income poverty among these same groups.

Direct job-creation measures — either public service jobs or employment subsidies — directly reduce the cost of hiring additional labor as perceived by potential public or private employers. Indeed, in the case of public service employment, a 100% subsidy of the wages of target group workers is provided, driving the cost of hiring additional such workers to zero. This reduced cost will cause employers to substitute workers in the target group for both capital inputs and workers who are not members of the target groups. Thus, employers have an incentive to accelerate plant and equipment maintenance or inventory accumulation (especially if the program is not a permanent one), or if confronting increased demand for output, to add a second shift of new workers rather than to increase overtime work. All of these reactions stimulate the demand for workers in the target group.

From an economy-wide perspective, a related effect will occur. If the direct job-creation program is targeted on workers who will increase their labor force participation in response to an increased labor demand, then potential output (GNP) will increase. Transfer program recipients, handicapped workers, and low-income youth would seem to be such groups, as large numbers of these workers are not employed — indeed, they are out of the labor force — because of unemployment, minimum wages, and other labor market constraints. In an inflationary situation, substantial increases in both the employment of these workers and GNP could occur without substantial upward wage pressure. Some economists have referred to this as "cheating the Phillips curve" by concentrating employment increases on sectors of the labor market experiencing excess supply.

The benefits of expanding GNP in this noninflationary way are even larger if these target groups are unemployed or out of the labor force involuntarily. In such a situation, the leisure foregone by the newly employed would be of small, zero, or even negative value. In economic welfare terms, the gain from employing such otherwise unemployed workers is the entire output that they produce, and not the output less the value of the inputs, as in the standard case.

Other gains also occur. Taxpayers will gain from the increased taxes paid by the newly hired workers, and the reduced welfare and other transfer payments. Thus, both the workers involved and society as a whole gain, as recipients work their way off welfare.

Two final effects should be noted: First, direct job-creation programs in the private sector may exercise downward pressure on prices by reducing total labor costs. This price-reducing effect complements the cheating-the-Phillips-curve effect mentioned above. Second, selective direct job-creation measures will tend to shift the composition of employment and earnings toward low-skill, target-group workers. If less inequality in the distribution of income is desired, this is a major benefit.

This economic case for direct job creation can be thought of in yet another way. If the key causes of excessively high unemployment and poverty among some groups are the constraints on the operation of the labor market due to discriminatory employer behavior, the power of trade unions, and minimum-wage and welfare policies, two approaches seem feasible. The first would be the elimination of the constraints — revamping or abandoning minimum-wage and income-conditioned transfer programs and eliminating restrictive employer and union practices. The second would be to ameliorate or offset the adverse side effects of these policies and practices. These side effects were described earlier as wedges between employer-borne gross wages and the perceived marginal product of low-wage workers, and between the net wage received by labor and the supply price of his/her working. It is precisely the reduction of these wedges that is accomplished by direct job-creation programs. To employers, the program reduces the wage costs of hiring low-wage workers, while to low-wage workers, the program increases the possibility of finding and the rewards of holding a job. In short, well-designed direct job-creation programs can serve to offset the adverse side effects of labor market constraints, and in so doing lead to increased employment and earnings of low-wage workers, and to increased output and aggregate employment with little or no inflationary pressure.

Clearly, then, the economic rationale for direct job creation is a strong one, and surely more substantive than that which has motivated political support for such measures. Unfortunately, the pattern that Henry Aaron documented for other areas applies to this policy approach as well. Both theoretical and empirical work has followed rather than guided direct job-creation policy.

While this rationale supported direct job-creation efforts prior to the 1980 election, it was apparently not persuasive for the new Administration taking office in 1981. CETA was included among the programs absorbing the $44 billion of budget cuts proposed for 1982; indeed, its elimination was recommended. Moreover, extension or renewal of the Targeted Jobs Tax Credit (TJTC) was not supported. One explanation for this position stems from the "supply-side economics" that motivated the budget proposals. This view envisions a revitalized private sector as yielding a sufficiently large increase in the demand for disadvantaged workers as to eliminate the need for direct job-creation measures. In addition, work effort is to be stimulated as a quid pro quo for the provision of income support through the imposition of work tests on the recipients of welfare programs. This policy change represents a major reversal of the past two decades of direct public sector concern with the employment status of disadvantaged workers. It also rests on a set of hoped-for supply-side responses, the economic evidence for which is scanty at best.

THE REALITIES OF DIRECT JOB CREATION

While the economic rationale for such a demand-side, direct job-creation strategy hypothesizes gains in both efficiency and equity, the effective design and implementation of such programs is not straightforward. Any ultimate appraisal of the role of a direct job-creation strategy must also confront several potential problems. (For a more full-blown discussion of the effectiveness of direct job-creation measures, see Haveman and Christainsen 1979).

The first problem associated with direct job-creation programs involves *displacement effects* — the reduction of employment somewhere as an offset of the job-creation impacts of the program. Because the primary objective for this strategy is employment creation, its evaluation must be in terms of its *net* job-creation impact, defined as the difference between the employment level in the economy with the policy and that without it. Clearly, because (1) the output produced by the subsidized workers competes with alternative outputs, (2) the financing of the program entails opportunity costs that represent displaced outputs, and (3) many of the subsidized workers would have been working even in the absence of the subsidy, the *net* job creation impact will be smaller than the *gross* number of workers hired or subsidized. The ratio of net to gross job creation is an indicator of these displacement effects.

Although several studies have estimated this ratio or its equivalent for public employment programs, estimates vary widely. For example, one evaluation of CETA, in which few constraints were imposed on the governmental units that administered the program, suggested that this net-to-gross jobs ratio approached zero in the long run. The implication is that fiscal authorities were able to divert nearly all of the CETA funds to expenditures that would have been financed alternatively in the absence of CETA. In general, the short-run net employment effects were found to be larger than the long-run effects (Johnson and Tomola 1977). Other studies evaluating public employment programs — and critiquing the above study — were more optimistic. They placed the ratio of net to gross employment at between 40% and 60% after one year — implying that about one-half of the funds were diverted from job creation through "fiscal substitution" (Borus and Hamermesh 1978).

It seems likely that public employment programs that constrain governmental units from diverting CETA funds to activities that would have been undertaken in their absence would yield net-to-gross employment ratios higher than those estimated for CETA. Moreover, for public service employment programs targeted on low-skill, high-unemployment groups, fiscal substitution is likely to be relatively difficult because the skill mix of target-group workers hired would not conform closely to that of regular public employees.

The only evaluations of direct job-creation programs aimed at the private sector are those of the NJTC. These studies measured the employment increases net of displacement within industries, but failed to consider the possible displacements in other sectors of the economy. In one study, the employment increases in the construction and retailing industries attributable to the NJTC were estimated by means of a variety of time-series regressions (Bishop and Haveman 1979b). The estimated NJTC employment stimulus over the 12-month period from mid-1977 to mid-1978 ranged from 150,000 to 670,000. For these industries, total employment growth over the period was 1.3 million. The preferred models attribute at least 20–30% of the observed employment increase in these industries to NJTC. This result is consistent with the observation that during the period of estimation in both industries, rates of employment growth substantially exceeded the rates of output growth.

Other studies, based on different data and techniques, also suggest a substantial effect of the NJTC. While these studies focus on the net intrasector employment effects, and hence fail to consider some possible channels of displacement, the employment effects attributed to the job-creation measure appear to be substantial (Perloff and Wachter 1979).

A second problem involves the resource and budget costs of the *net* jobs created by this approach. As indicated above, these costs are quite high. The most recent "guesstimate" of budget costs is based on the assumption that displacement is 20% in public employment programs and

80% in private sector job-creation programs. It suggests a cost per job
for private sector programs of about \$6,500 and a cost for public sector
programs of over \$9,000 per job.[5] Although these estimates do not con-
sider the increased tax revenues generated by the extra employment, or
the reduced transfer payments, they do suggest that the taxpayer cost
per job created is close to, if not in excess of, the net earnings of the
new employees.

This discussion of budget costs per job raises a third problem — the
valuation of the output produced relative to the real costs of creating the
jobs. The benefits attributable to such jobs involve not only the productivity of the worker while employed on the job, but also the contribution
of the work experience or on-the-job training to his/her earnings in the
future. The real costs of employing a worker in such a special public or
private program include both the value of the equipment and materials
with which he/she works and the value of what he/she would have been
doing if the program had not existed. This foregone productivity might
involve the worker's alternative market activities, or the home production
(e.g., child care) in which he/she would have been engaging, or simply
the value of the foregone leisure.

As with other effects, public direct job-creation programs are likely to
differ from wage subsidies to private firms in their efficiency impacts.
Economic theory suggests that the private sector approach will be the
more effective in meeting an efficiency, or *benefit-cost,* criterion. First,
private employers already have a known production process and a set
marketing channel for the products produced, whereas public employment programs are often undertaken with no clear definition of the expected output and no easy measure of productivity. Partially offsetting
this is the fact that through competition, privately marketed outputs are
more likely to displace other production than public outputs designed to
fill an unoccupied economic niche. Moreover, if private employers use
the subsidy to retain workers whom they would otherwise lay off, the
opportunity cost of the workers retained will be low. At least in principle,
direct public employment programs would appear better equipped to hire
very low skill, low wage workers with correspondingly low opportunity
costs. In practice, however, the managers of public service employment
programs have found that the hiring of such workers weakened their
efforts to develop productive and smoothly functioning work arrangements, and have not in fact targeted job slots on these workers (Nathan
et al. 1978). Finally, to achieve economic efficiency, actual wage rates
should equal the marginal opportunity cost of labor. Direct public employment programs, in effect, subsidize labor costs by at least 100% of

true marginal productivity. Wage subsidies toward the private sector are likely to come closer to subsidizing the difference between observed wage rates and real opportunity costs.

In any case, it should be emphasized that this economic efficiency criterion is a difficult one to meet for either private or public sector direct job-creation efforts targeted on low-productivity workers. While diverting such workers into a direct job-creation program is likely to entail relatively small losses from alternative activities (especially if the alternative to participation is involuntary unemployment), these workers do require associated inputs in the form of materials, equipment, and supervisory personnel, all of which comes at full cost. The key issue, then, is the value of the output produced. Because the output of public job-creation programs is not marketed, its value is hard to measure. This is especially true if the basic motivation for the program is to "keep occupied" members of the target groups or to provide them with work experience or training, rather than to use the public sector to achieve some defined objective or to produce some identifiable good or service.

The difficulties of meeting the efficiency objective have been illustrated in a recent study of a large, well-organized program of special workshops for handicapped and other less productive workers in the Netherlands. Little fault could be found with the internal organization of the factories in this job-creation program, and its clients are clearly less productive workers. Production from the workshops competed in the private market at market prices, and workshop managers were able to pursue any contracts for which they could assure delivery. The subsidy provisions, however, did little to encourage effective cost control in the program. An analysis of the benefits and costs of this program turned up a balance sheet that was not particularly favorable. The *net* economic costs of employment in the program are on the order of $4,000–$5,000 per year per worker (in 1979 dollars) — similar to taxpayer costs of U.S. direct job-creation programs. Only if the sociopsychological benefits to the workers are judged to exceed this value can the program be considered a socially efficient one (Haveman 1978).

Additional evidence on the economic-efficiency effects of direct job creation is found in evaluations of the Supported Work Experiment (Kemper, Long, and Thornton 1981). This evidence, like that of the Dutch program, is not encouraging. During the 18 months after participants were enrolled in the program, net economic costs ranged from $1,100 per participant for ex-addicts to $2,600 for youths. Only program sites employing AFDC recipients showed potential net economic benefits. This analysis, like the Dutch study, does not account for a number of potential intangible benefits from the program — in particular, the willingness of nonparticipants to pay for income redistribution through work rather than welfare, and the future employment and earnings increases of the participants attributable to the program.

A fourth problem of direct job creation concerns the effects on macroeconomic relationships if the programs are successful. Consider, for example, direct job-creation programs for the private sector. It was argued above that such programs, if effective, would increase employment at a substantially greater rate than output, and the NJTC results have suggested that this has occurred. A direct result of this unevenness is a fall in productivity — output per unit of labor input — as we measure it in the United States, as inputs grow faster than output. Similarly, if employment of target-group workers results in an increase in labor force participation from those in the group who are discouraged workers, employment may increase, but measured unemployment may remain relatively unchanged, or even increase.

One of the most widely accepted macroeconomic relationships is known as Okun's Law, which states that a 1 percentage-point reduction in the unemployment rate will be associated with a 3.2% increase in GNP. This relationship depends on several other macroeconomic responses in the economy as aggregate output changes — for example, the skill composition of employment, average hours worked per employee, and the utilization of capital. If the change in unemployment is induced by a wage subsidy targeted on low-skill workers, all of these standard macroeconomic responses will be altered, and Okun's Law will be repealed. Indeed, during recent years, it appears that just that sort of effect has been taking place — some recent estimates have placed the current Okun multiplier at about 2.0, down from the 3.2 figure of the original Law. (For a discussion of the changes in macroeconomic relationships due to employment subsidies, see Bishop and Haveman 1979a.)

Surely, it is an open question as to whether or not such changes in macroeconomic relationships are desirable. Declining productivity, for example, does have implications for economic growth and the maintenance of international competitiveness. On the other hand, the reduction in productivity may be evidence that low-skill workers are being removed from unemployment and idleness and transferred into the productive sector. In this case, these adverse side effects on macroeconomic relationships are evidence that direct job-creation efforts are indeed producing their intended effects, as well.

The final problem concerns the administrative and design problems associated with direct job-creation programs. Such programs are exceedingly difficult to design and administer — surely more costly than a general expansion of aggregate demand. The administrative difficulties of public service employment have already been referred to. As one critique (Danziger, Haveman, and Smolensky 1977) of the Carter PBJI jobs program stated:

> The mass creation of public service jobs for low wage–low skill workers is something with which this country has no previous experience. The effort is analogous to a private firm's promise to introduce a new product, the manufacture of which requires a technology which has not yet been developed. . . . The effort is fraught with uncertainty, and the possibility of an ineffective and unproductive program must not be neglected. [Consider these] potential problem areas. (1) Regarding the prime job sponsors, how would their competence and honesty be judged; . . . how would the limited number of jobs be allocated among them and would that allocation create inequalities and discrimination against the least skilled and least productive workers? (2) Can jobs be created which participants will not find demeaning and dead end; will they have a training component facilitating transition to regular employment; . . . what precautions would be taken to avoid competition with existing private and regular employment, competition which can lead to labor union objections and to displacement with little net job creations; . . . [would the wage paid in public service employment programs be sufficiently below the private sector net wage to encourage transition out of the program?] (3) How would the transition from special public sector jobs to private sector jobs be facilitated; if the available supply of public service jobs should prove greater than the demand would there be incentives for contractors to terminate existing holders of public service jobs or to encourage their transition to regular employment? (4) What problems would . . . [high expected job] turnover create for the administration and, especially, the productivity of the public jobs program? (Pp. 25–26)

The problems associated with employment subsidy programs are equally difficult, but of a quite different sort. For example, a marginal wage subsidy such as the NJTC will minimize displacement (and windfalls to employers), but will be relatively ineffective in targeting the additional jobs created. On the other hand, a program that is effectively targeted on low-skill workers may find recruitment costs high, employment goals unattainable, and output objectives difficult to achieve. Such programs may also result in the displacement of a more skilled worker who is a family's primary earner (e.g., a father) with a target-group individual (e.g., a youth) whose earnings position in the family is more peripheral. Moreover, programs with the highest potential for stimulating target-group employment may increase labor turnover, cause procyclical inventory accumulation policies, or stimulate additional growth in regions that are already the fastest growing. (For a discussion of the effective design of selective employment subsidy programs, see Bishop and Haveman 1979b.)

The realities of direct job creation must serve to temper the optimistic economic rationale for this strategy and dampen the apparent political enthusiasm for jobs programs designed to reduce unemployment and poverty. Yet, such tempering and dampening are not disastrous. One must, after all, consider the alternatives. And as has been suggested, the overall marks awarded supply-side education and training programs have not been high. And while income transfers have doubtless reduced income poverty, the administrative difficulties and the disincentives to work and advancement have discouraged even the most ardent supporters of the income support antipoverty strategy (Danziger, Haveman, and Plotnick 1981). Further, few would now argue that affirmative action, regional development, public works, or even a national service draft are likely to make great inroads into the unemployment problems of youths, minorities, or low-growth regions.

A balanced appraisal, it seems, would award a substantial role to direct job-creation efforts. The administrative problems are difficult, but not more so than those of training and transfer programs. And while displacement is a serious concern, even the most cautious appraisals suggest that the $6,000–$10,000 budget costs of creating jobs in direct job-creation programs are but one-third to one-half the costs of creating jobs via general tax cuts or public expenditure increases. Moreover, the targeting of effects on groups of greatest policy concern would appear to be more feasible under a direct jobs program — either public or private — than under alternative approaches. Perhaps the most telling consideration in support of a prominent role for direct job creation is its macroeconomic effect. In a period in which inflation is a serious concern, any strategy that holds out hope of increasing the employment of low-productivity workers, and thereby, of decreasing their income poverty with little or no upward wage and price effects, has to be awarded a relatively high grade. When the strength of the economic rationale is tempered by the hard realities of direct job creation, a nontrivial optimism must still remain regarding the potential role of this policy strategy.[6]

SOME NEXT STEPS IN DIRECT JOB-CREATION POLICY

Accepting this cautiously optimistic conclusion regarding the potential role of direct job-creation policy, the question is: Can we build on past experience and research to develop improved efforts in this area? What are some potential directions for policy, and what must be known in order to proceed efficiently?

One possibility concerns an *employee-based* employment subsidy arrangement. Until now, both of the major private sector job-creation efforts (the NJTC and the TJTC) have been employer-based. The employer verifies if a particular worker hired qualifies under the terms of the legislation for a subsidy, and if so, a claim for payment is filed. The worker need not know if he/she is generating a subsidy, nor will co-workers know. Moreover, in such an employer-based plan, the individual worker has little ability to influence his/her being hired, even if he/she has knowledge of being in the target population. Response to the incentive lies only with the employer, and as a result, any activities induced by the subsidy to match job to worker will be only on the demand side of the market. The labor supplier is a passive participant.

This incentive pattern would be altered if the subsidy were employee-based (see Bishop 1977). For example, assume that each worker certified as a member of the target group were given a card indicating that any employer hiring the worker would be entitled to a subsidy of a designated form. Indeed, the subsidy terms could be identical to those in any employer-based targeted program. Possessing the card would provide the worker with a labor market advantage and hence an incentive to search for a job. Knowing the rules of the program, the employer would have no less incentive to match job to worker than with an employer-based scheme. The advantage of such an employee-based plan, then, stems from the increased incentives on the labor suppliers to search for work, increasing the probability that they will be hired.

In evaluating such an arrangement, several questions immediately arise: (1) Would workers feel stigmatized if specially certified as card or voucher holders? (2) Would coworker resentment be generated if non-certified workers sensed special conditions or retention probabilities were associated with holding a certification card? (3) Would employers confront added (or reduced) administrative burdens if employee certification were handled in this way? (4) Are there possibilities for varying the terms of the subsidy depending on the circumstances (e.g., income level, age, or region) of the worker? (5) Would target-group members already employed be eligible for a certification card, and would their employers be eligible for the subsidy? (6) If the subsidy were paid only for hiring a new certified worker, would not artificially induced job turnover be created? Given the benefits from the increased job-seeking activities that an employee-based plan would induce, the answers to the above questions would have to be rather strongly negative to warrant abandonment of this idea without further consideration.

A second possibility related to a concern already expressed about public service employment — the apparently unproductive order of offering employment without a clear conception of the output or service to be provided. In the past, direct employment programs have had to look for an output, rather than for an output whose production matches the skills of target-group workers being clearly defined and accepted. Indeed, this was one of the criticisms of the public service employment component of PBJI — a criticism that carried weight. The suggestion here is that design of a new direct job-creation program be preceded by the clear specification of a public (or merit) good, the production of which would have gained public support, and be clearly visible and measurable. With such a clear delineation of output, the productive process could then be specified to maximize the employment of low-productivity, target-group workers.

The strategy being suggested, then, is the reverse of the procedure heretofore adopted in the United States. One example of this approach would be that of the Netherlands, where a clear national commitment to a neat, clean, well-trimmed landscape has now been established as a public merit good. To obtain this "output" has required municipalities, with national government support, to increase labor demands for sports field and playground improvement, roadway trimming and beautification, vacant field maintenance, and minor road repairs and clean-up. The provision of this output has entailed the employment of numerous low-productivity workers, including disabled and handicapped people. By focusing on attainment of this specific and visible output, public support is obtained, with the side effect of increasing the demand for low-productivity workers.

A third suggestion relates to the potential benefits of a combined training–job-creation effort. Existing private sector job-creation programs have neglected training relative to straight employment provision. Evidence suggests that private sector employment with on-the-job training over a continued period can have substantial long-run effects. If this is so, an explicit effort to link training and direct job creation may have merit.

Clearly, training provided by private sector employers will only be commensurate with the net benefits they perceive from such efforts. Hence if a training component (or requirement) were to be coupled with employment subsidies, the subsidy provision would have to be appropriately enlarged.

Such an employment-training program is not without precedent. In 1978, Sweden introduced a temporary marginal employment subsidy designed to stimulate a general increase in employment. The program originated in response to an expected decrease in industrial employment during the latter part of 1978 and was designed to expire on 1 July 1979. Any establishment that experienced a net increase in employment by that date above its 1 May 1978 level was eligible for the subsidy. Employers were required to satisfy the union involved that the relevant employees received a minimum of training (about two months' worth), with the amount of the subsidy being set to cover the additional costs incurred. There is little doubt that a subsidy arrangement that both paid training costs and subsidized employment could be made attractive to private business. Again, numerous questions of design and implementation can be raised, not the least of which concerns the verification of training quality, effectiveness, and costs. However, the potentials of such an approach would appear to warrant additional study and experimentation.

In conclusion, then, as we enter the 1980s, policies designed to create jobs directly would appear to have a strong economic rationale and, given concern with the employment status of disadvantaged workers, political appeal. As it now appears, the major problems of the 1980s will be continued inflation, structural unemployment of youths, women, and minorities, and economic dislocations due to energy prices and changing retirement patterns. Policies to enhance employment and earnings (in particular, employment subsidies) would appear to have an important role to play in such an environment. The Full Employment and Balanced Growth Act of 1978 already provides a legislative mandate to directly use such federal policies to meet these problems.

While this employment generation approach is basic to a more effective income support system, it in no way constitutes a complete reform of the transfer system. With a direct job-creation program in place, the work disincentives in the existing system could be reduced. Serious problems of program integration and administration, horizontal inequities among families of different types and in different locations, and incentives for migration and family break-up would still characterize the existing system. Making employment the core of the system, however, would influence the direction of future, more general reforms.

A reorientation of the support system that emphasizes earnings and employment can induce the low-skilled to increase their work effort and employers to increase their demands for such workers. It offers the potential for reducing poverty and dependence on government payments and increasing work, savings, and economic growth. The sacrifice of this potential in the interest of retrenchment would miss an opportunity for meaningful reform.

What is now necessary is that more be learned about the benefits and problems of alternative direct job-creation measures. Unless these measures can be designed so as to maximize their output and targeting potential, while avoiding their displacement and other adverse side effects, evaluation of them may ultimately be no more favorable than that of the education, training, and income support strategies of the 1960s and 1970s. Experimentation with both employee-based subsidy arrangements and subsidized employment-training arrangements contracted for directly with private sector businesses should be high on the policy agenda for the early 1980s. The results from such activities could serve as the basis for a renewed commitment to job-creation policies, an efficient expansion of employment subsidies, and perhaps, public employment programs.

NOTES

1. The concept of structural unemployment used here is that suggested by the Joint Economic Committee: "Structural unemployment consists of that margin of nonfrictional unused labor resources whose employment through conventional macroeconomic policies would result in an accelerating rate of inflation" (U.S. Congress 1979a, p. 27).

2. The emphasis in this definition is on structural unemployment, even though some direct job-creation policies are directed at cyclical unemployment problems (e.g., the New Jobs Tax Credit). As will be indicated below, the measures with a countercyclical objective also have a selective or targeted objective as well. For elaboration of a four-way public-private–countercyclical-counterstructural taxonomy of direct job-creation measures, see the testimony of Isabel V. Sawhill before the Joint Economic Committee (U.S. Congress 1979b).

3. Recent estimates place the number of such *discouraged workers* in the neighborhood of 750,000. Evidence on the labor force responsiveness of these groups is found in the testimony of Donald A. Nichols before the Joint Economic Committee (U.S. Congress 1979a).

4. The term *cheating the Phillips curve* was first introduced into the policy discussion in this area by Baily and Tobin (1977). A more pessimistic view of this possibility, which emphasizes the flexibility of wages and labor mobility, is found in the work of Johnson and Blakemore (1979).

5. See the testimony of Isabel V. Sawhill (U.S. Congress 1979b). The percentage displacement figures used are defended there. The per-job costs of private sector job creation would fall to $2,500 if the 80% displacement assumption were changed to 50%. Similarly, the cost per job in public sector job creation would rise to $14,300 if the same 50% displacement assumption were substituted for the 20% assumption used.

6. This tempered optimism also pervaded the evaluations of a direct job-creation strategy, as presented to the Joint Economic Committee. Several of these statements also emphasized

the existing imbalance in this strategy favoring public rather than private job-creation efforts.

REFERENCES

Aaron, H. J. 1978. *Politics and the Professors: The Great Society in Perspective.* Washington, D.C.: Brookings Institution.

Baily, M., and Tobin, J. 1977. "Macroeconomic Effects of Selective Public Employment and Wage Subsidies." *Brookings Papers on Economic Activity* 2:511–44.

Bishop, J. 1977. *Vouchers for Creating Jobs, Education, and Training: VOCJET, An Employment-Oriented Strategy for Reducing Poverty.* Special Report no. 17. Madison: Institute for Research on Poverty, University of Wisconsin.

Bishop, J., and Haveman, R. 1979a. "Selective Employment Subsidies: Can Okun's Law Be Repealed?" *American Economic Review* 69:124–30.

———. 1979b. "Targeted Employment Subsidies: Issues of Structure and Design." In *Increasing Job Opportunities in the Private Sector.* Washington, D.C.: National Commission on Manpower Policy.

Borus, M., and Hamermesh, D. 1978. "Study of the Net Employment Effects of Public Service Employment: Econometric Analyses." In *Job Creation through Public Service Employment,* vol. 3. Washington, D.C.: National Commission on Manpower Policy.

Danziger, S.; Haveman, R.; and Plotnick, R. 1981. "How Income Transfer Programs Affect Work, Savings, and the Income Distribution: A Critical Review." *Journal of Economic Literature* (September):975–1028.

Danziger, S.; Haveman, R.; and Smolensky, E. 1977. *The Program for Better Jobs and Income: A Guide and Critique.* Prepared for the U.S. Congress, Joint Economic Committee. Washington, D.C.: U.S. Government Printing Office.

Feldstein, M. 1974a. "Social Security, Induced Retirement, and Aggregate Capital Accumulation." *Journal of Political Economy* 82 (October):905–26.

———. 1974b. "Unemployment Compensation: Adverse Incentives and Distributional Anomalies." *National Tax Journal* 27 (June):231–44.

Haveman, R. 1978. "The Dutch Social Employment Program." In *Creating Jobs: Public Employment Programs and Wage Subsidies,* edited by J. Palmer. Washington, D.C.: Brookings Institution.

Haveman, R. H., and Christainsen, G. B. 1979. "Public Employment and Wage Subsidies in Western Europe and the U.S.: What We're Doing and What We Know." In *European Labor Market Policies,* edited by O. Ashenfelter. Washington, D.C.: National Commission on Manpower Policy.

Johnson, G., and Blakemore, A. 1979. "The Potential Impact of Employment

Policy on the Unemployment Rate Consistent with Non-Accelerating Inflation." *American Economic Review* 69:119–23.

Johnson, G., and Tomola, J. 1977. "The Fiscal Substitution Effect of Alternative Approaches to Public Service Employment Policy." *Journal of Human Resources* 12 (Winter):3–26.

Kemper, P.; Long, D.; and Thornton, G. 1981. *The Supported Work Evaluation: Final Benefit-Cost Analysis*. New York: Manpower Demonstration Research Corporation.

Levin, H. 1977. "A Decade of Policy Developments in Improving Education and Training for Low-Income Populations." In *A Decade of Federal Antipoverty Programs: Achievements, Failures, and Lessons*. New York: Academic Press.

Nathan, R., et al. 1978. "Monitoring the Public Service Employment Program." In *Job Creation through Public Service Employment*. Washington, D.C.: National Commission on Manpower Policy.

Perloff, J. M., and Wachter, M. L. 1979. "The New Jobs Tax Credit: An Evaluation of the 1977–78 Wage Subsidy Program." *American Economic Review* 69:173–79.

U.S. Congress, Joint Economic Committee. 1979a. *The Effects of Structural Employment and Training Programs on Inflation and Unemployment*. Washington, D.C.: U.S. Government Printing Office.

———. 1979b. Testimony of Isabel V. Sawhill, 21 February 1979. *Hearings*. Washington, D.C.: U.S. Government Printing Office.

11 THE EFFECT OF A NEGATIVE INCOME TAX ON WORK EFFORT: *A Summary of the Experimental Results*

Robert A. Moffitt

Among the many programs proposed for the reform of the welfare system, a negative income tax (NIT) is perhaps the most well known and the most durable. Despite this fame (or notoriety), an NIT signifies different things to different people and is not easy to define. To many observers, an NIT is a welfare program that would federalize the welfare system; simplify the benefit formula and streamline the payment procedures, thereby lowering administrative costs; raise the benefit level in many parts of the country to what would be regarded as a more humane level; extend coverage to families with an able-bodied male present and to families included in the *working poor* (i.e., those with a working head, but with an income below the poverty line). In addition, an NIT is most often thought of as a program that attempts to provide incentives to work purely by providing monetary incentives through the benefit formula, rather than by imposing a work requirement or a work registration requirement. So, an NIT attempts to provide work incentives by using a "carrot" rather than a "stick." Although all these different ways of

Most of this paper is a nontechnical discussion of material included in earlier papers by Moffitt (1979c) and Moffitt and Kehrer (1981).

thinking of an NIT are related to some degree, the merits of each are also intrinsically separable. For example, one could use a stick approach to work incentives, but still favor all of the other aspects of an NIT. Many of the recently proposed welfare reform bills, which use the stick approach, are in fact called NITs.

The pure form of the NIT has now been tested in several experiments across the country. Among other things, these experiments were intended to measure the degree to which the monetary incentives to work provided by an NIT are effective in encouraging work. It is the purpose of this paper to summarize the results of these experiments. To give the game away right at the beginning, I will state the main findings: the NIT programs tested in all these experiments reduced work effort, both relative to no program at all and relative to the existing welfare program (because of more generous benefit levels). Though the experiments have some problems of interpretation, as discussed below, this finding is as unequivocal as a technically complex research finding is ever likely to be.

In what follows, I will address several issues. First, I will summarize the results of the experiments and discuss what caveats must be added in light of some of their problems. Then I will consider the estimation of the expected work disincentives that would occur in the nation as a whole if an NIT were implemented. Following this, I will discuss the implications of these results and will consider the estimation of the effect of an NIT-stick on national work effort.

THE FINDINGS OF THE EXPERIMENTS

The four experiments testing an NIT have been set in a rather diverse set of sites across the country. The first experiment was in New Jersey and Pennsylvania; the second, in rural areas of North Carolina and Iowa; the third, in Seattle and Denver; and the fourth, in Gary, Indiana. The experiments also tested an NIT on rather diverse groups of people: on only husband-wife couples in New Jersey and Pennsylvania and in the rural experiment; on only blacks in the Gary experiment, although including both husband-wife couples and female-headed families; and on all races and all family types in Seattle-Denver. However, each experiment was alike in the most important respect, which was that each attempted to test an NIT by classical experimental methods. A sample of the low-income population was selected in each of the areas, and families were assigned to either an experimental group or a control group. The experimental group received the NIT and the control group did not, and the effect of the experiment was measured as the difference in the work effort of the two groups.

The experiments also varied the generosity of benefits of the NIT plans they gave to the experimental groups. This allowed the analysts to measure the effect of benefit generosity on work effort. The NIT plans tested, like all pure NIT plans, provided a positive benefit to families with no earnings at all, regardless of whether the head or anyone else was voluntarily or involuntarily unemployed. Thus, there was no work requirement in any of the experiments. However, to provide work incentives, benefits were not reduced by the full amount of any earnings that the family did receive. That is, the *tax rate,* or *benefit-reduction rate,* was less than 100%. The algebraic statement of the benefit formula is

$$B = G - tY \tag{11.1}$$

where B is the benefit paid to the family, G is the *guarantee level* — that is, the amount paid to a family with no other income — Y is the family's income level, and t is the tax rate. As is apparent from the benefit formula, an extra dollar of income, Y, reduces the family's benefit by t dollars, where t is some fraction between 0 and 1. Therefore, since an extra dollar of earnings lowers the benefit by only t dollars, total income does indeed increase (by $1 - t$ dollars). In the experiments, different levels of G and t were defined for different families in the experimental group. On average across the experiments, a tax rate of .50 and a guarantee level about equal to the poverty line ($6,191 per year in 1977 for a family of four) was offered. The guarantee level in all experiments was higher, the greater the family size.

It must be said at the outset that no economist familiar with the mechanics of an NIT ever really expected work effort to increase with an NIT, at least relative to no program at all. Other things being equal, one would expect that (1) the higher the tax rate — that is, the more the benefit is reduced if someone in the family works — the lower the work effort;[1] and (2) the higher the guarantee level — that is, the greater the payment to the family if no one works — the lower the work effort. This is illustrated in Figure 11.1, which shows the well-known NIT budget constraint. At zero hours of work, the NIT provides a guarantee equal to the distance $\overline{OD}$. As hours of work and earnings increase, if W is the wage rate, then income rises at the rate $W(1 - t)$, which is the (negative of the) slope of segment $\overline{DE}$. Benefits reach zero at point E. The indif-

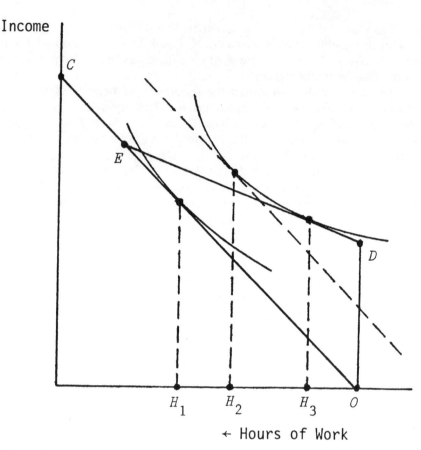

Figure 11.1. The Effects of a Negative Income Tax on Labor Supply

ference curves in the diagram show the response to the NIT as a movement from H_1 to H_3. This change is composed of a reduction in hours
worked from H_1 to H_2, resulting from a negative income effect, and a
further reduction from H_2 to H_3, resulting from a positive substitution
effect.[2]

This simple analysis shows why economists expect an NIT to decrease
work effort, at least relative to no program at all. If there were no welfare
program at all, the tax rate and the guarantee level would be zero; so
raising them both to some nonzero level is certain to reduce work effort.
However, relative to the current welfare program, the answer is ambiguous, for it depends upon whether the combined effects of G and t in the

NIT are greater or less than those in the present welfare system. More will be said on this topic later on.

The results of the four experiments are shown in Table 11.1. The table shows the difference in hours of work per week between the experimental group and the control group, broken down by the common categories of husbands, wives, and female heads of families. Although the measure of work effort shown is hours of work per week, I should note that most of the studies upon which the table is based actually measured differences in hours of work over longer time periods (per month, per year, per two years, etc.); I have merely standardized them all to a weekly basis. (See the discussion below of these work-effort reductions.) The unequivocal result shown in the table is that hours of work are reduced by the NIT. However, the range of reductions is disconcertingly wide, especially for wives (reductions of 2–55% and even one small positive effect) and female heads (12–28%). For husbands, the range is somewhat narrower (1–8%). Nevertheless, although the ranges may seem (and are) uncomfortably wide, they are actually *smaller* than those predicted for an NIT before the experiments were run. (For a detailed discussion of this point, see Moffitt and Kehrer 1981.)

Are these responses "large" or "small"? Fundamentally, this is an unanswerable question because these terms are too vague. The responses are small relative to some of the predictions that were made prior to the experiments of "massive" work-effort reductions. But they are definitely nonzero, and in this sense they are large.

In fact, an interesting footnote in the sociology of knowledge is provided by the history of the discussion of whether the experimental results are large or small. When the first results emerged from the New Jersey–Pennsylvania experiment, they were deemed to be small or nonexistent, and many observers concluded that indeed the poor would work just as hard under an NIT as in its absence. However, when the results of the Seattle-Denver experiment were publicized in late 1978, they were judged to be large (if not massive), resulting in a 180-degree reversal in public opinion concerning an NIT. Yet, as Table 11.1 shows, there was little quantitative difference in the actual results of these two experiments. Indeed, the Seattle-Denver experiment did *not* produce the largest responses for any of the three types of individuals in the experiments. However, the difference between the Seattle-Denver experiment and the others lies in the *significance levels* of the responses, for it showed statistically significant results, while the others rarely did so (largely because the sample sizes in the other experiments were so small). The common interpretation of the early experiments as showing zero or near-

Table 11.1. Adjusted Mean Experimental-Control Differences in Hours Worked per Week

Author	Husbands		Wives		Female Heads	
	Absolute Difference	Percentage Difference	Absolute Difference	Percentage Difference	Absolute Difference	Percentage Difference
New Jersey–Pennsylvania						
DHEW[a]						
White	−1.9	5.6	−1.4	30.6	—	—
Black	0.7	2.3	−0.1	2.2	—	—
Spanish-speaking	−0.2	0.7	−1.9	55.4	—	—
Hall						
White	−2.4[b]	7.1	−1.5[b]	32.8	—	—
Rural (Nonfarm)						
DHEW[a] and Bawden						
North Carolina blacks	−2.9[b]	8.0	−5.2[b]	31.3	—	—
North Carolina whites	2.1	5.6	−2.2	21.5	—	—
Iowa whites	−0.5	1.2	−1.2	20.3	—	—
Seattle-Denver						
Keeley et al.	−1.8[b]	5.3	−2.1[b]	14.6	−2.6[b]	11.9
Gary						
Moffitt	−1.6	4.7	0.2	3.7	−2.0[b]	27.8

SOURCE: Moffitt and Kehrer 1981.
[a]U.S. Department of Health, Education, and Welfare.
[b]Significant at 10% level (5% for New Jersey DHEW).

zero responses — although in accordance with well-established statistical tradition — demonstrates, in retrospect, the difficulties in generalizing from insignificant coefficients.

One of the interesting findings that has emerged in the experiments relates to the form this work-effort reduction has taken for males. There are strong indications that the reduction in total hours of work most often takes the form of reductions in the likelihood of being employed at all, rather than marginal reductions in the hours of work of those who remain employed. That is, the reduction in total hours of work shows up as a reduction in the employment rate in the experimental sample relative to that in the control sample. The policy implications of this finding are ambiguous. On the one hand, failing to work at all rather than simply working less each week is a much more major change in work effort, one that society is not likely to want to accept. On the other hand, this finding also implies that the total reduction stems from a rather large reduction by a small number of men rather than from a small reduction by a large number of men. Therefore, the NIT does not appear to have a pervasive effect on the work ethic of the entire low-income male population, but rather, appears to induce a small number of men to respond a lot — most do not respond at all.

The reason for this finding undoubtedly relates to the difficulty in changing marginal hours of work in the first place. Hours of work in most jobs held by prime-age males are institutionally fixed and difficult to change. This is less true of the low-income population than of the population as a whole, for low-wage workers are more likely to hold part-time and/or unstable jobs. But even low-income workers may be able to reduce work effort, mostly by not working at all. However, one way in which workers may be able to adjust hours marginally is by reducing overtime work. There has not been a great deal of attention paid to this possibility, but where it has (in the New Jersey experiment), it did indeed appear that part of the response was a result of a reduction in overtime.

A reduction in the employment rate of the low-income population can occur in several ways. It may take the form of a lengthening of time between jobs; longer periods of unpaid vacation and holidays; or just a permanent withdrawal from employment. It has appeared in some of the experiments that the first of these types occurred most often — a lengthening of time between jobs, often corresponding to an increase in the length of unemployment spells. For young workers, some data have also shown an increase in school attendance. Both of these uses of nonwork time have value in increasing the individual's human capital and are

probably more acceptable than increases in pure leisure. However, individual wage rates should presumably increase as a payoff to this investment; yet no such increases in wage rates occurred in the data, at
least during the period of the experiment.

The increase in unemployment spells took an interesting form in the
Gary experiment, where heavy layoffs from the local steel industry early
in the experiment increased unemployment rates in the Gary area and in
the experimental sample. The data on the participants showed that both
experimentals and controls *increased* their work effort over the period of
the experiment as unemployment rates in the area dropped, but that the
increase in the employment rate of the control group was greater than
that in the experimental group. Consequently, the "relative employment
reduction" that was taken as evidence of an NIT response resulted from
a slower return to work among experimentals, probably because they
were using the NIT payments as a form of unemployment insurance.
Members of the control group, who relied on the far less generous regular
unemployment benefits, were probably forced by economic distress to
return to work sooner.

As mentioned above, the experiments also tested NIT plans with
different tax rates and guarantees. The results in Table 11.1 should be
thought of as the responses to plans with about a tax rate of .50 and a
guarantee level equal to the poverty line, roughly the averages in the
experiments. In most of the plans currently before Congress, somewhat
different tax rates and guarantee levels (equal to 65% of the poverty line)
are being proposed, which would suggest a smaller work disincentive.
Therefore, the changes in work effort for different tax rates and guarantees are needed to be able to predict the responses to NITs with
different levels of tax rates and guarantees.

The results of the estimation of tax and guarantee effects in the experiments are shown in Table 11.2. The table shows the income and
substitution effects estimated in most of the major experimental studies.
The equation describing the basic response to an NIT can be written as
follows:

$$\Delta H = -\gamma W t + \delta B,$$

where H is hours of work, W is the hourly wage rate, t is the NIT tax
rate, B is the NIT benefit initially received by the family, γ is the
compensated wage effect, and δ is the income effect.[3] Economic theory
predicts that γ will be positive — that is, increases in the tax rate will
reduce work effort — and that δ will be negative — that is, increases in
the benefit level (indirectly proxying increases in the guarantee level) will

Table 11.2. Effects of an NIT on Hours Worked per Week

Authors	Experiment	Sample	Substitution Effect	Income Effect
Husbands				
Watts	New Jersey	White	−1.34	.012
			(.08)	(.03)
		Black	−.051	−.011
			(.03)	(.02)
		Spanish-speaking	3.26	.001
			(.18)	(0)
Horner	New Jersey	All races	1.45	−.016
			(.08)	(.04)
Hausman and Wise	New Jersey	White	2.77	−.007
			(.16)	(.02)
Bawden	Rural (Nonfarm)	N.C. blacks	0	.001
			(0)	(0)
		N.C. whites	0.18	−.002
			(.01)	(0)
		Iowa whites	−0.03	0
			(0)	(0)
Ashenfelter	Rural (Nonfarm)	All races	2.49	.005
			(.14)	(.01)
		All races	2.20	−.003
			(.12)	(.01)
Keeley et al.	Seattle-Denver	All races	1.07	−.023
			(.06)	(.05)
Robins and West	Seattle-Denver	All races	1.66	−.012
			(.09)	(.03)
Moffitt	Seattle-Denver	All races	0.04	−.007
			(0)	(.02)
Moffitt	Gary	Black	0.98	−.038
			(.05)	(.09)
Burtless and Hausman	Gary	Black	1.33	−.033
			(.08)	(.07)
Wives				
Cain et al.	New Jersey	White	−0.24	−.436
			(.01)	(.65)
		Black	−7.69	.028
			(.38)	(.04)
		Spanish-speaking	−3.88	−.081
			(.19)	(.12)

Table 11.2. *Continued*

Authors	Experiment	Sample	Substitution Effect	Income Effect
		White	8.84	.032
			(.44)	(.05)
		Black	1.27	−.339
			(.06)	(.51)
		Spanish-speaking	−7.65	−.335
			(.38)	(.50)
Bawden	Rural (Nonfarm)	N.C. blacks	.06	.001
			(0)	(0)
		N.C. whites	.14	0
			(.01)	(0)
		Iowa whites	.29	.002
			(.01)	(0)
Ashenfelter	Rural (Nonfarm)	All races	8.22	.005
			(.41)	(.01)
		All races	8.49	.012
			(.42)	(.02)
Keeley et al.	Seattle-Denver	All races	2.16	−.096
			(.11)	(.14)
Robins and West	Seattle-Denver	All races	3.65	−.083
			(.18)	(.12)
Moffitt	Gary	Black	7.30	.174
			(.37)	(.26)
Female Heads				
Keeley et al.	Seattle-Denver	All races	1.62	−.068
			(.08)	(.12)
Robins and West	Seattle-Denver	All races	1.90	−.065
			(.10)	(.11)
Moffitt	Gary	Black	3.55	−1.94
			(.18)	(.34)
Hausman	Gary	Black	2.00	−.040
			(.10)	(.07)

SOURCE: Moffitt and Kehrer 1981.
NOTE: All effects are in 1977 dollars. Elasticities are in parentheses (for income: total income elasticities). All elasticities in each group are evaluated at the same means as those of the experiments as a whole.

also reduce work effort. In other words, we expect a positive substitution effect and a negative income effect on hours of work.

The first column of numbers in Table 11.2 shows estimates of γ and the second column shows estimates of δ (numbers in parentheses are elasticities; for a detailed discussion of each study and the exact derivation of these numbers, see Moffitt and Kehrer 1981). As the table shows, there is tremendous variation in the size of the estimated effects. For husbands, substitution elasticities range up to 18% and income elasticities range up to 9%. Oddly, there are a few anomalous effects showing negative substitution effects and positive income effects, most of which occur in the New Jersey experiment. The most frequently cited explanation for those counterintuitive results relates to a series of unexpected and unfortunate changes in the local welfare environment in New Jersey over the course of the experiment. Specifically, the state of New Jersey introduced an AFDC–UF program toward the beginning of the experiment, and then substantially changed its benefit level midway through the experiment. Both of these changes affected the work effort of the control group, as well as that of the experimental group, many of whom left the experiment very early to take advantage of the higher benefits obtainable from the AFDC–UF program. This "contamination" of the experimental process could have resulted in the anomalous estimates. The rural results estimated by Bawden are also fairly low, possibly the result of small sample sizes and possibly the result of an equation specification that was not designed to estimate income and substitution effects (see Moffitt and Kehrer 1981).[4] Leaving aside the Watts and Bawden results for these reasons, the results show male income elasticities ranging from 0 to .09 and substitution elasticities ranging from 0 to .16.

The results for wives show even more variance. The results of Cain and Watts (1973) for New Jersey wives show frequent negative substitution effects and positive income effects of sizable magnitudes, resulting either from the same AFDC–UF problem just mentioned or from the low employment-participation rate of wives in the experiment (.1), or both. The same low-employment problem plagued the Gary experiment, where a sizable positive income effect was found. This was apparently a result of the Gary labor market, which provided very few part-time jobs for females and thus made marginal hour adjustments difficult. Again, Bawden's results are not ideal for present purposes for the same reasons mentioned above. Taking Ashenfelter's results along with those in the Seattle-Denver experiment yields a range of income elasticities from .01 to .14 and substitution elasticities from .11 to .42.

There have been only four studies of female heads, primarily because there were too few to analyze in any but the Gary and Seattle-Denver experiments. The results are all of the expected sign, and show income elasticities ranging from .07 to .34 and substitution elasticities ranging from .08 to .18.

These elasticities are considerably lower than those often found in the nonexperimental literature. In addition, they show that husbands and female heads have a much stronger guarantee effect than tax-rate effect. (The tax-rate effect is deducible from the uncompensated wage elasticity, which is the sum of the substitution and income elasticities.) For wives, tax effects are significant along with guarantee effects.

These results provide additional evidence of the disincentive effects of the NIT. The results are not as strong as those of Table 11.1, for there are some anomalous results that were not expected. That most of these occurred in the New Jersey experiment was another reason for the early suspicion that an NIT would not have strong work-disincentive effects, but the evidence from the other experiments plus the problems of experimental analysis in the New Jersey experiment are more than enough to negate such a conclusion. So the weight of the evidence does indeed suggest that increases in the tax rate and guarantee level have disincentive effects on work effort.

Statistical Problems in the Experiments.   Before accepting these results at face value, some mention of the statistical problems in the experiments is needed. The most important of the problems with the experiments was their limited duration. Most were only three years long. In a three-year experiment, one might expect that individuals would fail to respond as strongly as they would to a permanent program, such as would be enacted on a national level. However, as Metcalf (1973) has shown, this conclusion is only half correct, for there are forces at work that tend to make individuals overrespond to a three-year experiment as well. Specifically, since the NIT taxes earnings and thereby provides some work disincentive, there is a tendency for families to overreduce their work effort to take advantage of the short-run nature of the experiment; that is, to reap windfall gains in income for the three years of the experiment. On a priori grounds, there is no way to say whether this effect or the more obvious one suggesting an underresponse will be the stronger.

Fortunately, the Seattle-Denver experiment enrolled some families for five years as well as for three years, allowing a test of whether the duration of the experiment has an effect on the response. The results of analyzing these data (Burtless and Greenberg 1978; Moffitt 1979b) show that Metcalf was indeed correct and that there are two opposing forces at work in determining whether the estimates are overresponses or underresponses. Furthermore, these studies show that whether the response is, on net, too large or too small is different for plans of different guarantees and different tax rates, which should be expected, since a higher tax rate will cause individuals to overrespond more, and a higher guarantee level will cause individuals to underrespond more. At the levels of guarantees and tax rates chosen in the Seattle-Denver experiment, roughly those of the other experiments (perhaps a bit higher), the three-year experiment is an underestimate of the response. Moffitt (1979b) has estimated the difference in response to be about 2 percentage points. However, at lower guarantee levels, such as those provided by the plans recently before Congress (with guarantee levels of 65% of the poverty line), the responses predicted from the three-year experimental income and substitution effects are overestimates of true effects. In addition, the tentative evidence suggests that the substitution effects shown in Table 11.2 are about two times too large, and the income effects are about two times too small.

In addition to this problem of a three-year experiment, Robins and West (1978) have pointed out that individuals will adjust slowly to an NIT. However, using a partial-adjustment model, they found that the families in the five-year portion of the Seattle-Denver experiment had made most of their adjustments by the end of five years, though not all. Husbands had made 99% of their adjustments, wives had made 96%, and female heads had made 92%.

These two limited-duration problems represent the major difficulties in the experiments. When the substitution and income effects are adjusted for both of these problems, the ranges of substitution elasticities for husbands, wives, and female heads become (respectively) 0–.08, .06–.22, and .04–.10. The respective income-elasticity ranges become 0–.18, 0–.29, and .15–.74. Therefore, these adjustments, while changing the magnitude of the estimated effects, do not change their qualitative nature: substitution effects are generally positive and income effects are generally negative.

There are other statistical problems in the experiments, but no strong evidence that any of them would change these general conclusions. The experiments suffered problems resulting from attrition of the participants from the experiment; from adverse sample selection criteria used to draw the sample, which endangered the random assignment; from Hawthorne effects;[5] and from underreporting of income by the participants.[6] (Further details on the research on each of these issues can be found in Moffitt and Kehrer 1981).

GENERALIZATION TO A NATIONAL POPULATION

The estimated effects on hours of work shown in Table 11.1 above cannot be generalized to the national population or to other NIT programs for several reasons. First of all, as has already been discussed, those results apply roughly to an NIT plan with a tax rate of .50 and a guarantee level equal to the poverty line. To estimate the effect of NIT programs with different tax rates and guarantees, the estimated income and substitution effects must be applied to equation (11.1) above. This is particularly relevant because most of the programs currently pending before Congress have lower guarantee levels than those in the experiments.

Second, the experiments tested NIT plans in a particular group of areas around the country that are not, as a whole, representative of the entire United States. In particular, the distribution of income (as well as the distribution of wage rates and nonwage income) in these populations is likely to be different from that in the nation as a whole. Therefore, equation (11.1) needs to be applied to a national sample, not just a sample of families in the experiments.

Third, the experiments underestimated the response of middle-income and high-income families for the same reason, namely, that they enrolled (mostly) families from the low-income segment of the population. Since individuals who are in families initially with too high an income to be eligible for the NIT may reduce their work effort to become eligible, a national sample is necessary to simulate their response. However, for these individuals, equation (11.1) is not directly applicable. A somewhat more complicated simulation algorithm is required (see the appendix to this chapter).

The effect of an NIT plan with a tax rate of .50 and a guarantee level equal to 65% of the poverty line is shown in Table 11.3. These parameters are close to those currently being proposed before Congress. These estimates are obtained by applying the mean (adjusted) income and substitution elasticities in the experiments to a national sample of individuals. The national sample used is the Survey of Income and Education, a 1976 Census Bureau survey that obtained income information on a national sample. (This survey is often used for national simulations.)[7] As the table shows, the reduction in hours of husbands would be roughly 4%, about in the middle of the range found in the experiments. The reduction for wives would be about 27%, a larger reduction as should be expected. For female heads, a 16% reduction would occur. About 1 husband-wife family in 10 would participate in the program, and about 3 female-headed families in 10 would participate. More female-headed families would partic-

Table 11.3. Effects of a National NIT on Work Effort

	Husbands	Wives	Female Heads
Change in hours worked per week of participants	−1.0	−2.4	−2.1
As a percentage of initial hours	4.0	27.0	16.0
Fraction of population participating[a]	0.12	0.12	0.32

NOTE: Table based on a guarantee equal to 65% of the poverty line and a tax rate of .50.

[a]Assumes a 50% participation rate among eligibles.

ipate in percentage terms because of their lower income levels. Thus, although some of these figures are a bit lower than the experiments would lead one to predict, they still show significant work-effort reductions.

IMPLICATIONS

This evidence on the work disincentives of an NIT is so unequivocal that one is forced to reexamine the reasons that an NIT was ever thought to provide work incentives in the first place. As mentioned before, most economists studying the basic elements of the NIT benefit formula expected that the NIT would reduce work effort and believed that the only question was the quantitative one of *how much*. As Albert Rees (1974) once remarked, it is unfortunate that so few actually wrote down their expectations so that we could now say whether the actual findings are larger or smaller than expected. Nevertheless, there was certainly a widespread public opinion that an NIT would *increase* work incentives over the present system. It does indeed seem that something funny happened on this particular road to welfare reform.

At the outset, I should reiterate what was said in the introduction regarding the advantages and disadvantages of an NIT. Recall that an NIT is generally defined to include (1) a federalization of the welfare payment system, (2) a simplification of the benefit formula, (3) a streamlining of administration and a consequent reduction in administrative costs per case, (4) an increase in benefit-level generosity, and (5) an extension of coverage to male-present families and to the working poor. The evidence presented here has no direct bearing on these aspects of an NIT, and the merits of each can be debated largely independently of the work-effort question. Indeed, as far as benefit-formula simplification is concerned, it is not a question of whether we should have an NIT or not, but rather, whether we shall have a good one or a bad one. The present welfare system has a benefit formula that is of the same general form as that of an NIT, but is encumbered by many more restrictions than those imposed by an NIT.

Nevertheless, an NIT was supposed to provide incentives to work, but the evidence resoundingly rejects this hypothesis. Observers of the welfare system know that there are at least three reasons that the NIT generally shows a reduction in work effort rather than an increase.

First, most NIT plans provide more generous benefits than the existing system. Therefore, even if a national NIT were to encourage work effort by providing the poor with a lower tax rate than that in the current system, the increase in the guarantee level provided by most NIT plans is sufficiently large to generate reductions in work effort that outweigh the increases induced by the tax rate reduction. That is, there is a trade-off between benefit generosity and work incentives.

Second, most NIT plans extend coverage of the population. Therefore, even if the NIT were to increase the work effort of those currently on welfare, primarily female heads of families, one would still be providing benefits to families who were previously eligible for no benefits at all. The effect on their work effort cannot be positive. That is, there is a trade-off between breadth of coverage and work incentives.

Third, the tax rate in the AFDC program is no longer as onerous as it once seemed. In 1967, Congress mandated that states lower the tax rate on earnings in the AFDC program to .67. In addition, a number of recent studies have shown that the effective AFDC tax rate is probably considerably below this (see Lurie 1974; Hutchens 1978; Moffitt 1979*a*). The reason is that state AFDC programs often allow a number of income-related deductions in their benefit formulas, as well as often imposing certain maximums on benefits that effectively reduce the tax rate to zero. Therefore, the true AFDC tax rate is no doubt less than .67, although its exact magnitude varies from welfare family to welfare family (which raises separate problems of equity and administrative efficiency).

It is, of course, for all these reasons that most recent proposals for reform of the welfare system have not left work incentives to the carrot of the benefit formula, but have provided, in addition, the stick of work requirements, work-registration requirements, or (mandatory) public service employment. Occasionally, such a proposal is called an NIT, but it should probably be called an *NIT-with-stick*. The stick behind these proposals is the withholding of all benefits or some portion of benefits if the head of the family (ultimately) does not find a job or refuses to accept a suitable public service job.

To obtain some idea of the effects of such an NIT-stick on hours of work, I have simulated their effects on work effort, as shown in Table 11.4. An NIT-stick as simulated here would offer an individual zero benefits if he did not work, and would provide some different amount of benefits if he did work at a job requiring a certain number of hours per week (35). Given the number of hours required on the job, and given the level of benefits offered as a supplement to the job's earnings, the choice of work-effort response is simply whether to take the job, to work at an unsubsidized part-time job, or not to work at all. The methodology is discussed further in the appendix.

The results show that about 1% of the husbands in the population would participate in a plan with a tax rate of .50 and a guarantee level equal to 65% of the poverty line. The participants in the program would increase their hours of work by about 9% to take advantage of the subsidized jobs. At a tax rate of .70, fewer men would participate, and their hours would only increase by about 5%. At a tax rate of .50, but with a guarantee equal to the poverty line, about 4% of the population would participate, and their hours would increase by about 12%.

That an NIT-stick increases work effort rather than decreases it, as does a pure NIT, is of course to be expected. However, what these results indicate is that this gain in labor supply is bought at the price of a significant reduction in transfer of income to the poor. Only 4% of the men take the subsidized jobs, whereas 9% of the husband-wife families participate in the pure NIT. Moreover, benefits in the pure NIT are surely greater than those in the NIT-stick. Therefore, the society faces a clear trade-off between income redistribution and work incentives.

Table 11.4.   Effect of an NIT-Stick on Work Effort of Husbands

	Fraction of Population Participating	Change in Hours Worked of Participants	As a Percentage of Initial Hours Worked
Guarantee = 65%, Tax rate = .50	.012	2.9	.09
Guarantee = 65%, Tax rate = .70	.006	1.8	.05
Guarantee = 100%, Tax rate = .50	.038	3.7	.12

NOTE: Table based on a guarantee as a percent of the poverty line. A 50% participation rate of eligibles is assumed.

SUMMARY

The NIT experiments have added a great deal to our knowledge of the
disincentive effects of transfer programs. First of all, they have shown
unequivocally that a pure NIT will reduce work effort to some extent.
In addition, some idea of the magnitudes of these work-effort reductions
is provided by the experimental results. This makes possible reasonably
accurate estimates of the reductions in work effort that could be expected
on the national level if a pure NIT were implemented. The policy implications of the results are clearly to shift emphasis toward NIT-sticks,
which impose work requirements or work-registration requirements on
the recipients of benefits, although these programs would transfer less
income to the poor than a pure NIT.

APPENDIX

The simulation methodology is illustrated in Figures 11.A1 and 11.A2.
Figure 11.A1 shows a pure NIT budget constraint, AEC. An individual

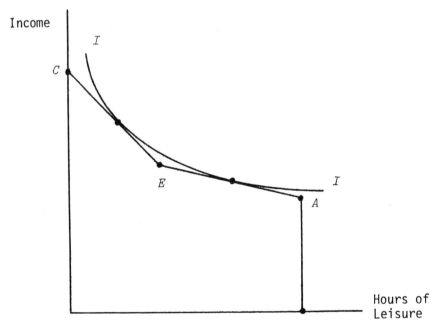

Figure 11.A1. An NIT Budget Constraint

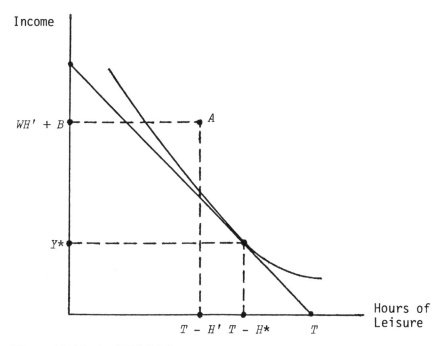

Figure 11.A2. An NIT-Stick

who is initially below the breakeven point, E, will definitely participate. His or her response will be directly calculable from equation (11.1) in the text. But individuals above the point will drop below only if the additional leisure compensates, in utility terms, for the loss in income. An individual with the indifference curve II shown in Figure 11.A1 is exactly indifferent between participating and not participating; a lower tax rate or a higher guarantee would result in participation. The response of the above–breakeven population is simulated by using the indirect utility function corresponding to the linear labor supply function discussed in note 3. Its indirect utility function is

$$V = [\alpha + \beta W + \delta N - (\beta/\delta)] \cdot (1/\delta) \cdot \exp(\delta W). \qquad (11.A1)$$

The simulation of an NIT-stick is illustrated in Figure 11.A2. It is assumed that the program pays a benefit of B if the individual works at a job for $H' = 35$ hours per week, resulting in total income at point A in the figure. The direct utility function corresponding to the above indirect utility function is used to compare an individual's utility at point A with utility at his initial hours point, H^*. If utility is greater at point A (as it would be for the individual shown in the figure), the individual is assumed to participate and therefore to increase his work week by $(H' - H^*)$ hours.

NOTES

1. This is not strictly correct, because income effects may dominate substitution effects. But the income effect of the guarantee will always outweigh the income effect of the tax rate.

2. The substitution effect is positive on *hours of work*. Hence a reduction in the net wage *reduces* hours of work.

3. A linear labor supply function under an NIT is

$$H = \alpha + \beta W(1 - t) + \delta[G + (1 - t)N],$$

where N is unearned family income. In the absence of an NIT, hours worked are

$$H = \alpha + \beta W + \delta N.$$

Therefore, the change in H is

$$dH = -\beta Wt + \delta(G - tN)$$
$$= -(\beta - \delta H_0)Wt + \delta B$$
$$= -\gamma Wt + \delta B,$$

where $B = G - tN - tWH_0$ is the initial benefit, and H_0 is initial hours of work.

4. Bawden included a treatment dummy in addition to the t and G variables.

5. Hawthorne effects occur when the participants in an experiment react to the act of being studied rather than to the treatment itself. This would occur, for example, if recipients intentionally did not reduce work effort because they knew they were being studied.

6. Underreporting of income is something of an exception. Greenberg, Moffitt, and Friedmann (forthcoming) found that underreporting income by female heads in the Gary experiment may have seriously inflated the estimated response shown in Table 11.1. See their paper for details.

7. The simulations are based upon decile distributions of W and N tabulated from the survey.

REFERENCES

Burtless, G., and Greenberg, D. 1978. "The Limited Duration of Income Maintenance Experiments and Its Implications for Estimating Labor Supply Effects of Transfer Programs." Technical Analysis Paper no. 15. Washington, D.C.: U.S. Department of Health, Education, and Welfare.

Cain, G. G., and Watts, H. W., eds. 1973. *Income Maintenance and Labor Supply: Econometric Studies.* Chicago: Rand McNally.

Greenberg, D.; Moffitt, R.; and Friedmann, J. Forthcoming. "The Effects of Underreporting on the Estimation of Experimental Effects of Work Effort:

THE EFFECT OF A NEGATIVE INCOME TAX ON WORK EFFORT

Evidence from the Gary Income Maintenance Experiment." *Review of Economics and Statistics.*

Hutchens, R. 1978. "Changes in AFDC Tax Rates, 1967–1971." *Journal of Human Resources* 13 (Winter):60–74.

Lurie, I. 1974. "Estimates of Tax Rates in the AFDC Program." *National Tax Journal* 27 (March):93–111.

Metcalf, C. 1973. "Making Inferences from Controlled Income Maintenance Experiments." *American Economic Review* 63 (June):478–83.

Moffitt, R. 1979*a*. "Cumulative Effective Tax Rates and Guarantees in Low-Income Transfer Programs." *Journal of Human Resources* 14 (Winter):122–29.

―――. 1979*b*. "Estimating a Simple Life-Cycle Model of Labor Supply: The Evaluation of a Limited Duration NIT Experiment." Mimeographed. Rutgers University, New Brunswick, N.J.

―――. 1979*c*. "The Labor-Supply Effects of an NIT: The Findings of the Income Maintenance Experiments and Their Implications for Aggregate Work Disincentives." Paper presented at the meetings of the American Economic Association, Atlanta (December).

Moffitt, R., and Kehrer, K. 1981. "The Effect of Tax and Transfer Programs on Labor Supply: The Evidence from the Income Maintenance Experiments." In *Research in Labor Economics,* edited by R. Ehrenberg. Greenwich, Conn.: JAI Press.

Rees, A. 1974. "An Overview of the Labor-Supply Results." *Journal of Human Resources* 9 (Spring):158–80.

Robins, P., and West, R. 1978. "A Longitudinal Analysis of the Labor Supply Response to a Negative Income Tax Program: Evidence from the Seattle and Denver Income Maintenance Experiments." Research Memorandum no. 59. Menlo Park, Calif.: SRI International.

12 A STUDY OF THE INTERACTION BETWEEN CASH TRANSFER PROGRAMS AND EMPLOYMENT PROGRAMS

David M. Betson and David H. Greenberg

In analyzing income maintenance issues, cash transfer policy and public jobs programs have usually been considered separately, with possible interactions between them generally ignored. Indeed, these two policies have frequently been viewed as competitive mechanisms for raising the incomes of those in need. As recent policy initiatives, including former President Carter's Program for Better Jobs and Income (PBJI) and proposals for workfare programs by the Reagan Administration, attest, however, future welfare programs in thc United States are likely to contain elements of both policies. Nevertheless, the implications of combining cash transfers and jobs programs have received comparatively little analysis.

These points may be illustrated by considering the effects of cash transfer and public jobs programs on hours of work and earnings. These effects are important because they help determine program costs and program success in augmenting incomes, as well as influencing the total output produced by the economy. For purposes of discussion, the particular form of transfer programs that we consider is a negative income tax (NIT) and the specific type of public jobs program that we consider is public service employment (PSE).[1]

230

As is well known, when an NIT program is considered in isolation, the usual prediction is that it will reduce the hours recipients work: the receipt of income engenders an income effect that should adversely affect work incentives, and the implicit tax associated with the program lowers the reward for market work, and consequently is expected to reduce hours through a substitution effect. If the negative income tax program is combined with a large-scale PSE program, however, the impact of the combined NIT–PSE system on work effort is much less clear a priori than the impact of the NIT alone, for the availability of PSE jobs also has two effects on hours: it allows some individuals to fill in periods during which they would otherwise be involuntarily unemployed, and it enables others to obtain employment at a higher wage than they could in a regular labor market. The first of these effects should unambiguously increase hours of work; the direction of the second effect depends on the shape of labor supply curves over the relevant range of wages. Thus, if the first effect is sufficiently strong and the second is either positive or small, a PSE could do much to offset the adverse influence of an NIT on work incentives. Because the PSE wage will exceed wages paid by some private sector employers, however, this mitigation of adverse work incentives will be associated with some hours being transferred from the private to the public sector, possibly resulting in a reduction in aggregate productivity.

A pure NIT and a combined NIT–PSE program not only have different effects on work incentives, but have differing distributional implications as well. Under a pure NIT, welfare expenditures are in the form of direct cash payments that have a strong inverse relation to household income from other sources. Under a combined plan, however, some welfare expenditures will be in exchange for labor services on public sector jobs and will not necessarily be closely related to households' positions within the income distribution. Thus—at least in the absence of work incentive effects—a dollar of transfer expenditure under a pure NIT should more effectively raise the incomes of those in need than a dollar expended under a combined NIT–PSE.

The various work incentive and distributional effects and interactions among them that have just been sketched are complex and make evaluation of combined NIT–PSE systems difficult. However, a natural and direct method that can be used to obtain information about such programs is to simulate their effects on individual households. This is the approach taken here.

The simulations that are reported on in this paper were conducted by means of a microsimulation computer model developed in the Office of

Income Security Policy Research within the Department of Health and Human Services.[2] This model has been used extensively within the government to develop and evaluate various welfare reform alternatives, including the Carter Administration's PBJI. The model treats various interactions among transfer programs, jobs programs, and the positive tax system, allowing for the labor supply adjustments that result from different combinations of these programs. The model can use data on a representative sample of the nation's households to simulate the effects of substantial changes in existing tax and transfer programs, including the guaranteeing of jobs to various subsets of the population.

This paper is divided into two main sections. In the first of these, we describe the microsimulation model; in the second, we use the model to simulate several alternative NIT–PSE systems. Simulation estimates are reported of the requirements for PSE slots under each system and the effects of each system on hours, earnings, transfer receipts, tax payments, disposable income levels, the distribution of income, and several other program outcomes.

THE SIMULATION MODEL

Simulation of alternatives to the existing welfare system proceeds in four major steps.[3] First, the Survey of Income and Education (SIE) is used to characterize the prereform economic status of a representative sample of the nation's families in 1975. Many of the variables required for this purpose, such as earnings, unearned income, and hours worked, can be directly obtained from the SIE. Others, such as tax payments and tax rates, are derived from schedules. Still others, including unemployment compensation amounts and benefit reduction rates associated with current transfer programs, are imputed from equations estimated from other data sources.

Second, the values of net wage rates and disposable income are adjusted to what they would be if the simulated reform measure were implemented, but work effort and earnings remained unchanged. For workers who are eligible for a public service employment job, it is necessary to compute what the values of the variables would be if: (1) the worker leaves the regular labor market to take a public employment job (a course of action that we characterize as the *pure strategy*); (2) he remains attached to the conventional job sector and takes a public employment job only when he is unemployed (the *mixed strategy*); or (3) he does not participate in public employment at all (the *private strategy*).

The third step consists of adjusting the values of the postreform variables to account for labor supply responses to changes in wage rates and disposable income under each public employment strategy. The values obtained from the first two steps are used to calculate the changes in net wage rates[4] and disposable incomes that would result from the welfare reform, prior to any labor supply responses. Predictions of the effects on work hours of the reform are then derived by multiplying these calculated changes by appropriate labor supply parameters that were estimated from the Seattle-Denver Income Maintenance Experiment.[5] Once these labor supply adjustments are computed, they are used to determine the number of hours individuals would work during the postreform period. Given these estimates of the hours family members would work, household earnings, transfer payment receipts, and tax payments can then be recomputed.

The first three steps of the simulation procedure, therefore, provide estimates of postreform income and hours for a sample of households. Where a household member is eligible for a public service employment job, it is necessary to compute alternative sets of postreform income and labor market measures for each of the three PSE strategies listed above. The final step in the simulation involves using these measures to determine whether an individual who is eligible for public employment will take such a job whenever he is in the labor force, only when he is unemployed, or not at all. Since this is probably the most novel feature of the simulation methodology, it is discussed in some detail.

Individual Decision on Participation in Public Employment. It seems reasonable to view an individual who is eligible for public employment as engaging in a comparison between the jobs program and his best opportunity within the regular job sector and as choosing the alternative that makes his family most well-off.[6] In general, one would expect that the chosen alternative offers the highest income level at a fixed number of hours worked.[7]

As indicated earlier, however, an individual is not confined to an all-or-nothing choice between public and regular employment. He may also participate in public employment during his weeks of unemployment, returning to the regular job sector when an opportunity becomes available. This mixed strategy seems, in fact, to be the possibility stressed by most advocates of large-scale public employment programs. Under certain circumstances, however, the mixed strategy may not be a viable alternative. Some unemployed persons may be unwilling to participate in public employment if the program wage is below their usual market wage, and some may be unwilling to relinquish unemployment compensation to accept a public employment job. Moreover, public employment programs may require a waiting period before an unemployed person becomes eligible for participation, and this waiting period may exceed the length of his spell of unemployment. These considerations are explicitly treated by the simulation procedure.

To determine whether or not various persons would participate in given PSE programs and whether they would select the pure or the mixed approach if they do participate, it has been necessary to develop participation tests. These tests assume that individuals will choose the strategy that maximizes the expected value of their family's stream of future disposable income after all labor supply adjustments have taken place.[8]

So far in our discussion of individuals' PSE participation decisions, we have ignored the demand side of the labor market. However, to retain some workers who would otherwise follow the pure strategy, employers may offer them higher wages. The number of such workers that employers would be willing to retain in this fashion (N^*) depends on (1) the number of workers they would have employed had the PSE program not forced them to pay higher wages (N), (2) the percentage increase in wage rates required to keep those who would otherwise follow the pure strategy ($\%\Delta w$), and (3) their elasticity of demand for these workers ($\epsilon_d < 0$). N^* may be computed as follows:

$$N^* = (1 + \%\Delta w \cdot \epsilon_d)N . \qquad (12.1)$$

Dividing equation (12.1) by S, the number of persons who would follow the pure strategy in the absence of any employer wage response, permits calculation of P, the proportion of these persons who will actually remain attached to the regular job sector. Thus

$$P = \frac{N^*}{S} = (1 + \%\Delta w \cdot \epsilon_d) \frac{N}{S} . \qquad (12.2)$$

Since from an individual worker's perspective the proportion P is viewed as his probability of staying in the private sector, equation (12.2) may be readily translated into the following expression for use in the simulation model:

$$P_i = (1 + \%\Delta w_i \cdot \epsilon_d) \frac{H_i}{h_i} , \qquad (12.3)$$

where P_i is the probability that a worker who would otherwise follow the pure strategy will be retained in the regular labor market once wages have fully adjusted, H_i is the hours he would have worked in the private sector in the absence of PSE jobs, and h_i is the hours he would have supplied to the PSE program in the absence of employer wage adjustments (the other variables were defined earlier). Based on the values of P_i, a random number generator is used to designate some workers, who would otherwise be classified as pure PSE participants, as remaining attached to the private sector.

The Components of Disposable Income. Since whether individuals will take PSE jobs depends on comparisons of family disposable income, it is obviously necessary to obtain information on its components. Moreover, in simulations of transfer and jobs programs, many of these components—such as transfer receipts from various sources and tax payments—are of direct interest in themselves. As was indicated earlier, the first step in the simulation of a welfare reform proposal is to find the values of these income components prior to the reform. Various provisions of the proposed reform—such as eligibility criteria, guarantee levels, and tax rates for NIT programs; wage rates and hours regulations for PSE programs; and any changes in the positive income tax system—can then be used in combination with estimated labor supply response parameters from the Seattle-Denver Income Maintenance Experiment to determine how the components would change were the reform implemented.

Because the SIE does not contain complete or reliable data on certain transfer receipts or tax payments under existing programs or on the tax rates that are associated with such programs, it was necessary to use various estimating procedures. In implementing these procedures, SIE data on nontransfer income, family size and structure, and personal characteristics were used in combination with the statutory requirements of existing programs and several predictive regression equations. For example, Social Security tax payments and tax rates were estimated from reported earnings in the SIE file and Social Security regulations. Similarly, measures of federal and state income tax payments and marginal tax rates were obtained from SIE data on nontransfer income and from the appropriate tax schedules.

Since transfer payments that are reported on the SIE file fall short of actual state outlays, it is necessary to use predicted amounts of AFDC and SSI for some families in order to reach control totals. Reported transfers are used whenever they are positive, and a fraction of those who reported no transfers are chosen randomly and assigned an imputed amount. AFDC tax rates are based on regression estimates of actual program experience in individual states. Food Stamps and SSI benefit-reduction rates and Food Stamp receipts were derived from schedules implied in the law.

Unemployment compensation amounts are derived from three regression equations that were estimated at the Urban Institute specifically for use in the simulation model. These regressions predict the probability for various workers of receiving payments when unemployed, their length of eligibility, and their weekly payment. Individuals are chosen randomly to receive payments on the basis of the probability estimates, and then the predicted length and predicted weekly payments regressions are used to compute their total payments.

It was pointed out above that the model assumes that an individual will choose the PSE strategy that yields him the highest future stream of disposable income. If he continues to work in the private sector, however, his future income will depend on how much unemployment he would incur, something he cannot know with certainty. For purposes of the model, we assume that he would make his choice on the basis of expected unemployment. Two regression equations from the Urban Institute Dynasim model, which predict the probability and length of spells of unemployment on the basis of individual characteristics, are used to determine the fraction of a worker's time in the labor force that he expects to be unemployed.

Market wage rates for workers are computed directly from the data by dividing annual hours worked into earnings. Those for nonworkers are imputed from regressions estimated on data from the Panel Survey on Income Dynamics. Each imputed wage includes a random error that maintains consistency with the acutal distribution of wages.

Annual hours worked prior to the welfare reform are directly available in the SIE. The number of hours that individuals would work during the postreform period, however, will be affected by a number of factors. To examine how these factors are treated in the simulation, it may be useful to consider the hours an individual would work if he (1) does not participate in public employment at all, (2) adopts the pure strategy toward public employment, or (3) takes the mixed approach.

Even if the individual does not consider public service employment, his hours will nevertheless be affected if the proposed reform would change his income or his marginal tax rate. As described earlier, the response to these changes are predicted through the use of estimated labor supply parameters from the Seattle-Denver Income Maintenance Experiment.[9]

The hours that a pure participant will work in public employment are estimated in three steps. First, since he would no longer be subject to involuntary unemployment, his reported hours of unemployment are added to the measure of the hours he worked during the prereform period.[10] Second, his labor supply response is calculated in much the same manner as for nonparticipants in public employment, except that any differences between his market wage and the PSE wage are taken into account. This yields an estimate of the hours he would be willing to supply to the program, given the program wage rate. His PSE supply hours are then compared to the maximum hours PSE participants are allowed to work, and the smaller of these two quantities is used as program hours worked.

The hours an individual would work under the mixed strategy are computed by summing his hours of conventional sector work — calculation of which has already been described — and the PSE hours he works while unemployed. In computing this latter figure, the simulation takes account of any differences between the individual's market wage and the program wage (for most mixed participants, the latter is likely to be smaller), and any losses in unemployment compensation that result from taking a PSE job. Losses in unemployment compensation are essentially treated in the simulation as if they reduce the public employment wage rate. The simulation also ensures that mixed-strategy hours conform to the limits on the number of PSE hours that may be worked each week and to restrictions on the number of weeks that workers must be unemployed before participating in public employment.

SIMULATIONS OF ALTERNATIVE NIT–PSE SCHEMES

Using the simulation model just described, several NIT–PSE plans were simulated in order to analyze the interaction between transfer policy and public employment programs. These plans are analyzed solely for households with children, since most PSE programs proposed in recent years would limit public job slots to the heads of such families. The first of the simulated plans, which we refer to as the *basic plan*, consolidates most existing federal welfare programs (including AFDC, AFDC–UP, SSI, the Earned Income Tax Credit, and Food Stamps) into a single NIT program that guarantees a minimum income of 75% of the federal poverty line to all households with children, but reduces transfer benefits at a rate of 50 cents for each dollar of earned or nonearned income. Since a number of states currently administer transfer programs that guarantee single-parent families more than 75% of the poverty line, many current recipients would be made worse-off by this reform unless the states supplemented their benefits. Believing that the high-benefit states would provide such supplements, we assume that single-parent families in states with high welfare benefits would be eligible for a combined federal and state income guarantee set at 100% of the poverty line. We further assume that in order to contain the costs associated with this higher guarantee level, transfer benefits received by single-parent families in these states would be reduced by 67 cents for each dollar of earned or nonearned income.[11]

The PSE component of the basic plan offers jobs that pay the 1975 minimum wage of $2.10 for up to 40 hours of work per week. These jobs, which are assumed to be available for all qualified persons who want one, are limited to primary earners in families with children who have been without work for a minimum of 5 weeks. Each PSE participant can remain in the program for a maximum of 1 year, but is then required to take a 5-week furlough, after which he may rejoin the program.

In addition to the basic plan, three other welfare reform alternatives were simulated. Each of these differs from the basic plan in a single major respect, allowing the effects of alternative policy decisions to be assessed. The first of these plans, the *NIT-only plan,* provides for only the implementation of the NIT portion of the basic plan. The second alternative, the *two-tier PSE–NIT plan* retains the PSE component, but differs from the basic plan by incorporating a two-tier NIT program that offers a lower guarantee to family units normally expected to work. This second plan maintains the NIT provision in the basic plan for single-parent families, but reduces the income guarantee for two-parent families from 75% to 50% of the poverty line. Benefits received by two-parent families under the two-tier plan are assumed to be reduced by 33 cents for each dollar of earned or nonearned income. The final alternative, the *PSE-only plan,* provides for the implementation of the PSE component of the basic plan, but leaves the existing welfare system intact.

The basic plan is considerably more expensive than its three alternatives. For example, its net cost in terms of tax expenditures is about 40% higher than either the NIT-only plan or the two-tier PSE–NIT plan, and more than three times higher than the PSE-only alternative, which leaves existing cash transfer programs unchanged.[12] Thus, comparing the basic plan with the three alternatives suggests the marginal value of spending additional tax revenues in various ways. For example, a comparison of the NIT-only plan and the basic plan indicates the value of adding a jobs component to a cash transfer program. Similarly, a comparison between the basic plan and PSE-only plan indicates the value of replacing the existing welfare system with an NIT program, once a PSE program is in place. A third comparison, that between the two-tier PSE–NIT plan and the basic plan, is of interest because it suggests whether the provision of less generous NIT benefits to two-parent families will provide greater encouragement to the heads of these families to participate in public employment.

In addition to the three comparisons just mentioned, a comparison between the NIT-only and the two-tier PSE–NIT plan should also be of considerable interest. These two plans have been designed so that their net cost in terms of the taxes required to finance them are approximately equal. Consequently, a comparison of their effects should indicate some of the trade-offs between using all of a given amount of tax revenue to finance cash transfer payments or using some of these funds to provide jobs.

Before presenting the results of the simulations of the welfare reform plans described above, it is useful to clarify some additional points. First, it is assumed in the simulations that all individuals eligible for transfer payments under the NIT components of these plans would actually receive them.[13] Second, the break-even levels of the simulated NIT plans (that is, the income level at which eligibility for NIT benefits ceases) are all set at 150% of the poverty line.[14] Thus, comparisons among the simulated plans are facilitated because the families who are eligible to receive NIT benefits under the different plans are similar. Third, it is assumed that any individual who is otherwise qualified can obtain a public employment job regardless of his family income level. Hence, some PSE participants will be from families with incomes that are above the NIT break-even level.

Table 12.1 reports simulation estimates of the number of households that would be eligible for cash transfers and the number of persons that would participate in PSE jobs under each of the welfare reform plans described above. Since many PSE participants — especially those following the mixed strategy — would not remain at a public service job for the entire year, the number of full-time equivalent PSE job slots that would be occupied are also reported. The estimates indicate that about 7.2 million households with children would be eligible for transfer payments under the NIT component of the basic plan, and around 2 million households would have a member employed at a PSE job at least some time during the year. A little over 1 million job slots would be required for these PSE participants, with three-quarters of the slots going to persons who also receive NIT benefits. To place these estimates in perspective, consider that in 1975 there were 31.2 million households

Table 12.1. Number of Persons Participating in the Cash and Jobs Components of Alternative NIT–PSE Systems (in thousands)

Simulated Plans	Number of Households Eligible for Cash Transfers	Number of PSE Participants			Number of PSE Slots		
		Transfer Recipients	Nonrecipients	Total	Transfer Recipients	Nonrecipients	Total
Basic plan	7,218	1,470	539	2,009	794	224	1,018
NIT only	7,379						
Two-tier NIT with PSE	7,056	1,486	542	2,028	804	224	1,028
PSE only[a]	7,079	1,638	435	2,073	820	233	1,053

[a]Existing welfare system remains intact.

with children. Had the basic plan been in existence in that year, 7.8 million (or about one-quarter) of these households would have received either NIT benefits or PSE wages or both.

Table 12.1 provides some evidence of interactions between transfer programs and PSE, but these interaction effects appear to be rather small. For example, a comparison of the basic plan with the NIT-only plan indicates that adding PSE jobs to the NIT program would reduce the number of households receiving cash transfer payments by about 2%, by enabling 161,000 families to work their way off welfare. Similarly, a comparison of the basic plan with the PSE-only plan suggests that replacing the current welfare system with an NIT program would reduce the number of required PSE slots by about 3%. This occurs, as will be seen shortly, because of the NIT's influence on work incentives.

The estimates in Table 12.2 show the predicted changes in earnings under each of the simulated plans. As may be seen, the private sector earnings of transfer recipients are predicted to decline. However, slight increases are predicted for nontransfer recipients whenever the current welfare system is replaced by an NIT. The changes in private sector earnings that are reported in Table 12.2 are attributable to both the NIT and the PSE programs. Indeed, the table indicates that the NIT-only and PSE-only plans would cause approximately equal reductions in total private sector earnings. Private sector earnings decline under the NIT because of changes in work incentives that would induce many transfer recipients to reduce their hours of work. (These reductions by transfer recipients would be slightly offset, however, by increases in work effort by some families who receive benefits under current welfare programs, but who would no longer be eligible under the simulated NIT.) The PSE engenders a reduction in private sector earnings because some workers would leave the private sector jobs they currently hold to work at a PSE job. Thus, the program causes public work to be substituted for private work.

Table 12.2 also indicates that the two equal-cost plans (that is, NIT-only and two-tier PSE–NIT) would be associated with virtually identical reductions in private sector earnings. However, earnings from the PSE component of the two-tier PSE–NIT plan would be almost three times the size of this reduction in private sector earnings, and consequently, total earnings in the economy would actually rise under this plan. The NIT-only plan, which does not contain a PSE component, would, by contrast, cause a reduction in total earnings.

Table 12.3 provides a somewhat different perspective on the work-incentive effects associated with the simulated welfare reform plans. This

Table 12.2. Aggregate Changes in Earnings under Alternative NIT–PSE Systems (in billions of dollars)

Simulated Plans	Change in Total Private Sector Earnings			PSE Earnings			Change in Total Earnings		
	Transfer Recipients	Nonrecipients	Total	Transfer Recipients	Nonrecipients	Total	Transfer Recipients	Nonrecipients	Total
Basic plan	-2.7	.2	-2.5	3.5	1.0	4.5	.8	1.2	2.0
NIT only	-1.9	.3	-1.6				-1.9	.3	-1.6
Two-tier NIT with PSE	-1.9	.2	-1.7	3.5	1.0	4.5	1.6	1.2	2.8
PSE only[a]	-1.3	-.2	-1.5	3.6	1.0	4.6	2.3	.8	3.1

[a]Existing welfare system remains intact.

Table 12.3. Percentage Changes in Hours and Earnings under Alternative NIT–PSE Systems

Simulated Plans	Total Hours Worked			Total Earnings			Private Sector Earnings		
	Transfer Recipients	Nonrecipients	Total	Transfer Recipients	Nonrecipients	Total	Transfer Recipients	Nonrecipients	Total
Basic plan	1.3	.7	.8	3.7	.3	.5	-12.4	.1	-.6
NIT only	-7.4	.0	-.7	-8.8	.1	-.4	-8.8	.1	-.4
Two-tier NIT with PSE	5.0	.7	1.1	7.4	.3	.7	-8.8	.1	-.4
PSE only[a]	10.8	.6	1.5	12.5	.3	.8	-5.1	-.1	-.3

[a]Existing welfare system remains intact.

243

table suggests that transfer recipients would make substantial proportional adjustments in their total hours, total earnings, and private sector earnings in response to most of the simulated plans. However, because transfer recipients comprise only a minority of all families, the proportional effects on total hours and earnings in the overall economy are relatively small.

Table 12.3 further implies that work incentives tend to be minimized by welfare reform approaches that provide relatively generous transfer payments, such as the basic and NIT-only plans, and maximized by approaches that stress public service jobs and provide relatively ungenerous cash transfers, such as the two-tier PSE–NIT and PSE-only plans. However, all four of the simulated plans are predicted to cause declines in private sector earnings, suggesting that such declines are inevitable, whatever the mix between cash transfers and public employment jobs.

The estimates reported in Table 12.4 indicate how transfer payments and disposable incomes would be changed by the simulated plans and what the net cost to the government of the simulated plans would be.[15] The three plans that contain NIT components would increase cash payments to families with children by 20–48%. The PSE-only plan, by contrast, is associated with a reduction in transfer payments. This reduction occurs because PSE earnings would be "taxed" by current welfare programs. Thus, outlays for public service jobs would be partially offset by reductions in welfare payments to PSE participants. A similar offset is also apparent in comparing transfer payments under the basic plan with payments under the NIT-only plan.

It is evident from Table 12.4 that there is considerable variation in the net cost of the four simulated plans. And as one would anticipate, the more costly a program is, the greater is the increase in disposable income that it produces. To normalize for variation in program costs, we have divided the change in disposable income associated with each plan by the plan's net cost. The resulting *efficiency ratio,* which is reported in Table 12.4, suggests that per dollar of expenditure, the four simulated plans are all roughly equal in their effectiveness in raising participants' incomes.

This finding may be surprising at first. It is well known that reductions in labor supply and earnings that result from cash transfers mean that a dollar of transfers will raise disposable income by less than a dollar. But since public service jobs are associated with increases in earnings, it might appear that adding a PSE component to an NIT program should raise efficiency ratios. However, as a comparison of either the basic or the two-tier PSE–NIT plan to the NIT-only plan indicates, this does not occur. In fact, the ratio slightly falls!

Table 12.4. Aggregate Changes in Net Transfers and Disposable Incomes under Alternative NIT–PSE Systems (in billions of dollars)

Simulated Plans	Change in Transfer Payments			Change in Disposable Income			Net Cost	Efficiency Ratio
	Transfer Recipients	Nonrecipients	Total	Transfer Recipients	Nonrecipients	Total		
Basic plan	4.91	−.46	4.45	5.62	.17	5.79	8.26	.70
NIT only	6.32	−.40	5.92	4.72	−.39	4.33	5.97	.73
Two-tier NIT with PSE	2.55	−.48	2.07	3.98	.18	4.16	5.83	.71
PSE only[a]	−.71	−.20	−.91	1.17	.59	1.76	2.32	.76

[a]Existing welfare system remains intact.

The explanation for this finding resides in the fact that PSE programs cause some persons to substitute public work for private work. To see this, consider a worker who leaves a private sector job that pays $2 an hour for a PSE job that pays the 1975 minimum wage of $2.10 per hour. The efficiency ratio associated with the PSE program for this particular worker is only .05 (i.e., at a net cost to the government of $2.10, the individual's income only increases by a dime). Given the large estimated amounts of substitution of public for private work indicated by Table 12.2, it is hardly surprising the PSE programs do not succeed in raising efficiency ratios.

Table 12.5 reports several indices that measure the effects of the four simulated plans on the income distribution and on poverty. The measures of target efficiency, which are reported in the first two columns of the table, indicate the percentage of PSE earnings and NIT transfers that would be received by the pretransfer poor.[16] Thus, these measures are intended to reflect the extent to which public expenditures on the PSE and NIT components of the various plans would be concentrated on households with the greatest needs. As is evident, there is very little variation among the four alternative plans in terms of the target efficiency of either their NIT or PSE components. However, it does appear that target efficiency is considerably higher for transfer expenditures under any given plan than for PSE wage expenditures. The relatively greater target efficiency of transfers occurs because, by design, the size of payments received under an NIT is inversely related to income levels. Some public expenditures under a PSE program, by contrast, will inevitably be received by relatively high-income persons who become unemployed.

The remaining five columns in Table 12.5 present several measures that may be used to assess the extent to which the simulated plans reduce income inequality and poverty. The first of these measures indicates the number of households whose annual disposable incomes would be increased or decreased by a minimum of $240 if each plan were implemented. The next measure is an estimate of the percentage decrease in persons below the poverty line that would result from implementation. The final two measures are based on a proportion known as the *welfare ratio*, which is computed by dividing a household's disposable income by its poverty line. The mean of the logarithm of the welfare ratio is reported in the sixth column of Table 12.5, and the variance of the logarithm of the ratio, which indicates how the plans affect the size distribution of disposable income, is reported in the seventh column.

The number of households made worse-off by the first three plans is at first blush surprisingly large. These estimates, however, point out one

Table 12.5. Effects of the Alternative NIT–PSE Systems on the Income Distribution and on Poverty

Simulated Plans	Target Efficiency of		Number of Households (in thousands) with		% Change in Poverty Population	Mean of Log of Welfare Ratio	Variance of Log of Welfare Ratio
	PSE Earnings	Transfer Payments	Higher Incomes	Lower Incomes			
Basic plan	75%	88%	5,374	1,223	−49.2	.704	.210
NIT only		88	4,772	1,368	−37.1	.694	.218
Two-tier NIT with PSE[a]	74	91	4,471	1,365	−27.5	.691	.231
PSE only[a]	74	85	1,413	0	−9.4	.664	.274
Current system		90				.653	.275

[a] Existing welfare system remains intact.

247

of the hard facts of welfare reform: it is difficult, if not impossible, to construct a transfer program of moderate cost that does not make some households worse-off. This problem is further exacerbated by the demands of state governments that they not be asked to bear any additional cost of the reform and, in fact, that they be relieved of some of their present welfare burden.

As might be anticipated, the basic plan, which is the most expensive of the simulated welfare reform alternatives, is predicted to have the largest impact on income inequality and poverty, and the PSE-only plan, which is the least expensive proposal, has the smallest impact. In fact, the results for this plan suggest that in the absence of reform of existing welfare programs, a program that provides minimum-wage jobs will have only a very modest effect on either income inequality or poverty.

The most interesting implications of Table 12.5 are suggested by comparing the NIT-only and two-tier PSE–NIT plans, the two equal-cost alternatives. This comparison implies that poverty and income inequality can be more effectively reduced by a welfare reform package that does not include a PSE component than by an equally expensive package that does — a finding that reflects the fact that expenditures on transfer payments are relatively more target efficient than expenditures on jobs. Thus, it appears that welfare expenditures on public service jobs must be justified on grounds other than their effectiveness as antipoverty tools. As pointed out earlier, one possibly important justification is that PSE programs tend to increase total work effort. Consequently, improvements to the incomes of poor persons are received as earnings, rather than as unearned transfers, a distinction that may be important to many taxpayers. In addition, PSE programs *may* result in the production of socially useful output and provide their participants with valuable work experience. The production of socially useful output in the public sector would, of course, counter production losses in the private sector resulting from reductions in hours worked at conventional jobs. At least partially offsetting these potential benefits, however, is the fact that because of larger requirements for physical capital and supervisory personnel, PSE programs are generally more expensive to administer than NIT programs.

SUMMARY

In the previous section, we presented results from simulations of various combinations of NIT and PSE plans in order to analyze relations between these two welfare strategies. Our findings can be summarized by the following observations:

- A program that entails only a guarantee of cash will lead to reductions in work effort when compared to the current system.
- Coupling a PSE program with a cash program will increase total work effort and total earnings in the economy when compared to the current system.
- A guaranteed-jobs program, even one paying the minimum wage, will lead to reductions in private sector work that can be as large or larger than reductions resulting from an NIT scheme.
- The demand for PSE slots does not vary substantially as transfer benefits increase. However, guaranteeing jobs does reduce the amount of transfer benefits somewhat.
- The efficiency of PSE in raising recipients' incomes is no greater than that of cash programs.
- An NIT plan that does not have a PSE component will have a somewhat greater impact on income inequality and poverty than an equal-cost plan that does have a PSE component.

Given these observations, the trade-off facing policymakers interested in alleviating poverty seems clear. On one hand, they can proceed by relying mainly on cash transfer programs that maximize reductions in poverty, but minimize work incentives among recipients. Or on the other hand, they can adopt a strategy of guaranteeing households both cash and jobs, an approach that engenders greater work efforts, but per dollar of tax expenditure has a less favorable impact on the poverty population. Either course of action, it appears, will reduce private sector earnings among low-income persons.

Since reduction in private sector employment, earnings, and output is a major shortcoming of both cash transfer programs and public jobs programs, it seems important to develop policies that will be helpful in mitigating these effects. Such policies would either make the private sector jobs that are available to disadvantaged workers more attractive to these persons or would make such workers more attractive to potential employers. Specific examples of such policies include wage vouchers, employer tax credits, wage subsidies and earnings supplements for low-wage workers, and job-search assistance and job training for the disadvantaged. Programs of this type are likely to receive increasing emphasis over the next several years.

NOTES

1. In PSE programs, individuals who are unable to secure conventional employment are paid some fixed wage (often the minimum wage) by the government to perform services that are presumed to be socially useful, but of less value than the cost of providing them. Under an NIT, families without any other income are allowed a certain fixed amount of transfer benefits, known as the *guarantee* or *basic benefit level,* which increases with family size. As family income from other sources (including PSE wages) rises, NIT transfer payments are reduced by an implicit tax rate, often referred to as the program's *benefit-reduction rate.* When income from other sources is so high that the benefit reduction exactly offsets the income guarantee — a point known as the *break-even level* — payments under the program cease.

2. The model has become known as the *KGB model,* after its three developers: Richard Kasten, David Greenberg, and David Betson.

3. Because of space limitations and the complexity of the model, the model is only sketched here. Greater detail, as well as an examination — and in some cases, sensitivity tests — of major assumptions that underlie the simulation methodology, may be found in Betson, Greenberg, and Kasten (1980).

4. An individual's *net wage rate* is simply his nominal wage times one minus the cumulative tax rate he faces.

5. These parameters are estimated by two variables that represent the net changes caused by the various payment plans in the experiment. The first variable measures the change in family income resulting from the experimental treatment in the absence of any adjustment in hours worked. The second is the change in an individual's net wage rate due to the program's benefit-reduction rate. The estimates produced by this procedure indicate how individuals will adjust their work effort in response to changes in the amount of transfer payments they receive or in the size of the benefit-reduction rates they face. The regression model that was used to obtain these estimates was developed by Keeley et al. (1978).

6. The simulation methodology assumes that this choice is made on the basis of perfect information about the alternatives, an assumption that probably results in an overstatement of the public employment supply population. Unless persons are aware of public employment and know something about it, the program is not a viable alternative for them. Knowledge of the program is likely to be positively related to the publicity given the program, the length of time the program has been in operation, and the size of the program.

7. For purposes of the simulation, it is assumed that an individual will participate in public employment whenever he sees it as marginally superior to his best conventional-sector alternative. In actual practice, however, a substantial differential between public and conventional employment may be necessary, if only to overcome inertia. Nevertheless, many of the frictions that exist in labor markets would be reduced over the long run. For example, many persons may not actively consider voluntarily leaving their present jobs to participate in public employment; but once they have been terminated or laid off, they may seriously examine PSE as a possible alternative to available regular employment opportunities. Thus, the methodology is best viewed as being based on a static model of economic behavior; the adjustments to the introduction of a PSE program would not take place instantaneously, but only over time. The larger the comparative advantage of public employment, the more rapidly the adjustments would be expected to occur.

8. This procedure does not allow for the fact that individuals may not always be able to choose freely the total number of hours they work, at either a regular or a public employ-

ment job. In such cases, income might be higher if an individual picks one strategy over the other, but only because he would work longer hours. If so, the individual must trade off a higher family income against lower hours, and his choice will only be clear with knowledge of his utility map. For this reason, we plan to implement shortly a procedure developed by Betson (1980) that utilizes income and substitution-effect estimates, such as those from the Seattle-Denver experiment, to derive the information we need about households' underlying utility surfaces. Preliminary tests of this utility technique suggest that it produces results that are very similar to those produced by the simpler procedure we currently use.

9. Two separate sets of labor supply estimates are actually used to make these calculations. The first, which is based on a logit regression equation, predicts changes in the probability of participating in the labor force. Based on these predicted changes, a random number generator is used to reassign some nonworkers to a worker status. Then the second set of Seattle-Denver estimates are used to predict adjustments in annual hours for both the new workers and previous workers.

10. This implicit assumption — that reported unemployment accurately reflects the involuntary loss of time to the labor market — appears consistent with the premise underlying most proposals for public employment programs.

11. In addition to the District of Columbia, the states that were simulated to supplement the federal benefit for single-parent families were Alaska, California, Connecticut, Illinois, Iowa, Kansas, Massachusetts, Michigan, Minnesota, New Jersey, New York, New Hampshire, Oregon, Pennsylvania, Rhode Island, Vermont, Washington, and Wisconsin.

12. All the plans we examine in the text are assumed to be deficit financed, an assumption that is implicit in most previous simulations of various welfare alternatives. We have maintained this assumption in order to highlight the interaction between the NIT and PSE programs. However, we have also conducted a simulation that finances the basic plan by adding a surcharge to the federal income tax. Under this plan, non-NIT recipients would face substantially higher tax rates, and in response to this change in work incentives, they would apparently increase their earnings. In fact, this predicted increase in private sector earnings is about three times larger than the estimated reduction in the private sector earnings of transfer recipients. Although this result may be surprising at first, it is quite consistent with the backward-bending labor supply curves that are implied by the Seattle-Denver work-response parameters used in this study. At first, we thought that this result might merely have been a consequence of basing our simulations on labor supply parameters from the Seattle-Denver experiment. However, we have conducted a number of sensitivity tests with labor supply parameters estimated with nonexperimental data (see Betson, Greenberg and Kasten forthcoming) and have consistently found that earnings increases among the higher-income persons who would finance various income redistribution schemes, such as NITs, would more than offset decreases in earnings among recipients. One implication of this finding is that reductions in private sector output resulting from work disincentives are not a major obstacle to large-scale comprehensive transfer programs — at least, if these programs are financed through the income tax system.

13. In practice, receipt of cash transfer benefits would depend on how the plans were administered, but would undoubtedly be under 100%. Thus, the simulation estimates of the size and costs of the NIT components of the various plans contain an upward bias of unknown magnitude.

14. In 1975, 150% of the poverty line for a family with two parents and two children corresponded to an annual income of $6,183.

15. The net cost to the government is equal to the PSE wage bill, plus the sum of the

changes in transfer payments, tax revenues (including Social Security taxes), and unemployment compensation. Neither administrative costs nor the value of PSE output is included in these cost estimates.

16. The term *pretransfer poor* refers to households that would be counted as poor in the absence of either the existing welfare system or the simulated programs.

REFERENCES

Betson, David. 1980. "Labor Supply Functions and Their Implicit Expenditure Functions: Theoretical Deviation and Application to Micro-Simulation Analysis." Ph.D. dissertation, University of Wisconsin (Madison).

Betson, David; Greenberg, David; and Kasten, Richard. 1980. "A Micro-Simulation Model for Analyzing Alternative Welfare Reform Proposals: An Application to the Program for Better Jobs and Income." In *Microeconomic Simulation: Models for Public Policy Analysis,* edited by Robert Haveman and Kevin Hollenbeck. Madison: Institute for Research on Poverty, University of Wisconsin.

———. Forthcoming. "A Simulation Analysis of the Economic Efficiency and Distribution Effects of Alternative Program Structures: The Negative Income Tax versus the Credit Income Tax." In *Universal versus Income-Tested Programs,* edited by Irwin Garfinkel. Madison: Institute for Research on Poverty, University of Wisconsin.

Keeley, Michael C.; Robins, Philip K.; Spiegelman, Robert G.; and West, Richard W. 1978. "The Estimation of Labor Supply Models Using Experimental Data." *American Economic Review* 68 (December):873–87.

LIST OF CONTRIBUTORS

WILLIAM P. ALBRECHT, Department of Economics, University of Iowa, Iowa City, Iowa

DAVID M. BETSON, Institute for Research on Poverty, University of Wisconsin, Madison, Wisconsin

SHELDON DANZIGER, Institute for Research on Poverty, University of Wisconsin, Madison, Wisconsin

J. FRED GIERTZ, Institute of Government and Public Affairs, University of Illinois, Urbana, Illinois

DAVID H. GREENBERG, SRI International, Menlo Park, California

DANIEL S. HAMERMESH, Department of Economics, Michigan State University, East Lansing, Michigan

ROBERT H. HAVEMAN, Department of Economics and Institute for Research on Poverty, University of Wisconsin, Madison, Wisconsin

G. WILLIAM HOAGLAND, Human Resources and Community Development Division, Congressional Budget Office, Washington, D.C.

JAMES R. HOSEK, The Rand Corporation, Santa Monica, California

ROBERT J. LAMPMAN, Department of Economics and Institute for Research on Poverty, University of Wisconsin, Madison, Wisconsin

ROBERT A. MOFFITT, Department of Economics, Rutgers University, New Brunswick, New Jersey

LARRY L. ORR, Office of Technical Analysis, Department of Labor, Washington, D.C.

MORTON PAGLIN, Department of Economics, Portland State University, Portland, Oregon

ROBERT PLOTNICK, Department of Economics, Dartmouth College, Hanover, New Hampshire

FELICITY SKIDMORE, Madison, Wisconsin

PAUL M. SOMMERS, Department of Economics, Middlebury College, Middlebury, Vermont

DENNIS H. SULLIVAN, Department of Economics, Miami University, Oxford, Ohio